THE TRUTH
about the legendary drinking, the wives, the mistresses, the children, the family in-fighting, the little rich boy whose hunger for both power and pleasure never stopped growing.

THE TRUTH
about the most savage and costly act of corporate violence in Detroit history, when Lee Iacocca, Ford's "golden boy," was sacked, and the plans for the car that could have saved Ford's future were scrapped.

THE TRUTH
about the Byzantine company intrigue and ultimate executive squeeze that at last made Henry Ford II step down.

THE TRUTH
that only America's most feared biographer could tell.

Victor Lasky
Never Complain, Never Explain

NEVER COMPLAIN, NEVER EXPLAIN

THE STORY OF

HENRY FORD II

VICTOR LASKY

BERKLEY BOOKS, NEW YORK

NEVER COMPLAIN, NEVER EXPLAIN

A Berkley Book / published by arrangement with
Richard Marek Publishers

PRINTING HISTORY
The Putnam Publishing Group edition / July 1981
Berkley edition / November 1983

ISBN: 0-425-05750-X

A BERKLEY BOOK ® TM 757,375
Berkley Books are published by The Berkley Publishing Group,
200 Madison Avenue, New York, New York 10016.
The name "BERKLEY" and the stylized "B" with design
are trademarks belonging to Berkley Publishing Corporation.
PRINTED IN THE UNITED STATES OF AMERICA

To My Wife Pat

Contents

And one of the things I want to make sure of before I'm so crippled up I can't do anything [is] that I've destroyed as much of my paperwork as I possibly have so that nobody will ever know anything about me, or as little as possible.

Henry Ford II,
interviewed
by Barbara Walters on
ABC's *World News Tonight*,
April 30, 1980

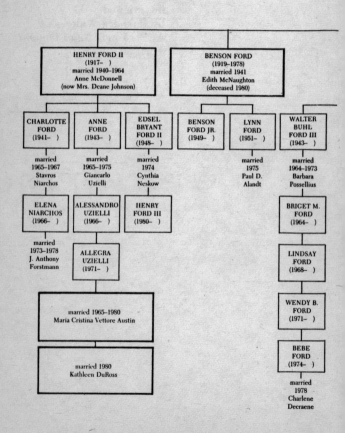

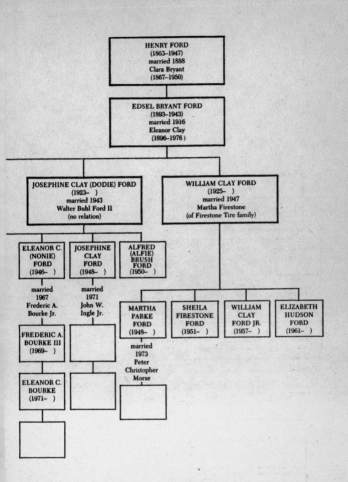

1

1979
ANNUAL MEETING

IT WAS, OBSERVERS SAID, THE MOST COLORFUL ANNUAL MEET-
ing ever held by the Ford Motor Company. And it was undoubtedly the longest one in the seventy-six-year history of the
company that helped change the industrial face of America.
On Thursday, May 10, 1979, a warm, hazy morning in downtown Detroit, nearly 3,000 stockholders, newsmen, local celebrities and out-of-town critics lined up for a block to get into
the meeting at the Ford Auditorium, which is within walking
distance of the city's spectacular Renaissance Center, whose
very existence owed much to the man who was the day's center
of attention—Henry Ford II.

It was, as the *Wall Street Journal* reported the next day,
"the greatest show in town." From the moment Henry II called
the meeting to order, the packed city auditorium seemed to be
set for an old-fashioned melodrama. The highly partisan crowd

didn't hesitate to cheer the heroes and hiss the villains.

The principal hero was the Chairman of the company, Henry Ford II, who had previously announced that this would be the last annual meeting over which he would preside. And the principal villain was Roy Cohn, the controversial New York lawyer who had been hounding Ford with a dissident-share-holder suit, all the while raising embarrassing questions about the Chairman's high living, allegedly at company expense.

Also on hand was Ford's rebellious nephew, Benson Ford, Jr., who was conducting the first revolt of a Ford heir in the history of the family. Among other things, young Ben was suing his mother for control of his deceased father's voting stock, alleging that his father had been an alcoholic and had not known what he was doing when he assigned voting rights of his stock to his brothers Henry and William Clay Ford. In addition, Benson Jr. was seeking his father's seat on the company board.

Even more embarrassing was the spreading gossip about the rather messy divorce battle Henry Ford was having with his Italian-born second wife, Cristina Vettore, who had let it be known she was good and angry about being spurned for a younger woman. The new liaison had become public knowl-edge after Henry II was arrested for drunk driving in California some years before while in the company of Kathleen DuRoss, a comely ex-model then thirty-four years old. It was on that occasion that the Chairman of the Ford Motor Company uttered those immortal words "Never complain. Never explain."

Also troubling were business problems. The company's share of the domestic market was declining. Even more important, the company was afflicted with what Henry II called "repu-tational degradation," stemming in part from its Pintos, whose gas tanks, it was alleged, tended to explode in rear-end colli-sions. At first Ford insisted there were no defects in the sub-compact cars, but just prior to government hearings the company agreed to recall the Pintos.

On top of everything else, Henry II was not feeling well. Years of high living plus long hours of company business had finally caught up with the sixty-one-year-old Chairman. In 1976 he had suffered an attack of angina pectoris, a heart condition aggravated by stress, and he decided the time had come to slow down. The realization that he was mortal like everyone else hit him particularly when his brother Benson, two years his junior, died in 1978 of the same disease.

When he began making noises about wanting to hand over the scepter, Ford was greeted with disbelief. "Nobody wants to believe what I say," he had told *Business Week,* almost plaintively. And for good reason. For thirty-four years Ford had been synonymous with the Ford Motor Company. As chief executive officer, he had been the very visible ruler (some Detroiters said "monarch") of the nations's third-largest company. He had been power personified. And he knew how to crack the whip, as a long series of ousted executives could and did attest.

Now, at the annual meeting, the grandson of the founder of the Ford Motor Company appeared to be ready to close out a remarkable family dynasty. "After thirty-four years on the job," he said simply and stoically, "I am ready to stand aside. The period I have closely identified with is nearing its end. For the company, a great new era is just beginning." When he finished reading what had been billed as his "farewell" speech, Henry II beamed his appreciation at the standing ovation given him by the shareholders. And several—including his oldest daughter, Charlotte—made brief statements thanking him for his service with the company. Charlotte had come from New York, accompanied by her sister, Anne Ford Uzielli, and her brother, Edsel B. Ford II, who was working for the company in Australia. Also, there was Henry's sister, Mrs. Walter Buhl Ford II, whose husband, though a Ford, was not of the automobile family.

But not everyone applauded. The wife of Lee A. Iacocca, arriving in a chauffeur-driven Chrysler, announced she had come because she believed Ford "has management problems." Of course, her husband had been cavalierly dismissed as company president the previous summer by Henry Ford, who told him, "I just don't like you." And Iacocca, who until then had been widely regarded as Henry's heir apparent, soon became president of the ailing Chrysler Corporation.

But in standing aside, Henry II made clear he would continue as Chairman "for an indeterminate period." Still, it was a touching moment in the annals of American industry. And it was one fully recorded by the media. Excerpts of the annual meeting were televised that evening on all the network news shows. And across the country newspapers referred editorially to the event as the "end of an era." But was it really? Was Henry Ford serious about handing over the reins of power to Philip Caldwell, whom he anointed as his supposed successor? Or, as was widely suspected with some justification, was the mild-mannered Caldwell merely to preside over the interregnum, awaiting the eventual crowning of Ford's son, Edsel, as chief executive officer?

The meeting had begun with Henry II asking for a moment of prayer for his brother Benson, who had been a Ford Motor officer and director when he died. But that moment of silence was about the only one in a session that lasted over four hours. At times Ford had to plead with the audience to remain quiet when Roy Cohn hurled more than a dozen pointed questions at the auto magnate. Some of the questions raised by the New York attorney had to do with allegations that Henry II had misused company funds and that the company had paid a bribe to an Indonesian official for a government contract. The charges, all of which had been denied, were the subject of a lawsuit filed by Cohn on behalf of a number of dissident stockholders. As we shall see later, the suit was settled out of court. And the alleged bribe, denied by the company, was the subject of a probe being conducted by the Justice Department in Washington. This too was later dropped.

Cohn, who had been greeted with catcalls when he rose to speak, politely thanked Henry II for having restored quiet in the cavernous auditorium, then proceeded to flail him. Among other things, the attorney noted that one allegation in his lawsuit on behalf of dissident shareholders—namely, that Henry II had squandered company funds on himself—had been proved accurate when the Chairman repaid $34,585 to the company for personal use of an apartment in New York's Hotel Carlyle.

"Why did you withhold those facts a year ago?" Cohn demanded.

"I did not withhold any facts a year ago," a flustered Ford

replied, referring to his responses at the previous annual meeting. "I told the facts as I knew them."

According to Ford, most of the restitution was "for beds that were slept in by friends I didn't even know about . . . some of them my wife's." And, as far as he knew, everything had been paid back, "and I don't owe Ford Motor Company one thin dime."

Cohn wasn't having any of the explanations. He accused the Chairman of having arranged a pay increase, canceling out the $34,585 he had repaid the company and leaving stockholders with a "net loss of $11,050." Henry did not respond.

Beads of perspiration appeared on Ford's brow as Cohn kept hammering away. Finally Henry had had enough. When Cohn raised some questions about some severance payments provided Lee Iacocca, Ford ended the inquisition with a suggestion: "Why don't you put your money in Chrysler and go to their meeting. Okay?" The audience responded with cheers.

There was silence, however, when Ford's nephew, Benson, rose to speak. Here he was, in person, the twenty-nine-year-old rebel who had sent shockwaves through his otherwise close-knit family by going public with claims he was being rooked out of his rightful inheritance. And young "Ben" had made no secret of his feeling that he was being done in by Uncle Henry's machinations. Uncle Henry meanwhile had let it be known that his nephew's bid for the seat on the board held by his father had been rejected by the directors' nominating committee.

As all eyes were riveted on him, Benson Ford, Jr. called himself "a successful businessman" and added, "I know something about cars." He also spoke of his father's desire that "I follow in his stewardship as a director of Ford Motor." As for being rejected for that post, Benson noted that the only member of the nominating committee who had interviewed him was his uncle, Henry Ford II, and that he had never even met any of the other committee members.

"I do not intend to fade away," added Benson. "I intend to contribute to Ford's growth in the twentieth century."

But Uncle Henry insisted that Benson was "not qualified" to sit on the board of directors and that being a member of the family or owning class B family stock no longer constituted an entrée into the hierarchy of the Ford Motor Company. "If any member of my family achieves a senior position in the company, it will be through merit and by decision of the board of directors," he said. "There are no crown princes in the Ford Motor Company and there is no privileged route to the top."

Of course this was a new state of affairs in the Ford Motor Company. After all, Henry II and his brother William Clay, eight years his junior, had both been named to the board before they were thirty years old. And, as one stockholder noted, they were then probably far less qualified than was Benson Ford, Jr. This Henry II did not exactly deny. But he insisted that times had changed. "When I was named a director," he said, "it was a family company. The board meetings were held in my grandfather's head."

Charlotte Ford's appearance was unexpected. It came after Benson Jr. had left the hall to appear in a courtroom several blocks away in connection with litigation he had filed to contest his father's will. Trim, well-dressed and looking very much like her mother, the thirty-eight-year-old daughter of Henry Ford II arose to say that Benson was alone among thirteen cousins in his fight with the family. She said she was speaking "on behalf of the family, especially our generation," in tribute to her father and what he had done for "the company, its stockholders, employees, the city of Detroit and the world in the past 38 years."

"You are a great human being," she told her father. "Generous, loyal and, above all, honest."

"I appreciate that from the bottom of my heart," her father replied, "and I love you."

It had been a trying four hours. But when the annual meeting was over, Henry Ford II greeted the press with a smile, cigar in hand. "I'm feeling pretty good," he said. He had conducted the session without a mishap. And he had handled the pugnacious Roy Cohn, whose very name gave him the willies, with considerable aplomb. He was concerned, however, that his nephew Benson Jr. had hired the New York attorney to handle some of his litigation. All of which surely spelled trouble. And more trouble was the last thing the still embattled Henry Ford II needed.

2

THE
FAMILY MEETING

JUST PRIOR TO THE SHAREHOLDERS' MEETING, A GATHERING OF
the Ford clan took place at the fashionable Grosse Pointe Shores
home of Henry II's younger brother, William Clay Ford. There
was nothing unusual about the conclave. The family, which
consisted of the three living grandchildren and thirteen great-
grandchildren of the company's founder (and their husbands
and wives), routinely gathered for a meeting every spring.
These were private affairs, conducted away from the prying
eyes of the press. The main purpose was to keep everyone
informed of the family's investments and financial transactions.
Another purpose was to keep family members informed about
what everyone else was doing. Except for weddings and fu-
nerals, this annual gathering was practically the only time most
of them saw one another. In the past most of these meetings
had occurred at Henry's home, but Henry was no longer living

there. His grand mansion in Grosse Pointe was now occupied by his second wife, Cristina, from whom he had been separated since 1976.

Cristina of course had not been invited to this family gathering. The "pizza queen," as Benson Jr.'s mother referred to her, was now a nonperson, about whom the less said the better. Benson's mother, Edith McNaughton Ford, had been invited, but she decided not to attend, apparently because she knew that her son would come under bitter attack. And though she was opposed to what her son was doing, Benson Jr. still was her son. What Benson was doing, among other things, was contesting his father's will. The will, though providing Benson with a trust fund valued at $7.5 million, gave control of the trust to his ailing mother and, successively, to his uncles Henry and William. Benson's legal battles, needless to say, were proving embarrassing to a family that had always sought to keep its internal problems private.

Benson had been invited by Uncle Henry. But the original telegram contained the wrong address. This was straightened out in a follow-up letter in which his uncle apologized. Nevertheless Benson was suspicious. "I thought they might be setting me up to go to the wrong house so I would look like an idiot." Benson had not forgotten that he was unable to go to his father's final interment because he had not been informed in time. "It hurt me deeply and it gave rise to stories in Grosse Pointe that I was an ungrateful son."

Benson reports today that he has never forgotten that, following his father's death, Uncle Henry had slipped into his dad's sitting room and stuffed his pockets full of expensive jewelry. Benson's sidekick Elliot Kaplan had reported the incident to him—alerted by Benson's mother who had observed it herself—and Benson then went to complain bitterly to his mother.

"Do you want me to do anything about it?" he asked her.

"No," she replied, "you'll only make matters worse."

"But, Mom, we can't allow such things to happen in this house."

"Benson, please don't argue," she said. And the matter was dropped.

Benson Jr.'s arrival at Uncle Bill's home was not exactly

greeted with joy. He could sense what he later described as the "anxiety level" of those present. "When I walked into the foyer," he recalls, "I could hear everyone laughing and yelling at each other. Those old houses have marble floors and the echoes are deafening. I said to myself, 'It sounds like a convention going on here.'" But when his assorted relatives saw him enter, they hushed up. "I had the feeling they were amazed I would dare to show up."

After a while several of his cousins did come up to greet Benson. Among them was Henry's son Edsel, who shook Benson's hand and asked how things were going in California. Benson was a partner in several California enterprises, including an auto-parts manufacturing business. "Fine," said Benson, who asked how things were going in Australia, where Edsel was a junior Ford executive. Seeing his sister Lynn, Benson greeted her warmly. But Lynn did not respond. After mouthing a few pleasantries, Benson went into the living room to await the beginning of the family conclave.

Before the meeting began, however, Benson's uncles approached him. They seemed upset. "We'd like to speak to you for a moment," said Henry. "Would you please come with us?" Benson rose from his seat and accompanied his uncles to the library. Once the door was closed, Henry got to the point. "Our electronic surveillance says you're wired. Is that true, Benson?"

Benson was dumbfounded. He had indeed been "wired" with a Fargo unit strapped to his chest. The monitoring device had been provided by some friendly West Coast police officers, one of whom was sitting at that very moment in a limousine parked on a nearby side street, listening to and taping the conversation. What Benson had forgotten was the extraordinary security that surrounded the Ford family. Uncle Billy's home, for example, had an electronic screening device embedded in the doorframe. Benson had been there many times, usually for parties. But he had thought that the screening was aimed at people carrying weapons. Uncle Billy, like most Fords, was fearful of possible violence aimed at the family. This was a carry-over from the days of the founding father, Henry Ford, who, because of fear of kidnapping, usually carried a gun and was surrounded by bodyguards.

"Benson," his uncle repeated, "is it true?"

Benson at first hesitated. He frankly did not know what to say. But then he decided: the hell with it. "Yes," he said, "it's true."

Benson Jr. thought his Uncle Billy was about to go into shock. Henry, however, was outraged. "Benson, I just can't understand you. After all, this is your house too. There are no lawyers here. Why in hell did you come in here wired?"

"Uncle Henry, I really didn't know what I was coming into—whether this was going to be a hostile or a friendly environment. After all, I have to look out for my interests."

"Well, I see your point," said Henry, adding, "You're smart, Benson. You don't take us for granted."

But Uncle Billy was not that sanguine. "Why, Benson? Why? Why are you doing this to the family? It's only family, and it's your family."

"Okay, okay," Benson retorted. "I'll turn the damn thing off."

But that wasn't good enough. The uncles wanted to dismantle the device. Benson said, "No, it isn't mine. It's someone else's property." He agreed to remove the instrument, and placed it in a drawer. After Benson put his shirt on again and adjusted his tie, he returned to the living room and Uncle Henry began the meeting.

Not a word was said about what had just taken place.

The first subject under discussion was Henry II's impending resignation and the elevation of Philip Caldwell to the presidency of the company. Caldwell of course was an outsider in a company that had always been headed by a Ford. And it was the consensus of those present that sooner or later another Ford would have to take over the reins of leadership. There was even talk about Uncle Billy's eventually becoming the chief operating officer of the company. And everyone, including Benson Jr., thought that was a good idea. In all, this discussion took about five minutes.

The rest of the evening was devoted to Benson Jr., although Henry II never mentioned his nephew by name. At first he presented what turned out to be a preview of what he would say at the shareholders' meeting—namely, that there were no crown princes in the company and no privileged routes to the top. He said that now that he was removing himself from company affairs, he did not want to see a lot of blood shed in family disputes. He then called for family unity, insisting that otherwise the family could not survive as it had in the past. Any disputes should be settled within the clan, he said, without recourse to publicity-seeking outsiders, meaning of course Roy Cohn. If there were any problems to be solved, why not lay them on the table right now? That's what these family meetings were all about.

But Benson Jr. said nothing. And eventually the meeting was concluded.

Benson was about to leave when Charlotte Ford approached him with fire in her eyes. "Why in hell did you hire Roy Cohn?" she demanded.

Benson had been prepared for hostility, but not from the distaff side of the family. However, he replied using similarly hard words, "I hired him because he's one mean, tough son-of-a-bitch."

"Don't you see what it's doing to my father?"

"Yeah, I can see what it's doing to your father, but I'm not going after your father. I hired Cohn to represent me in personal actions, which I would much rather have settled amicably."

"Well!" Charlotte responded, turning away in disgust.

And that unloosed a torrent of abuse from others in the family. Particularly shrill were William Ford's daughter, Martha, and her husband, Peter Morse. Also sounding off were Benson's sister, Lynn, and husband Paul Alandt. Hiring Roy Cohn was tantamount to committing treason, they insisted. And they wanted to know why Benson was also demanding more than $2 million in damages and an audit of Ford Estates, the organization that handled Ford family money.

"Look," Benson finally said, "I'm not trying to hurt you guys. All I want is a proper accounting of what I'm entitled to. I don't believe I've been getting it. As for Roy Cohn," he went on, "I couldn't care less. If you don't like him, it's okay with me. It's no big deal."

After which, according to Benson Jr., there was a sharp change in the atmosphere. His cousins changed the subject. Several, in fact, suggested having a party. "That was their way of apologizing, I guess," said Benson. Only Charlotte Ford continued to glare at him. "She had that vengeful look in her eyes, like 'You're killing my father and I hate your guts.'" Her father meanwhile had not said a word. He had listened to the entire dispute with a smile on his face. Unlike Charlotte, he did say goodbye to his nephew.

Benson did not stay for the party, which lasted well into the night. He called for his driver and drove back to his hotel. There he told his business associates what had occurred. He had come away with the feeling that what was most troubling his relatives was the extraordinary publicity he had lately been receiving. "Six months before, I was an unknown, and everybody was happy," he recalled, "but then I began coming on like gang-busters, getting my name in the papers, and all of a sudden they felt threatened." Some of the publicity had not been pleasant, he concedes. Being forced to label his father a drunk, in order to contest the will, had not been one of his happiest moments. And neither was his having been busted for possession of a small amount of cocaine and hash, which resulted in his being put on a parole program. The incident had occurred at the San Francisco International Airport when he and a girl friend deplaned from a trip to the Far East. Though Benson has his own suspicions about the timing of the arrest, all he would say publicly about it—recalling the drunk-driving arrest of Uncle Henry—was "Never complain. Never explain."

The family meeting did not resolve anything, as far as Benson Jr. was concerned. The schism was further intensified at the stockholders' meeting when Uncle Henry publicly described his nephew as "not qualified."

"It's practically irreparable now," a source close to the Fords told the *Detroit Free Press* several days later.

3

THE FOUNDER

ALL DAY LONG THEY FILED SLOWLY PAST THE BODY OF THE MAN who had put America on wheels and had fathered automotive mass production. It was the spring of 1947. It was estimated that over one hundred thousand people had come to take their final look at the pinch-faced, fragile remains of Henry Ford lying in state in the lobby of the recreation hall of Greenfield Village. The next day thousands waited in the rain to watch the auto city's elite arrive to attend the funeral rites at St. Paul's Episcopal Cathedral. A hush fell on the throng crowding the sidewalks of Detroit's Woodward Avenue as the widow, Clara Bryant Ford, leaning on the arm of grandson Henry Ford II, stepped out of a maroon Lincoln limousine.

Inside St. Paul's, the Very Reverend Kirk B. O'Ferrall bade Henry Ford godspeed on his way to "his long home which shall know no end, in the infinite Eternity of God." The crowd filed out and the body was driven, in a Packard hearse, to his family's small cemetery on Joy Road. The old man would not have liked that, since he had never ridden comfortably in any but a Ford vehicle. Then, as the rain came down in buckets, Henry Ford was buried in a muddy grave.

Ford had lived until his eighty-third year. His passing was front-page news around the world. Thousands of messages of sympathy poured into Dearborn. And as usually happened in the case of a great man's death, his virtues were accentuated while his faults were conveniently forgotten. Thus Ford's life-long friend Edgar A. Guest could assert, "His was a sensitive heart . . . an understanding mind. . . . He had sympathy and pity for the woes of others."

But not everyone who had known Henry Ford would have agreed. For in many of his dealings he could be mean, tough, and irascible. He ruled the River Rouge plant—seat of the mighty empire he had reared out of sweat and ingenuity—with an iron fist, brooking opposition from no one. His enforcer, Harry Bennett, was an ex-navy boxer who knew how to break heads and who, at Ford's insistence, operated a network of informers throughout the Ford plant. All his life Henry Ford lived in fear of enemies, real and imaginary. At various times he imagined that "international Jews," the Catholic Church and, particularly, the Catholic DuPonts were out to get him. Ford's home at Fairlane, his secluded 1,369-acre estate at Dearborn, was honeycombed with tunnels through which he could escape or where he could hide in the event of danger. And he rarely traveled anywhere without packing a revolver.

Yet paranoid and bigoted as he was, Henry Ford remains a giant of the twentieth century, an ambiguous, flaky, Janus-like figure who, to the dismay of his numerous biographers, simply cannot be pinned down or pigeonholed. Stubborn and cantankerous, he had opinions, mostly ill-informed, on every conceivable subject. "If you study the history of almost any criminal," he once stated, "you will find that he is an inveterate cigarette smoker." He made a fetish of eating raw carrots and soybeans. He was a teetotaler who fully supported Prohibition. And he had his own private religion, believing strongly in reincarnation. As "proof" he would cite this example: "When the automobile was new and one of them came down the road, a chicken would run straight for home—and usually get killed. But today when a car comes along, a chicken will run for the nearest side of the road. That chicken has been hit in the ass in a previous life."

Coming from a nineteenth-century farm in the Middle West, Henry Ford believed in the small-family enterprise, distrusted Wall Street and the world of corporate finance. Many ordinary people who identified with his outspoken dislike of the eastern Establishment wanted him to run for President of the United States. And for a time he was sorely tempted. In fact, in the summer of 1923 he published an article in *Collier's* entitled "If I Were President." One public opinion poll at the time showed him a leading favorite for the Democratic nomination. But after a talk with Calvin Coolidge, then filling the unexpired term of Warren G. Harding, Ford withdrew and announced his support of the even less articulate Republican.

One reason for Ford's popularity was his seeming "folksiness." He was not given to putting on the airs of a *nouveau riche*. Though a billionaire, he couldn't have cared less about high society. He did not hobnob with the superwealthy. In fact, he distrusted almost anyone who was unable to work with his hands. Once he did visit Morgan partner E. T. Stotesbury at his hundred-and-forty-five-room, fourteen-elevator home in Philadelphia. "The Stotesburys are charming," he said afterward. "It's a great experience to see how the rich live." Dirt farmers would write to him as if he were a country cousin. One biographer has estimated that over a twenty-year period he received at least two thousand letters a day on almost every topic. Though most were serious, some were funny indeed. A woman from Georgia wrote: "Boozy girls are hauled about by drunken men screaming with laughter over pinches by promiscuous hands on any part of their bodies. Now Henry, I want you to do something about all this."

Significantly, the last letter Bartolomeo Vanzetti wrote before going to the electric chair went to Henry Ford thanking him for his efforts on behalf of the anarchists Sacco and Vanzetti. "Just this morning," wrote Vanzetti, "I accidentally learned that you had asked or suggested the commutation of our death-sentence to life imprisonment so as to give us an opportunity of presenting eventual new discovered evidence.... I am sure a new trial would vindicate my innocence; this is the only reason why I would prefer commutation to my execution... consider me as very grateful to you for your request or suggestion in our case—also for my family."

Outspokenly antiwar, Ford fulminated against capitalist "warmongers" like any Populist or Socialist agitator. And although he was probably the richest capitalist in the United States, he told the *Detroit News:* "Do you want to know the cause of war? It is capitalism, greed, the dirty hunger for dollars. Take away the capitalist and you will sweep war from the earth." On December 4, 1915, during World War I, he chartered the *Oscar II* to transport him and a group of pacifists to Europe in order "to get the boys out of the trenches by Christmas." The ignominious failure of the "Peace Ship" brought Ford home sickened, humiliated and disillusioned. But he continued to speak out against war, telling the radical journalist John Reed, whose *Ten Days That Shook the World* later glorified the Bolshevik Revolution, that flags were "silly rallying points" for "crooked politicians" and profiteers. Once the war was over, he pledged, he would haul down the American flag from his factory and raise instead a "Flag of All Nations" which he would have designed. Moreover, he said, should the U.S. enter the war, he would burn down his plant rather than manufacture one piece of military equipment. But he was to forget that resolve when the U.S. entered the conflict. In fact, he made another huge fortune on war contracts.

Meanwhile, Ford was involved in a million-dollar defamation suit against the *Chicago Tribune,* which, in a 1916 editorial, had referred to the auto magnate as "an ignorant idealist" and "an anarchistic enemy of the nation." The *Tribune* had taken umbrage at Ford's opposition to the government's mobilization of the National Guard for duty along the troubled Mexican border. Three years later the case finally came to trial in the tiny county seat of Mount Clemens, Michigan. To prove that Ford was indeed "an ignorant idealist," the *Tribune's* lawyers hammered away at his intellectual capacity, knowledge of history and comprehension of current events. And what was developed by Ford's replies was indeed startling. Asked to identify Benedict Arnold, Ford said he was a "writer." The American Revolution, he thought, had taken place in 1812. And he didn't have the slightest idea of what the Monroe Doctrine was all about. Nevertheless the jury found the newspaper guilty of libel and fined it six cents. Both sides claimed victory and vindication.

For Henry Ford it had been a humiliating experience. He had been laughed at in the courtroom. And newspapers across the land commented on his lack of erudition. The *New York Tribune* concluded that Ford was "deliciously naive and preposterous" and *The New York Times* observed, "He has not received a pass degree." In Iowa, the *Sioux City Journal* claimed Ford was "a man with a vision distorted and limited by his lack of information." In 1918 Ford ran an unsuccessful race for the U.S. Senate as the Democratic candidate. *The New York Times* editorialized that Ford's election "would create a vacancy both in the Senate and in the automobile business." Reminded during that 1918 campaign of a previous boast that he had rarely bothered to vote, Ford claimed that in 1884, at the age of twenty-one, he had indeed voted, marking his ballot for President Garfield. The problem was that Garfield had been assassinated three years earlier.

An infuriated Ford, seeking to strike back at his critics, attempted to do so through the pages of the weekly Dearborn *Independent*, which he had converted to the *Ford International Weekly*, dedicated to "social justice" and opposed to "Wall Street" and capitalists.

"Why, you're a capitalist," aide Harry Bennett told him.

"No, I'm not, either," Ford insisted.

By the standards of the time, Henry Ford had been a progressive and benevolent employer; his policy on racial discrimination was well ahead of its time. On his death the *Journal of Negro History* described him as "a great benefactor of the Negro race, probably the greatest that ever lived . . . When other manufacturers restricted Negro workers to the drudgery of the shops or to the brush and the broom around the plants, Ford employed Negroes to do skilled labor and put them on the production line alongside the white workers. . . . Henry Ford never posed as any special friend of any race; but he gave Negroes along with others the chance to help themselves, and in so doing he met the highest test of being a friend of man."

Also adding to his progressive image was the fact that in 1914 he had established an unheard-of $5-a-day wage and a profit-sharing scheme in his plant. Ford's argument was that good pay makes good workers; and well-paid workers could buy more cars. Ford's seeming altruism wasn't greeted happily in all quarters. The publisher of *The New York Times,* for example, blew up. "He's crazy, isn't he? Don't you think he's crazy?" And Edward L. Doheny, the oil tycoon who later came to grief in the Teapot Dome scandal, branded Ford a "Bolshevist." All of which only confirmed Ford's impression that "powerful enemies" who resented his "strong stand against exploitation of labor for the benefit of speculative capitalism" were seeking to discredit him and his enlightened policies.

Among those "powerful enemies" were the Jews, who, Ford had come to believe, dominated both international banking and revolutionary movements. In fact, Ford thought the Jews were so powerful that Catholics were their tools. To obtain material backing up his thesis, Ford hired a pack of detectives. Communicating in code and identified by numbers such as 101X, the sleuths hung around synagogues and infiltrated Jewish organizations looking for Jewish "secrets." So convinced was Ford that the Jews were behind President Lincoln's assassination that he spent a small fortune seeking to discover John Wilkes Booth's body in order to prove his theory. Just as weird was Ford's discovery of *The Protocols of the Learned Elders of Zion,* a notorious forgery purporting to reveal the inside facts of worldwide conspiracy for Jewish conquest. Portions of this document, which had in fact been used to foment pogroms in czarist Russia, were published in the Dearborn *Independent,* as were other articles, over a period of seven years, excoriating "the chosen people" for virtually every misfortune ever experienced by man.

Remarkably, Henry Ford could not understand why his Jewish friends were turning against him. After all, he was not against them personally; he was only against evil "international" types. With his typically inconsistent outlook, Ford used as the chief architect of many of his plants Albert Kahn, who was Jewish; and he was absolutely dismayed when a prominent Detroit rabbi whom he admired returned a gift of a brand-new Model T. He was flabbergasted when protest marches and even riots occurred outside Ford showrooms where the *Independent* was on display. A Jewish boycott cut into Ford's sales.

Still Ford refused to relax his anti-Semitism, even when Hearst editor Arthur Brisbane, an old friend, appealed to Ford to cut out the nonsense. The problem with Brisbane, the *Independent* countered, was that he "has not studied the [Jewish] Question." And when 121 prominent non-Jewish Americans, including two former Presidents, William Howard Taft and Woodrow Wilson, also protested to Ford, he kept on running the articles, contending that there was nothing in them that could conceivably hurt anyone.

In 1926, Ford was slapped with two libel suits brought about by his anti-Semitic accusations. The last thing he wanted was to go into court and repeat his *Chicago Tribune* experience. And the last thing his company needed was a new flare-up over Ford's anti-Semitism. His son, Edsel, among others, urged a settlement. Finally Ford agreed to a public apology:

> Trusted friends with whom I have conferred recently have assured me in all sincerity that in their opinion the character of the charges and insinuations made against the Jews, both individually and collectively, contained in many of the articles which have been circulated periodically in the Dearborn *Independent* and have been reprinted in the pamphlets mentioned, justifies the righteous indignation entertained by Jews everywhere toward me because of the mental anguish occasioned by the unprovoked reflections made upon them. . . . I deem it to be my duty as an honorable man to make amends for the wrong done to the Jews as fellow-men and brothers, by asking their forgiveness for the harm I have unintentionally committed, by retracting so far as lies within my power the offensive charges laid at their door by these publications, and by giving them the unqualified assurance that henceforth they may look to me for friendship and goodwill.

The apology was accepted, and the fiction spread that somehow Ford's anti-Semitism had been imposed upon him by aides who had fed him false information. That was true, too, but the fact remains that the motor magnate never got around to sacking those underlings. And as the Richmond *Times-Dispatch* noted, "In denying knowledge of the anti-Semitic policy, he has set himself up as a target for ridicule." His old editorial adversary, the *Chicago Tribune,* observed, "Mr. Ford advances an empty head to explain his cold feet." Nevertheless, Jewish leaders viewed Ford's recantation as a major victory.

But was it really? In 1938, on the occasion of his seventy-fifth birthday, Henry Ford received the Grand Cross of the German Eagle from the Nazi vice-consul. Deluged with protests, Ford told reporters that his acceptance of the second-highest German decoration did not "involve any sympathy on my part with Nazism." Moreover, he insisted, he felt that stories about Nazi persecution of the Jews had been vastly exaggerated.

Despite his highly publicized apology, Ford was still perceived as being anti-Semitic. Ford told of a meeting he had with President Roosevelt: "He took up five minutes telling me of his ancestry. He wanted to prove to me that he had no Jewish blood." And certain Republican political fund-raisers felt they could do well with the old man by reciting the names of Jews who surrounded FDR, their Jewishness often fictionalized. In fact, according to Harry Bennett, Wendell Willkie, running for President in 1940, tried this tactic in seeking a $500,000 contribution from Ford. In time Ford became wise to the gambit. When told about the "Jews around Roosevelt," Ford pulled a surprise. "Well," he said, "that's all right. If 'they' weren't around Roosevelt to handle the money, this country would go broke in a hurry."

Ford's antagonism toward the Jews did not sit too well with his only son. For one thing, his father's crude anti-Semitism offended Edsel as being preposterous. Moreover, it was bad for business. The feeling was that many Jews were refusing to buy Ford products.

Toward labor old Henry had been more ambivalent. By setting the $5-a-day wage, he felt he was sharing his profits with the workers. And later on, in the twenties, he led the way in approving a five-day workweek, a move that led the president of the National Association of Manufacturers to assert, "Ford may try to amend the Decalogue, but any general acceptance of the five-day week means a surrender to easy and loose living." And in two depression years he even raised salaries when his rivals were cutting them. Yet the rise of the unions caused him such personal grief that he authorized head-cracking when organizers sought to storm his industrial fortress. Revealing a good deal of his personal philosophy, he said: "The average employee in the average industry is not ready for participation in management. And industry at this stage of our development must be more or less of a friendly autocracy."

And autocratic he most certainly was—even with his only son. Edsel was totally unlike his father, and this infuriated old Henry. He was amiable and self-effacing, in contrast to the rambunctious, abrasive old man. Though his father had prevented him from going to college, Edsel was intellectually inclined and an omnivorous reader. This, too, infuriated old Henry, who never read books because, he claimed, "books muddle me." Edsel's views on the future of the car market were different too. The old man believed that engineering was the key, but his son felt that styling would be paramount. And the son proved to be right.

The father desperately sought to dominate the son. And Edsel sought to fight back—quietly. One way was to avoid living near the old man's Dearborn estate. Instead, after he married Eleanor Clay in 1916, he built a home across town in Grosse Pointe, a Detroit suburb where the city's "aristocracy" lived. Old Henry did not like Edsel's neighbors, many of whom worked for the hated rival General Motors Corporation. And he kept his son under surveillance not only at the plant but even in his home. He arranged, for instance, to bribe Edsel's servants for information. Once, when Edsel was out of town, Harry Bennett drove Henry out to his son's estate on Lake St. Clair, where, uninvited, he barged in and destroyed a stock of whiskey and champagne.

Edsel found it impossible to reason with his father. Even though old Henry had named Edsel president of the company when he was twenty-six, he made life miserable for his son, countermanding his orders and rehiring men Edsel had dismissed. Once Edsel, over his father's objections, decided to build a row of coke ovens. Old Henry told Bennett, "Harry, as soon as Edsel gets those ovens built, I'm going to tear them down." And Henry did precisely that.

When Edsel protested the close surveillance of employees—every fourth man on the assembly line was said to be an informer—his father gradually withdrew from him, both professionally and personally, and gave increasing powers and recognition to his devious little chief of "internal security," Harry Bennett. And according to Bennett, it was old Henry's inordinate fear of robbers and kidnappers that led the company to employ thousands of former criminals. Thus, by retaining lines of communication to the underworld, Bennett said he could be kept informed of any plots against Ford or the company. To this end he turned over the plant's fruit-supply concession to Chester LaMare, reputed boss of Detroit's underworld, defending the arrangement as an experiment in rehabilitation. Some years later LaMare was slain in a typical gangland execution.

Then there was the time old Henry, who loved children, ordered Bennett to recover a kidnapped child. Before anything could be done, the father paid $20,000 and the child was returned. Some hoodlum acquaintances of Bennett got the ransom back by torturing the kidnapper. The kidnapper then waylaid Bennett and shot him in the leg. Bennett, who asked the police not to interfere, observed offhandedly, "The gunman was later shot and killed on a Detroit street—in some gang feud, I suppose."

Came the Depression, and Bennett—with old Henry's full approval—tightened his grip on the company. He ruled with fear, forbidding all conversations between workers in the factory, seeking to suppress all talk of unions. "Mister Ford"—as he was always addressed—was determined never to recognize any union, thundering, "I have never bargained with my men. I have always bargained for them." And Mister Ford's solution for the economic crisis that had left sixteen million unemployed across the land was for people to leave the cities and go back to the farms. As the bread lines lengthened, Ford said that the Depression was "wholesome" and that "these are the best times we ever had." The populist millionaire was not prepared for the avalanche of criticism that greeted him. No longer were his admirers urging him to run for President. In fact, the number of his admirers sharply decreased. One letter he received in Dearborn had this to say: "Stick to your pistons and gear grease. As a prophet of the Lord you never would have got out of old Egypt land."

As the Depression deepened, the Ford company was displaced as the world's biggest auto maker by General Motors, which created better styling (at a higher price) and believed in corporate decentralization instead of Ford's autocratic one-man rule. Ford's business losses were extraordinary. On the eve of Pearl Harbor, production was half as high as the 1929 record of 1,870,000 vehicles, and profits had been practically nil for a decade. Ironically, there were Depression years when the Rouge plant was in full operation only because of work for the Soviet Union. Despite the old man's abhorrence of communism, his company built thousands of tractors for shipment to the U.S.S.R. Besides that, Ford authorized the training of hundreds of Soviet technicians in Ford methods of production. When, during World War II, he sent greetings to Joseph Stalin through an intermediary, the Soviet dictator responded: "Thank you. I am surprised at this, but pleased because I consider Mr. Ford one of the world's greatest industrialists. Will you please give him my best regards and may God preserve him." For the atheistic Stalin to invoke the deity in Ford's behalf was even more astounding.

World War II saved the company. This despite the fact that Ford—true to his pacifist convictions—had spoken out against the war in Europe as evil. And while he was willing to build aircraft engines for U.S. defense, he at first refused to build them for the embattled British. All of which was forgotten when Pearl Harbor was attacked. The Ford Motor Company then went all out in support of the war. Though theoretically Henry Ford had handed the business over to his son Edsel, he was still the real boss, keeping close watch on the great assembly lines. By this time, however, the United Automobile

Workers was succeeding in organizing Ford workers. Rather than capitulate to the hated union, old Henry threatened to shut down the plant. Edsel, however, was opposed to his father's tantrum. And he convinced his mother, Clara, to step in and argue with her husband of fifty-three years. Mrs. Ford, who had had enough of her husband's stubbornness, went so far as to threaten to leave him if he did not sign with the union. For one of the few times in his life, Henry Ford listened to reason.

Old Henry, however, never forgave his son for acting against his deeply ingrained prejudices. And Edsel, by now ailing, knew that his father thought more of brass-knuckled Harry Bennett, who always followed orders, than he did of his own son. And that hurt the extraordinarily sensitive Edsel more than he cared to admit. For, though nominally the leadership of the Ford Motor Company rested with Edsel, it was Bennett who was viewed as the more powerful by the other executives. And old Henry, the real boss, wanted it that way. On one occasion Edsel talked seriously about resigning the presidency of the company. But with his sons Henry II and Benson in the armed forces, that would have left Bennett in complete control. Edsel decided to remain, realizing he was the only one in the company who could act as a brake against his father and Harry Bennett.

In May 1943, Edsel Ford died of stomach cancer and undulant fever, the latter apparently contracted from drinking unpasteurized milk from his father's farm. It was also said that Henry Ford's only son died of a broken heart. His physical strength had been sapped by continual bickering with his father and Bennett. Edsel Ford's death—he was only forty-nine—sent a wave of sorrow throughout the automobile world, for he was loved and respected by most of those who knew him. His passing also caused concern among those troubled about the future of the company. Bennett, however, when asked whether he would attend the funeral, told Henry Ford he would not. He would not be that hypocritical. He knew, he said, that Edsel "despised me" and the "honest thing to do was to stay away."

The day before Edsel's funeral, Henry Ford reassumed the presidency, even though he was nearly eighty and had had two strokes that left him with large mental gaps. From time to time he had had hallucinations and held conversations with people who had long been dead. The Ford family was worried, as was the Roosevelt administration. The war had reached a crisis stage, and Washington had no intention of allowing the company's vast production facilities, so vital to the war effort, to be crippled. For a time there was talk of seizing the company or putting it under the aegis of the Studebaker Corporation. But the family and the government put their hopes on Henry Ford II, then not quite twenty-six years of age.

In the last two years of his life, after he was forced to hand over control of the company to his grandson, old Henry appeared to have lost his zest for life. He was continually haunted by memories of his conflicts with Edsel. Only his belief in reincarnation sustained him. "Well, Harry," he once told Bennett, "you know, my belief—Edsel really isn't dead." He just couldn't stay away from the subject. "Do you honestly think I was ever cruel to Edsel?" he asked Bennett.

"Well, cruel, no; but unfair, yes," replied Bennett. "If that had been me, I'd have got mad."

The old man now rarely appeared to be mad about anything. According to Bennett, Edsel's death had worked a profound change in Mister Ford. He was no longer anti-Semitic, anti-Catholic or anti-anything. He was just a tired old man who wanted to live in peace. An attack of indigestion almost finished him off. He puttered around his Georgia plantation and Greenfield Village, the magnificent collection of Americana that he had financed. On his last day at his Dearborn estate, Fairlane, old Henry seemed to have improved considerably. He asked his chauffeur to drive him around the Rouge plant and Dearborn. And then, strangely, he asked to be driven to the family's small cemetery on Joy Road.

"Well," he told his chauffeur, "this is where they're going to bury me when I die. In among the rest of my folks."

Then back to Fairlane. The river had overflowed its banks and had flooded the powerhouse. His big house was without electricity or telephone service, heated only by open fires. At about nine o'clock Henry Ford went to bed. Two hours later Clara Ford heard her husband's voice. She roused the chauffeur and had him drive to a nearby phone to call for the doctor. But by the time the doctor arrived, Henry Ford was gone. He had

died as he had entered the world eighty-three years before—
by the light of old-fashioned kerosene lamps and flickering
candles.

4

TAKEOVER

As BENSON FORD, JR., NOW RECALLS IT, THERE WAS VERY little discussion in the family about Henry Ford I. "To us he was almost a historical figure, someone we would occasionally read about but rarely talk about." Young Ben, who was born in 1949, two years after his great-grandfather's death, did seek to familiarize himself with the legacy. And he did so by visiting Greenfield Village, where many Ford artifacts were collected for exhibition. What particularly delighted Benson as a lad were photographs showing his great-grandfather's friendship with such people as Thomas Alva Edison and George Washington Carver. Carver of course was the famous black scientist who had discovered hundreds of useful substances in the peanut as well as in the sweet potato. Both Carver and Ford shared their eccentricities in food, delighting in partaking of such delicacies as dandelion and grass sandwiches.

One of the founder's eccentricities that continued to embarrass the family, even after his death, was his anti-Semitism. "We knew, of course, that my great-grandfather had apologized to the Jewish people," says Benson Ford, Jr. "But we had also heard that the apology was not all that convincing. There were jokes in the family that the reason why Cadillacs were outselling Lincolns was because Jewish people were refusing to buy Ford products."

Following Ford's death, the family sought to undo the damage wrought by the old man's provocative views. His grandsons Henry and Benson participated in various community enterprises aimed at combating religious prejudice. Eventually the anti-Semitic issue was laid to rest, as far as the family was concerned. As recently as May 1980, Henry Ford II was given the Anti-Defamation League American Heritage award, with many notable speakers paying tribute to his "genius in building America," including his contribution to the Anti-Defamation League's ideal of seeking "to end the defamation of the Jewish people and to secure justice and fair treatment for all citizens alike." Ford, who made no reference to his grandfather in his remarks, was deeply appreciative.

By 1980, of course, Henry II was no longer playing a major role in the company his grandfather had founded. A year before, knowing that dire times were ahead, he had left its day-to-day operations in the hands of Philip Caldwell. Within months the company was forced to deal with its worst crisis since the calamitous years shortly after World War II. Faced with ever-rising gasoline prices, Americans were no longer interested in LTDs, Continentals, Thunderbirds and other Ford gas guzzlers. So these big cars sat rusting in dealers' lots. Ford's North American automobile division lost at least half a billion dollars in the first quarter of 1980 alone.

"The last part of the 1970s has been tough from a product standpoint," said Henry II, in an interview with *Newsweek*, April 28, 1980. "And boy, the '80s are going to be *really* tough!"

Who was to blame? Was it the government for holding down

gasoline prices, thus creating a demand for big cars, which ended with price rises and gas shortages? Now the demand was for small, fuel-efficient vehicles, and this the Ford company was not immediately prepared to meet. The reason simply was a decision on the part of Henry Ford not to down-size as quickly as General Motors. This was in 1975, when Lee Iacocca, then the company president, had proposed the financing of a small, front-wheel-drive car. Henry vetoed the idea, maintaining it was too risky a financial gamble. "I said it's wrong," Iacocca later recalled. "We were drowning in cash. It was the greatest tactical error in automotive history. They get an F for management."

By "they," of course, Lee Iacocca meant his old boss Henry Ford II. But even Henry has conceded he made a serious mistake in misreading the market. It was perhaps an understandable, though expensive, error. After all, memories of the 1973–74 Arab oil embargo had generally faded and people were buying big cars. Nevertheless, it had been primarily Henry's mistake, and he was forced to live with it. His resolution of the problem was simple. He dumped the ensuing mess in the lap of Phil Caldwell, who succeeded him as chairman. Still, as a major shareholder and as chairman of the finance committee, Ford maintained an inordinate voice in the affairs of the company, though his vantage point was no longer the twelfth floor of the Ford Administration Building—Dearborn's "Glass House"—but a sumptuous suite in the sprawling Renaissance Center on Detroit's riverfront.

The heir to a classic American industrial fortune, Ford was in many ways unlike the company's founder, his late grandfather. The original Henry was a better mechanic than anyone else around; his grandson was no mechanic at all. And the feeling persists in Detroit that, unlike his grandfather, HFII (the monogram on his shirts) never really cared all that much about automobiles and could have done just as well making something else. Also, unlike his grandfather, Henry II preferred the good life of an international jet-setter, partying in the far corners of the world, drinking to excess and, as he once put it, "fooling around with the broads." In only one way, according to a former Ford Motor sales manager, was he the exact image of his grandfather. "The only thing to understand about Henry and the old man," said John Davis, "is their utter inconsistency. Complete chameleons, both of them."

Over the years, Henry II's antics often attracted the prying eyes of the press. He became a favorite subject of gossip columnists. But in more recent times, the thought of an intensive probing into his life, both private and professional, disturbed him. He couldn't care less about what people thought of him, he told Barbara Walters in a 1980 interview. Which is why, he said, "I've destroyed as much of my paperwork as I possibly have so that nobody will ever know anything about me, or as little as possible."

His grandfather had also remained closemouthed about his personal life. But the founder of the family fortune never destroyed anything. In 1953, as part of the company's fiftieth anniversary celebration, his private papers were opened to the public. It appeared that Henry Ford I had saved almost everything. In dusty shoe boxes, old desks, bureaus and closets, without system or order, were old rent receipts, grocery bills, letters from crackpots and U.S. Presidents, train tickets, and a vial supposedly containing Thomas Edison's dying breath. Voluminous files were discovered too, containing the Ford Motor Company's records over the years, including the first tiny payroll. Mixed in with all this were thousands of mostly unpublished photographs. All of this material was carefully assembled by archivists for the benefit of scholars and authors. Approval for this monumental task was given by the founder's heirs, including Henry Ford II.

But Henry II has not been as willing to cooperate with scholars and journalists as far as his own life is concerned.

"Why not?" asked Barbara Walters.

"I don't know. It's just an attitude of mine."

"No diaries, no books, no papers?"

"No diaries, no books, no papers, no nothing."

"Professionally, as well as personally?"

"That's right," Ford replied. "I...I...I've always thought—and I found out how stupid I was—that I could separate my private life from my business life. And I found out a long time ago I couldn't do that, so now I want to make sure that nobody knows anything about me except what's in the public domain. They'll never find anything about me from going through my files."

Walters, who seemed perplexed, changed the subject. "Many people," she said, "are wondering why you are divesting yourself of some of your beautiful possessions, paintings and other lovely things. And also why are you selling Ford stock?"

"Well, I would tell them it's none of their business."

It hasn't always been that way. There was a time when Henry Ford II courted attention. A vast public-relations machine kept the public aware of his comings and goings, his speeches and his philanthropic activities. But as time went on he began to change his mind about publicity. Even friendly writers were bluntly informed he wasn't interested in talking to them. He couldn't care less about setting the record straight on anything, he insisted. All he wanted was to be left alone. His attitude was expressed to Booton Herndon, author of an adulatory biography, some years ago. During a luncheon interview, Ford announced he had written a "whatchamacallem— a preface" and handed it to Herndon, who published it as a passage in the book. It read: "I'm not interested in this damn book. I'm only cooperating because I've been asked to. I don't care if anybody reads it or not. [Signed] Henry Ford II."

Henry II was born in Detroit on September 4, 1917, the first of the four children of Edsel and Eleanor (Clay) Ford. It is recorded that at the age of three he held the torch that lit the blast furnace at the new River Rouge plant. A photograph of the occasion shows a chubby youngster in the arms of his derby-wearing grandfather. Wearing a beaver hat and a little fur coat, young Henry seemed somewhat apprehensive as a foreman, standing nearby, led a lusty cheer from assembled workingmen. But rarely was he allowed to attract public attention in his early years. Fear of kidnapping kept photos of the Ford children out of the newspapers, and they were constantly guarded by husky men provided by the Ford Service Department, headed by Harry Bennett. Thus the young heir's boyhood passed in relative seclusion with his brothers and sister, Benson, William and Josephine.

During the twenties the Edsel Ford family lived in a brownstone Italian Renaissance-style house at 7930 East Jefferson Avenue in Detroit. A back lawn running down to the edge of the Detroit River provided a playground for the children. Years later the spacious grounds were purchased by the United Automobile Workers of America for the union's international headquarters.

In 1924, in spite of Ford's antiroyalist sentiments, he entertained the Prince of Wales, who was touring America, at a private reception at the Detroit Club, the fifty guests personally selected by Henry Ford, then sixty-two years old. Later there was a dinner party and dance hosted by the Edsel Fords at their East Jefferson Avenue mansion. All of Detroit society vied for invitations, the Duke of Windsor being one of the most glamorous persons ever to visit the motor city. Among those invited was Edsel's mother-in-law, Mrs. William Clay, who was so shy she refused to be presented to the prince. Instead, desiring a peek at the handsome Englishman, she hid behind a screen in the nursery when he was brought up to be introduced to the children. The excitement proved too much for Josephine, then only one year old. She got sick to her stomach. None of which fazed seven-year-old Henry, who, when asked by the prince how things were going, responded, "My sister just threw up and grandmother is hiding behind the screen."

Grandfather Ford doted on the children. All during their early years Henry would drive over to Edsel's house and almost steal them back to Fairlane. He couldn't do enough for them. He kept buying them toys fit for royalty. And he thought it imperative that they learn something about farming. Thus he personally taught them how to sow seed and make hay, providing them with elaborate miniature machinery to do the job properly. An inveterate shutterbug, Ford took numerous pictures of them in the fields doing their chores. One photograph, retrieved from the archives, shows the children in their own tiny automobiles touring the roads at Fairlane. Another is a photograph of a Santa Claus house, made of logs, which Ford had had built for them behind his mansion. It had a Santa Claus and real reindeer. As they grew older, Ford built them their own tiny steam locomotive, which they operated on rails at the Rouge plant. A photograph shows a knicker-clad Benson polishing the bell while Henry, also knicker-clad, climbs into the engine's cab.

Meanwhile, young Henry attended the old, all-boy Detroit University School (chauffeur-driven both ways), where he showed himself to be reserved, good but not outstanding in football, and no ball of fire in his studies. Nor did he show any academic flare at Hotchkiss, the select Connecticut prep school that he entered in 1933 at the age of sixteen. Books still bored him, though he was again better on the playing field than in the classroom. A course in Cicero proved too much for young Henry. He had to take it over in summer school. But his grades were generally fair and he liked Hotchkiss. (By his side at most times was a bodyguard who doubled as a swimming instructor.) When he graduated in 1936 his yearbook said of him, "You've got something there if you handle it right."

But whatever Henry II had, it most certainly was not scholastic brilliance. He entered Yale with the class of 1940, where he was known as "T," after grandfather Henry's Model T, belonged to Zeta Psi fraternity and the Book and Snake Club, meanwhile managing the Yale crew. Majoring in engineering and finding it difficult, he gave it up after a year for sociology—mainly, he said, because he found in Professor Albert Keller a teacher who "did not use highfalutin professorial language, but the people's own language." But in his senior year, just weeks before he was to graduate, Henry II handed in a ghost-written senior thesis. Unfortunately he had forgotten to remove the bill from "Rosie's," the tutoring service that had prepared the paper. Called to account, Henry dropped out of the university without receiving a diploma. (Eighteen years later, addressing the Yale Political Union, Ford began to read a prepared speech, stopped, grinned and said, "I didn't write this speech either.")

Henry's years at Old Eli were marked by another episode, which could have been more serious. On November 18, 1937, while driving through the small Connecticut town of Oxford, he struck and injured a twelve-year-old girl as she alighted from a school bus. A $25,000 suit, filed by the girl's attorney, was settled out of court by a phalanx of lawyers dispatched by the Ford Motor Company. It was not to be the first time that the power of the family enterprise would pull Henry Ford II out of a jam.

Just before he entered Yale in 1936, Henry II had met Anne McDonnell, the third of fourteen children of New York investment banker James Francis McDonnell and granddaughter of Thomas E. Murray, the inventor whose patents were topped in number only by those of his friend Thomas Edison. They met in the best tradition of the American Rich—aboard the French liner *Normandie*. Henry II had been visiting Europe with his parents and brother Benson. They had toured Ford plants in England and France, and Henry II later confessed that he was not particularly overwhelmed. But he was most definitely overwhelmed by Anne McDonnell, then seventeen, pretty and blond. Henry was all of nineteen. And he was smitten. He couldn't keep his mind off Anne. And apparently Anne couldn't keep her mind off the chunky, jolly young man from Grosse Pointe. They began to date, Henry often driving down to New York from New Haven in his elegant yellow Lincoln-Zephyr roadster. During the summers Henry would spend considerable time in Southampton, where the McDonnells had a fifty-room mansion amid fifty acres rolling down to the Atlantic. In Manhattan the McDonnells owned a three-floor, twenty-nine-room apartment on upper Fifth Avenue which contained separate kitchen facilities for the children. There too Henry was a frequent visitor.

It was at about this time that Henry II met a Harvard man named John F. Kennedy, who was seeing Anne's sister Charlotte. In fact, for a time Jack was engaged to her. But the engagement was short-lived, largely because the McDonnells disapproved of the young Bostonian. They regarded Jack as a "moral roustabout" and his father, Ambassador Joseph P. Kennedy, as a "crook and thorough bounder." Years later, when then Senator Kennedy ran into Mrs. James Francis McDonnell, he said, "Did you know I almost married your daughter?"

"Yes, I did," replied Mrs. McDonnell, "and I'm happy you didn't."

Henry Ford II was something else. The McDonnells liked him very much, considering him a "regular guy." And he delighted in their company, their informal beach suppers and songfests. Early in 1940, after three years of courtship, Anne and Henry announced their engagement. There was one fly in the ointment, however. Anne was a Roman Catholic while Henry was raised a Methodist, though he professed no religion. The problem was resolved when Henry agreed to accept religious instruction and embrace the Catholic faith. There had been some minor objections from Henry's father, but Edsel soon overcame his qualms. Henry Ford I proved more intransigent, the Church of Rome long being one of his bugbears. For a time, it was said, old Henry even toyed with the idea of disinheriting his grandson. But he too, in time, became reconciled, though never entirely.

No sooner had the engagement been announced than newspapers across the country heralded the approaching marriage as "the wedding of the century." The forthcoming nuptials, uniting two of the nation's wealthiest families, provided entertainment and a welcome relief for Americans fearful they soon would be drawn into the war that had broken out in Europe the previous summer. Every detail, including those concerning the religious conversion of young Ford, was appropriately recorded. And no less a personage than Monsignor (later Bishop) Fulton J. Sheen gave him instruction. Sheen, the proselytizing professor of fundamental theology at the Catholic University of America, was famed for having converted columnist Heywood Broun, among other celebrities, to Catholicism. On the morning of July 13, 1940, the wedding day, Henry Ford II was baptized by the monsignor in the private chapel on the McDonnell estate at Southampton.

Three days before the ceremony the Edsel Fords sailed into Southampton aboard their yacht, the *Onika*—Hawaiian for "Kiss me quick"—joining in the prewedding gaiety honoring their son and his fiancée. The senior Henry Fords arrived in their private railroad car, the *Fairlane,* and stayed on the *Onika,* which was anchored at the yacht club. For a time it had been feared that old Henry would not attend. But a few sharp words from his wife had convinced him to do otherwise. And so here he was, smiling, jovial and gracious, posing for picture after picture with his grandson's beautiful bride, finally leading her onto the dance floor at the wedding reception. The photogra-

phers even recorded the elder Ford in deep conversation with
Monsignor Sheen. It was reported that the cleric had sought to
discuss theology with the famous Methodist, who put him off
with an oblique but cordial observation. "Well, now," he said,
"you've got the best religion in the world," after which he
changed the subject.

The wedding, at the Church of the Sacret Hearts of Jesus
and Mary, a gray stone edifice on Hill Street in Southampton,
went off without a hitch. Among the bridal attendants were the
sister of the bridegroom, Josephine Ford, and the sister of a
future President of the United States, Kathleen Kennedy, who
later became the Marchioness of Hartington and died in a plane
crash in 1948. Both of Henry's brothers played roles at the
wedding. Benson was the best man and fifteen-year-old William was one of the ushers. Among the guests were many of
Southampton's summer residents, all of them very rich and
very social. The automobile business was represented by the
Harvey Firestones and the William S. Knudsens. Also there
were the Alfred E. Smiths. The arrival of the "happy warrior"
and former Democratic presidential candidate set off cheers
from the large crowd in the street. Slipping into the church
was a future President of the United States, John F. Kennedy,
then of course known only as a son of the U.S. Ambassador
to the Court of St. James's. Not only was every one of the
church's five hundred seats occupied, but there were many
standees in the back and side aisles.

At noon Monsignor Sheen celebrated the nuptial mass, which
was distinguished by the apostolic blessing of Pope Pius XII
for the bride and groom. After the service came the reception,
held in the living room of the McDonnell mansion overlooking
the ocean. A buffet was served in a large pavilion that had
been erected for the occasion. Wedding gifts were displayed
in two white satin-decked rooms. Sixteen armed guards were
on hand to protect the treasures, which included jewelry, silver
and crystal of all sorts, worth at least a million dollars.

When the newlyweds departed for a two-month wedding
trip to Hawaii, where the Edsel Fords had also honeymooned,
a carload of gifts remained unopened. A special gift the bride
was most anxious to see awaited her upon her arrival in Grosse

Pointe that September—a handsome Georgian house on Provencal Road, a private street near Lake St. Clair, the gift of the Edsel Fords. The Fords had also transferred to their son 25,000 shares of Ford Motor Company stock, "in recognition," wrote Edsel, "of the fact that you are finishing your college career this month, and after being married will join the Ford Motor Company as your future business, and also because of the fact that you are at the present time a Director of the Company." Of course Henry II had finished his college career, but in a somewhat awkward manner, hanging around, however, long enough to handle arrangements for the Yale-Harvard race. Later he told friends that if he had known what his "destiny" was going to be, he would never have gone to college, considering it largely a waste of time.

His "destiny" of course was the Ford Motor Company. For several months, after he returned from his honeymoon, Henry worked in the Rouge plant with his younger brother Benson. Benson, then twenty-one, had gone to Princeton. Like his older brother, Benson did not take easily to scholastic pursuits. He tried such subjects as Spanish, French and geology. "I signed for courses I thought would be easiest," he said later, "but I miscalculated—they were tough. Still, I wasn't worried. I figured I could always get a job at Ford." In September 1940, with his father's permission, Benson dropped out of Princeton. He could always get a job at Ford; and he did.

Both brothers worked as grease monkeys in the dynamometer rooms and experimental shops. Neither, according to chief engineer Laurence Sheldrick, showed any great mechanical aptitude, but they "didn't pull any punches about getting their hands dirty . . . and their clothes all messed up." They started work at 7:00 A.M. and quit at 4:00 P.M., earning the going rate. And their father loved it. Aware of his sons' academic limitations, Edsel Ford was eager for them to get involved in company activities. He himself had never gone to college; his father didn't believe in it. After a while Edsel arranged for Henry and Benson to join the crew experimenting with a new vehicle, requested by the army and called the jeep. When the first model was completed, Sheldrick took Edsel to watch the tests. Sheldrick also arranged for Henry and Benson to drive the new

vehicle out of a patch of tall grass and underbrush right up to
their dad. "That was the one time that I saw Edsel when he
was thoroughly enjoying himself," said Sheldrick. "He was
awfully proud of his boys."

Early in 1941 Benson became engaged to Edith Mc-
Naughton, daughter of Lynn McNaughton, a onetime sales
manager of G.M.'s Cadillac division. Ben had met "Edie" in
kindergarten at Detroit's exclusive Liggett School. When he
moved on to Detroit University School, Edie attended the nearby
Country Day School. And when he went east for further school-
ing, winding up in Princeton in 1938, Edie began to attend
Miss Finch's School in Manhattan. Three years later Ben proposed to Edie on the deck of his father's houseboat in Hobe
Sound, Florida. They were married on July 9, 1941. The marriage, at Christ Church in Grosse Pointe, five months before
Pearl Harbor, marked one of the last social appearances of his
father. Even then, friends who knew Edsel well were concerned
about his health and saw in his drawn countenance evidence
of impending illness.

Meanwhile, both Henry and Benson were ordered to report
to their draft boards. Their grandfather was beside himself. He
was opposed to the war in Europe and argued against those
who favored U.S. involvement. There was nothing new about
Henry Ford's position. Over two decades before, he had incurred the displeasure of prowar elements, who had publicly
labeled him a "Hun-lover." But he had done something else
that was infuriating. He had used his clout on all levels, including the White House, to keep Edsel from service in World
War I, even though his son, then twenty-four, was willing to
enlist. Ford had told friends that had Edsel been drafted, "certain interests" that disliked "the Ford system" would "have seen
to it" that his son would never return. News that Edsel had
been exempted, ostensibly because he was a key man in a war
industry, set off a wave of bitter criticism. Republican Congressman Nicholas Longworth of Ohio, who was married to
Theodore Roosevelt's daughter Alice, declared that of the seven
people in the world who were certain to go through the war
unscathed, six were sons of the kaiser and the seventh was
Edsel Ford. One Michigan newspaper nominated Edsel as the

leader of the "office-chair cavalry," while another declared, "All his life he will be singled out as a slacker and a coward."

And all his life Edsel Ford did live under that cloud. Which was why, despite the qualms of his father, he insisted that his sons should not ask for deferment. When it looked as if he were about to be drafted into the army, young Henry enlisted in the navy. Commissioned an ensign, he was assigned, not inconveniently, to the Great Lakes Naval Training Station in Chicago. Meanwhile his brother Benson was drafted, after being rejected twice because of near blindness in his left eye. "They were getting to the bottom of the barrel," he said later, "and they took me because I could see thunder and hear lightning." After receiving his basic training at Selfridge Field, near Detroit, he entered Officers Training School and came out a second lieutenant in the air force. When his father died in 1943 he was assigned to Detroit, where his job was to swear in inductees.

At Great Lakes, Henry II at first was assigned to instruct enlisted men in mathematics. But he soon was reassigned as assistant to the director of the training office of the Ninth Naval District, in which capacity he helped establish and equip schools under the naval training program. For the first time in his life young Ford felt he was really on his own. No longer did he live the protected existence of his youth, constantly watched by guards and servants because of his grandfather's fear of kidnappers. Once, when Harry Bennett began making inquiries as to whether he needed anything, young Henry got angry, accusing him of keeping track of his movements as in days of old. Intervening, Edsel Ford wired Bennett from Florida, asking him to please leave his son alone. Old Henry's reaction was, "Now, don't you do another damn thing for him."

Young Henry had been transferred to duty at a navy school in Dearborn when his father died in the spring of 1943. Edsel's death posed a dilemma for Washington, for he had been a steadying influence in a company overrun by crackpots, ex-convicts and suspected Nazi subversives. Edsel had worked closely with the Pentagon in producing a considerable amount of the military equipment, including much needed planes, which were being used in the war effort, then reaching its crescendo.

Still ahead was the invasion of Europe, while, in the Pacific, Allied forces were beginning to close in on the Japanese empire. And though the senior Henry Ford had ostensibly resumed the presidency of the company, he was ailing and, to all intents and purposes, it was Harry Bennett who was running the gigantic enterprise.

At this juncture the administration moved swiftly. Henry Ford II was placed on the inactive list and released from the navy. But even though he had been hustled into the Ford management picture by none other than the Secretary of the Navy himself, after reportedly consulting with President Roosevelt, there was no special job waiting and nobody to report to particularly. Thus when young Henry turned up at the Rouge plant to report to work, he found that "everybody was away." "So," he later explained, "I picked myself half a desk in somebody's office. I didn't know what all the buildings were for."

That his grandfather was irate about the government's intervention in the affairs of the company he had founded was no secret. And young Henry felt the backlash. The grandfather was still incensed at "Henry's turning Roman." And he was particularly dismayed that the proud Ford name was now being associated with such organizations as the Sacred Heart Academy and Archdiocesan Council of Catholic Women. For Mrs. Henry Ford II, after giving birth to two daughters, Charlotte and Anne, was devoting much of her time to promoting Catholic good works. Old Henry came to believe that his grandson was still under the "influence" of Monsignor Sheen. Once when his grandson did something old Henry didn't like, he said to Bennett, "Don't pay any attention to what he says anymore. Someone's talking to him."

Somehow or other the rumor spread that old Henry was himself considering conversion. In fact, Walter Winchell broadcast an item to that effect on his nationwide Sunday-night radio program. Old Henry could hardly contain himself. He was talked out of suing Winchell, but for days he could hardly talk about anything else. Finally he got an idea. "How far can I go in Masonry?" he asked Bennett, who didn't know but said he would find out. Which he did. The Masons were amenable to giving Ford the thirty-third degree. It took some days to run

Ford through all the degrees, but he participated in the rituals cheerfully. Every time he would drive downtown to take some more degrees he would say, "I'm going down to take care of Winchell."

Old Henry's paranoia reached even into such areas as his grandson's friendships. One night, as was his wont, he telephoned Harry Bennett. This time he was more excited than usual. "I'll be out to pick you up first thing in the morning. I've got some startling news. I'll show you I'm right about those DuPonts!" Even after all these years the old man still had a phobia about the DuPonts' plotting to undermine the Ford Motor Company. The next morning Ford told Bennett his "startling news." Which was that his grandson had become friendly with a young man, newly arrived in Grosse Pointe, who was a DuPont!

Bennett tried to calm his boss. "I never heard Henry mention a DuPont!" he said. But Ford was not to be calmed. So Bennett said he would look into the matter. At lunch that day he did ask young Henry about his new friend. Henry admitted the friendship, adding that, whatever his grandfather thought, he intended to continue it. Needless to say, that only served to infuriate the old man even more. And there was nothing he could do about it.

And there was little he could do about young Henry's friendship with Ernest Kanzler, whom twenty years before he had ordered fired as a company executive. Kanzler was Edsel Ford's brother-in-law, his wife being Eleanor Ford's sister. Old Henry thought Kanzler a "perverse influence" on Edsel, and he sought to break up the friendship. Old Henry resented the brilliant Kanzler's dreams of bringing the company into the twentieth century. At one point Eleanor Ford went to her father-in-law weeping, trying to resolve the dispute. But old Henry would not cave in. Kanzler had to go. Kanzler's severance of direct connection with the company marked the parting of the ways between father and son. Things were never the same again between them.

And now young Henry was seeing a good deal of Kanzler, seeking "Uncle Ernie's" counsel on company matters. As he later recalled, he was "green" and "reaching for answers." And he wasn't getting much help from a grandfather who by now viewed young Henry's activities as almost beyond the pale. By now, too, young Henry had begun to make public speeches. One of them, back east, acquiesced in the government's wartime controls over the industry. The speech, which was opposed to everything his grandfather believed in, sent the old man up the wall. On Henry's return Bennett told him, in the grandfather's presence, he should not make speeches like that. Old Henry, still furious, said, "Aw, I don't care. Don't tell him anything. I don't want him to agree with me on anything."

Old Henry then did something that eventually was to cause a crisis in the family—except that no one in the family knew about it at the time. The senior Ford, in a secret codicil to his will, wrote over the company upon his death to a Bennett-dominated board of trustees. Not one of the four Ford grandchildren, let alone Henry II, was named to the board, which was supposed to control the Ford company for ten years following the old man's death. The lawyer who drew up the codicil, I. A. Capizzi, later said he had been informed that "Mr. Henry Ford was concerned that Henry Ford II would come too much under the control of Kanzler in the operation of the company and that therefore Mr. Henry Ford was interested in setting up a means whereby the operation of the company would vest in others until Henry II and the other grandchildren were old enough to manage the company themselves."

Meanwhile Henry II was trying to learn the automobile business. He later recalled:

In a way, not having a job was a good thing for me. It left me free to roam around and find out a lot of things about production that I didn't know, and it also gave me time to find out a lot of things about Bennett. When an important policy matter came up, Bennett would get into his car and disappear for a few hours. Then he'd come back and say, "I've been to see Mr. Ford and he wants us to do it this way." I checked with my grandmother and found out that Bennett hadn't seen my grandfather

on these occasions. In fact, he hadn't seen my grandfather in months.

Significantly, young Henry hadn't checked directly with his
grandfather. In fact, he himself rarely saw his grandfather. Still,
young Henry sought to keep up appearances. Addressing Ford
dealers in Massachusetts in the summer of 1944, he spoke thus
of his grandfather: "He is in excellent health. He puts in a full
working day, including Saturday. He goes to Willow Run practically every day, and has put a lot of his effort into that plant,
and I believe the outstanding results accomplished at Willow
Run reflect his personal supervision."

All of this of course was nonsense. Far from being in excellent health, the senior Ford was in poor physical condition,
his mind constantly wandering. And his "personal supervision"
of company activities was practically nil. But young Henry was
not about to say anything that could be carried back to his
grandfather and create further misunderstandings. For he knew
that every statement he made was being monitored by Harry
Bennett. And Bennett was the old man's major source of information. He trusted no one else. Bennett, moreover, was the
old man's only hope of resisting his numerous, mostly imaginary, enemies. "The Jews and Communists," Ford said once,
"have been working on poor Harry until he's almost out of his
mind." What Bennett needed, old Henry told an interviewer,
was a good vacation. "Then he'll come back all ready to keep
on fighting the ones who are trying to take over our plant."

Actually, the only fight Bennett was involved in was with
Henry Ford II. Early on he had set out to cut him down, but
young Henry was soon to win powerful allies through the magic
of his name and his own developing call-me-Henry magnetism.

Among those allies was John Bugas, a tall, rangy, Wyo-
ming-born former agent in charge of the FBI's Detroit office.
His investigations had included thefts and other malpractices
in the Ford plants. They had also included an investigation of
Harry Bennett, apparently at Edsel Ford's behest. And this,
needless to say, annoyed Bennett no end. So what did Bennett
do? He hired Bugas away from the FBI to be his assistant in
handling labor relations. "Maybe," Bugas later said, "he fig-

ured it was the best way to keep his eye on me."

Young Henry couldn't have been more delighted. For Bugas transferred his allegiance from Edsel to Henry II. Bennett soon realized he had blundered. "I thought that if Bugas were around the plant, young Henry would in time see him as I did," he wrote in his memoirs.* "Unfortunately, that didn't happen." What did happen was that young Henry had a trained intelligence operative sitting right smack in Bennett's office. All the time, however, Bennett was expecting old Henry to fire both Bugas and his grandson. "And," he wrote, "I firmly believe that if Mr. Ford had kept his health only a little while longer, he would have done just that."

Meanwhile Henry II was biding his time. He knew that, sooner or later, he would have to confront Harry Bennett and his "bunch of thugs." The question was when. The major problem of course was old Henry, who could not comprehend the muddled situation in the management of the Ford empire. Once, when young Henry sought to discuss Bennett with him, the old man flared and said, "I won't hear a word against Harry." And that was the biggest asset Bennett had going for him in his struggle to control the company. The other problem was the fact that Bennett had placed his own men in key positions in the company. In addition, he had begun firing top executives whose loyalties he suspected. Others quit in disgust, among them sales manager Henry C. Doss. In resigning, Doss had told young Henry, "I don't like to leave you and I wouldn't leave you if something could be done with this Bennett situation."

"I don't blame you a damn bit," Henry had replied, "but there is nothing much I can do about it now. Some day I will!"

Of course young Henry was not without some strengths of his own. Among many in the lower echelons of management, being a Ford gave him a leg up in his struggle with Bennett. At the same time, he was being cheered on by war-production leaders in Washington, who considered Bennett an impediment to the war effort. But probably his most important asset was

---

*Harry Bennett, as told to Paul Marcus, *We Never Called Him Henry* (New York: Fawcett, 1951), p. 175.

the backing by the women in his family. His mother, Eleanor, who had seen her husband brutally treated for decades, was not about to let control of the company slip into the hands of Edsel's persecutor. And she was joined in her determination by her mother-in-law, Clara, tenacious in her defense of family interests. The two strong-willed women, needless to say, controlled large blocks of voting stock.

So tense was the atmosphere in the plant that both young Henry and John Bugas took to carrying guns. Bennett was never without a weapon either. In addition, he controlled the plant police, seeded with bruisers, ex-cops—some shady, some not—football players and ex-cons. No one could have guaranteed that a shoot-out would not explode at the River Rouge.

The tension was further exacerbated when young Henry learned about the codicil to his will old Henry had signed and which, in the event of his death, would turn over control of the company to a ten-member board of directors—not including Henry Ford II—for ten years. The board, he also learned, would consist largely of Bennett's friends. Shaken and angry, young Henry rushed over to see Bugas. This, he said, was the last straw. He was ready to quit the company, sell his stock, and inform Ford dealers of the company's condition.

"I tried to calm him down," Bugas said. "Finally he agreed not to do anything drastic until I talked to Bennett and found out what it was all about."

Bugas went to Bennett's office and told him what Henry II had learned. According to Bugas, Bennett was visibly agitated. "Is that what's been bothering him?" he asked. "You come in here tomorrow and we'll straighten the whole thing out."

The next morning, bright and early, Bugas was in Bennett's office. Bennett showed the former FBI agent the original type-written codicil as well as a carbon copy. Then, in a dramatic gesture, Bennett touched a match to the original. Both men watched the document burn on the floor. When the flames subsided, Bennett scraped up the ashes, placed them in an envelope, and handed them to Bugas.

"Take this back to Henry," he said.

Later Bennett told I. A. Capizzi, the lawyer who drew up the codicil, that the document "wasn't any good anyway." The reason, according to Bennett, was that old Henry had so encumbered the "codicil" with biblical verses, scribblings, and other evidence of a disintegrating mind that it never would have stood up in court. Capizzi concluded that Ford may not have signed the document.

Whatever the case, the codicil, drawn up without their knowledge, moved young Henry, his family and a few trusted executives into urgent action. Young Henry began to meet with Bugas, John Davis, sales manager, and Meade Bricker, a production expert, in the downtown Detroit Club. There, in a corner of the high-ceilinged private establishment, safe from eavesdroppers, they plotted their strategy. Finally a fateful decision was made: Henry Ford II had to take over the presidency.

For some time Clara Ford had been urging her husband to transfer the presidency to his grandson. But old Henry, stubborn as usual, had refused. Then came the turning point. Young Henry's mother, Eleanor, a forceful, intelligent woman, who had not fully recovered from her husband Edsel's death, insisted on the presidency for her son. "If this is not done," she told her father-in-law, "I will sell my stock!" That did it. On September 20, 1945, Ford summoned young Henry to Fairlane. "My grandfather told me he was planning to step down and let me be president of the company," Henry later recalled. "I told him I'd take it only if I had a completely free hand to make any changes I wanted to make. We argued about that—but he didn't withdraw his offer."

Returning to the Ford Administration Building, young Henry directed Frank Campsall, old Henry's secretary, to prepare his grandfather's letter of resignation and to call a meeting of the board of directors the next day to elect him president. On September 21, 1945, the board met. Among those present were Henry Ford, young Henry, Mrs. Edsel Ford, Harry Bennett and two longtime Ford executives. As Henry Ford's resignation was being read, Bennett, who knew what was coming, watched bitterly. Unwilling to go through with what he later described as a "charade," Bennett rose abruptly, congratulated young Henry, and made for the door. But he was prevailed upon to remain until the decisive vote was taken.

Following the meeting, young Henry met briefly with Bennett. "I told him," said Henry, "that I had plans for reorganizing the company and that he didn't fit into them. I told him that John Bugas was taking over his job as industrial-relations director as of the next day. As a matter of fact, although I fired Bennett immediately from his job and from his position of authority, I told him he could stay with the company if he wanted to."

But Bennett declined. Instead he bitterly told young Henry, "You're taking over a billion-dollar organization here that you haven't contributed a thing to!" Then, as an afterthought, he added, "I've tried awfully hard to like you, and had hoped to part friends."

Later that day Bugas went to Bennett's office. There was an embarrassed silence. Suddenly, according to Bugas, Bennett shouted, "You dirty son of a bitch, you did this to me!" Reaching into his desk drawer, Bennett pulled out a .45 in a shoulder holster and strapped it on. "I thought he was going to try to kill me," said Bugas. "He seemed to be out of his head." But Bugas was ready. He had come armed with a .38. "I was sure something bad was going to happen and I could see myself and Bennett and the company all over the newspapers. Then he slumped down in his chair, exhausted." Bugas began to talk to him. "I told him it wasn't my fault and it wasn't Henry's fault. I said it was the fault of the no-good characters he had surrounded himself with during his years with Ford. He pulled himself together and we shook hands. All that afternoon his office was filled with smoke. He was burning papers in his wastebasket. That night he went away and we never saw him again."

The next day young Henry drove to Fairlane to inform his grandfather that he had fired Bennett. "I went to him with my guard up. I was sure he'd blow my head off." Listening quietly, old Henry said nothing. As his grandson was about to leave he finally murmured, "Well, now Harry is back where he started from."

But Harry remained on his mind. In the twilight of his life Henry Ford repeatedly called for Harry and wondered where he was. Harry had ceased to communicate with the old man. But that wasn't the end of the saga. Bennett found himself under constant surveillance. "Although I was now separated from the company," he wrote, ". . . some person or persons set a gang of junior G-men to checking on me and tailing me everywhere I went. . . I further learned that though I went unarmed, all the men following me around carried guns. I can't say I was much frightened."

Nevertheless Bennett decided to go to his northern Michigan ranch for a rest. While there he received an urgent message from Harry Wismer, the noted sportscaster married to a niece of old Henry. Wismer wanted to see him. When they met, Wismer said he had arranged the clandestine meeting because Henry Ford wanted to talk to him. Bennett said he would be glad to talk to old Henry.

Some time later Henry Ford reached Bennett by telephone. Somehow he had managed to call from a phone outside his home. What Ford wanted him to do was "go into the plant and shut it down." Then, according to Bennett, old Henry began to weep, becoming incoherent. Bennett, after checking with the old man's physician, disregarded the order. Old Henry tried to reach him several more times, but Bennett refused to take the calls.,

Bennett was in California when Henry Ford passed away. He decided not to go to the funeral of the man he had served for twenty-nine years. He knew that the family felt bitter toward him and would not welcome his presence. He knew too that if he went, the newspapers "would make a show of it." Instead Harry Bennett announced he couldn't get reservations to go back east.

Bennett was not the only one to feel the swish of the new broom. At least one thousand others were swept out of their jobs following young Henry's accession to the throne. They included the superintendent of the Rouge plant, a half dozen other factory division heads and various major and minor supervisory people. Also dismissed was William J. Cameron, Ford "voice of the air" and onetime editor of the defunct Jew-baiting Dearborn *Independent*. Young Henry showed no mercy. The purge was thorough and uncompromising. Informed that one executive had fitted himself up with a cozy hideaway at the Rouge plant for his private entertainment, he descended on the executive's office with a raiding party. The door was locked. Henry picked up a wrecking bar and smashed down the door. He fired the executive the next day.

All of which surprised Detroit, now full of rumors about who would feel Henry's axe next. There was also much speculation as to who was advising the new boss of the Ford empire.

"I think Henry II's principal adviser," said one intimate at the time, "is the memory of his father."

5

INDUSTRIALIST

EVEN BEFORE HE TURNED THIRTY YEARS OF AGE HENRY FORD II had become one of the most publicized men in American industry. He was the subject of numerous articles in both newspapers and magazines. One of the most perceptive was published in *Life* magazine* shortly after he became president of the Ford Motor Company. In it Gilbert Burck wrote that young Ford

> does have his grandfather's bluntness and impatience with diplomatic protocol, and it is possible to imagine his becoming as arbitrary as his grandfather when he gathers experience and confidence. It is easier, however, to imagine his combining his frankness with knowledge

*October 1, 1945.

and experience in a way that will make him an unusually able practitioner of human relations. . . . He perhaps has a little of his grandfather's habit of devising oversimple solutions to complex problems and he gets very enthusiastic about new ideas very easily. But it is hard to imagine his going off half-cocked so long as he retains his present ability to value other people's knowledge more highly than his own.

And among those whose opinions he valued most highly was Ernest Kanzler, who now headed the Universal Credit Corporation, originally created to handle the paper on Ford's installment sales. Kanzler had left the Ford Motor Company, of which he had become production manager, following a dispute with Henry Ford I. Nevertheless he maintained a close relationship with his brother-in-law, Edsel Ford, and kept up with company affairs. When World War II began he was named chief of the automotive branch of the War Production Board in Washington and rose to be director general. As such, he had much to do with the retooling of the motor industry for war work.

It was Kanzler who first suggested, following Edsel's death in 1943, that Henry Ford II be returned to the company from the navy. And it was he who became one of young Henry's principal advisers. In fact, Henry rarely made a major move without consulting "Uncle Ernie." Later, when asked about their relationship, Kanzler said, "We talked a lot."

There was a lot to talk about.

They talked a great deal about the company, of which young Ford had become president and chief executive officer on September 21, 1945, just two weeks past his twenty-eighth birthday. At best, the company could be described as a stumbling giant. Management morale was low, what with resignations and dismissals. Worker efficiency was estimated at one-third below normal. And the books were burdened with soybean farms, Brazilian rubber plantations, mineral and timber tracts, as well as other nonautomotive, nonprofitable ventures. No one knew how much it really cost to make a car. "Can you believe it," Ford remarked later, "in one department they figured their costs by weighing the pile of invoices on a scale." Moreover, because of old Henry's aversion to paperwork, there had never been a proper audit of the company. The payroll carried people who had been dead for some time, and at least one supposed employee was discovered serving time in a penitentiary. Competent executives were few and far between. "The upper echelons of the company were woefully inadequate," a former Ford executive recalled. "Essentially, there were no university graduates in the upper five hundred people in the company." The reason, of course, was old Henry's aversion to employees with academic credentials.

The job of bringing Ford Motor into the mid-twentieth century was an enormous one, and Henry II was smart enough to know he could not do it alone. Describing himself as "a young man reaching for answers," he was grateful for the counsel willingly provided by Kanzler. As early as 1919 "Uncle Ernie" had begun to plan an efficient organizational structure for the company. But old Henry would have nothing to do with it. Now Kanzler had a more willing listener for his reorganization proposals. And the first step was finding proven managers capable of rebuilding the company.

In 1946 Kanzler suggested that Ernest R. Breech, a former General Motors executive, then president of the Bendix corporation, be asked to lead the Ford rebuilding effort. It was probably Kanzler's most important recommendation, but it nearly came a cropper. Breech, though willing, was concerned about lines of command. What would happen, he asked, if he and young Henry did not agree on some proposal? Kanzler's solution was a contract setting Breech "up for life," along with other safeguards. Kanzler thought he had gotten Henry to agree to the deal. But then Henry balked. "My lawyer says I'm abdicating when I make Ernie vice-president," he told Kanzler. Advising his nephew to relax, Kanzler said he would talk to Breech. Breech then assured Kanzler there would "certainly be no misunderstanding in that direction." On July 1, 1946, Ernest Breech formally joined the company as executive vice-president.

The situation at Ford was worse than Breech had expected. "For a modern business, it was pitiful," he recalled. "They had financial statements like a country grocery store." The chief engineer, he said, "knew as much about designing cars as a pig did about Christmas." Breech immediately began bringing in his own people. They included Lewis D. Crusoe, a former G.M. assistant treasurer; Harold T. Youngren, chief engineer at Borg-Warner Corporation; Albert J. Browning, former merchandising manager for Montgomery Ward; Delmar S. Harder, former production supervisor for G.M.; and John Dykstra, another former G.M. executive.

In his own efforts to strengthen management, Henry had already made a package deal that brought a group of newly retired military officers into the company. Their leader, Colonel Charles B. (Tex) Thornton, who had headed the Office of Statistical Control in the air forces, had wired Ford, advising him that he and his team of logistical experts were interested in applying military management techniques to a civilian company. After consulting with Kanzler, Henry hired all ten of them. Two of them—Robert S. McNamara, later Secretary of Defense and head of the World Bank, and Arjay Miller, later dean of the Graduate School of Business at Stanford University—were to become presidents of Ford Motor Company. Thornton, who stayed with the company only briefly, was to become board chairman of Litton Industries.

Since none of the group knew anything about the automobile business, they spent their first four months moving from department to department, asking questions. They became known, ironically, as the "Quiz Kids" (the real Quiz Kids answered questions rather than asking them), a title that was annoying because, as one later observed, "We weren't kids, and we weren't quizzing anybody. We were asking a lot of questions because it was the only way we could get the information we needed." What they found in the course of their investigation was disturbing. Conditions at Ford were more chaotic than they had imagined. One supervisor, asked the cost of a project under his direction, replied that he didn't know. "We don't talk about costs around here," he said. A large Ford fund deposited in a bank was drawing no interest. "The bankers must have loved it," said Arjay Miller. Once settled in, however, the former military men became known as "Whiz Kids."

Like the "Whiz Kids," Henry Ford II was trying to learn

the business. Moving about the plant a good deal, he was rarely in his office, which in those days was small, plainly furnished and glass-enclosed like all the rest. He was usually home by seven in the evening.

Home was a Georgian brick house with four bedrooms, comfortably furnished with early American pieces but far from palatial. Still worried about kidnappers, he did not permit the house to be photographed. Nor did he allow the press to take pictures of his two young daughters, Charlotte and Anne. In those days he rarely went to nightclubs or expensive restaurants, preferring to entertain at home.

On occasion he would accept outside speaking engagements on behalf of Ford's public relations, about which so much needed to be done when he took over. Robust, straightforward and emotionally uncomplicated, he was good on his feet. One of his early appearances was at a dinner of the Off the Record Club, where he was subjected to questions by Detroit newsmen on matters concerning his company. Henry handled himself well, conceding he didn't know all the answers to their questions. Then, as the ordeal drew to a close, Henry said, "Now I want to ask *you* a question." Why, of course, said the moderator. "Where's the men's room?" he asked with a smile. The question brought down the house. From then on Henry Ford II could do little wrong in the eyes of most Detroit newsmen.

Still, young Ford realized he would need professional help if he were to succeed in getting the message of the "new" Ford Motor Company across to the public. He hired Earl Newsom, a top New York public-relations man, who, among other things, supervised the writing of Henry's speeches. Newsom also helped stage young Ford's well publicized bout with the Office of Price Administration and its director, Chester Bowles. This occurred when the Ford company was seeking to bring out a postwar car, a 1946 Ford that was actually an improved 1942 model. The OPA had set price ceilings that seemed too low to young Henry. Bowles said he was seeking to curb inflation and that, anyway, the automobile companies had profited enormously from the war.

Henry's impetuous decision was to launch a nationwide ad campaign blasting the OPA. Newsom, who thought this tactic "counterproductive," argued Henry out of the plan. Instead, he talked Henry into issuing a series of statements explaining why it was necessary for Ford to get higher prices. He argued that strikes had slowed production and his company was experiencing heavy losses because of rising costs. Bowles, unimpressed, accused Ford of "selfishly" seeking to "undermine the American people's bulwark against economic disaster," namely the OPA. But finally, following the intervention of President Truman, the battle of press releases ended. Ford won several price increases. But more important, in his confrontation with Chester Bowles young Henry emerged as a spokesman for the entire motor industry.

All of which was heady stuff indeed for a young man whom few of his competitors had originally taken very seriously. They had felt, with a certain glow of satisfaction, that he had a lot to learn about the business. After all, only a few years before he had been, as *Life* described him, "a quiet, pleasant, blue-eyed, apple-cheeked young student with a disposition to put off crossing bridges until he got to them." Now he was building himself a team whose consuming ambition was to make the Ford Motor Company a postwar powerhouse. And in the process Henry II was quickly learning a great deal about modern corporate organization and operation.

"And he worked hard at it," Ernie Breech recalled later. "He was there early every morning. He just did it the hard way, learning by sitting in meetings, listening." To keep production men alert, he was driven to and from work in a new car each day. On his way Henry wound windows up and down, bounced in the seats and tested all the gadgets. Once, when a closing car door sounded tinny, he went down the production line slamming doors with the angry comment, "Don't you know that Chevrolet salesmen take prospects over to a Ford salesroom and slam a car door? When it sounds like this, they just say 'See, tin,' then take them back and sell them a Chevrolet."

And while Henry II was learning the ropes, it was actually Ernie Breech who was running the show. In Ford's newly acquired team-conscious ways, Ernie was called "the quarterback." And like some quarterbacks in those days, Breech was on the small side physically, smart as a whip, tough and cocksure. In 1947 Breech made a bold move. He put the team to work on a brand-new automobile for 1949, the first major innovation in the postwar period. At a meeting of the top brass he declared, "I have a vision. We start from scratch. We spend no time or money phonying up the old Ford, because this organization will be judged by the market on the next car it produces, and it had better be a new one. So we'll have a crash program, as if in wartime. Any questions?" There were none, and work was begun.

With great fanfare the new car was introduced to the public at New York's Waldorf-Astoria on June 8, 1949. For six days, tens of thousands of potential customers jammed the gold-and-white ballroom where it was displayed. In all, sales of the new model that year amounted to over 800,000 units, making 1949 the biggest year Ford had had since 1929. In 1950 the company made a profit—after taxes—of $265 million. In 1953 Ford moved past Chrysler into second place. The Ford Motor Company was well on its way back.

Asked how the turnaround was accomplished so quickly, Henry, referring to his immediate postwar production, told an interviewer in 1978, "We didn't have the money we needed to bring out really good products, but . . . the damned market had had no vehicles at all for several years so you had a seller's market for a long period of time. You could sell almost anything you could make, regardless of whether it was any good or not. People just wanted to buy transportation and admittedly we didn't make a terribly good product."

But by itself, Henry conceded, the seller's market was not enough. "Really," he added, "the credit for pulling this place together and operating and making it tick and getting us onto an even keel belongs to Ernie Breech. He really did a superb job here and it pulled us through."

By then, too, the company had done much to improve its labor relations, which had reached such a dismal level under Henry Ford I and Harry Bennett. In his labor policy young Ford, more sophisticated than his grandfather, leaned heavily on Elmo Roper, the public-opinion analyst, who had long recommended a more liberal approach. Roper conducted surveys among Ford employees on what bugged them about the company. He found that many workers had no feeling of "belong-ing," or felt that the company had made little effort to explain what it was trying to do. Quite a number believed it would be too "dangerous" to say what they really thought. Fear of re-prisals was only too evident. Studying the results, Breech called in all superintendents and division heads and warned them against continuing harsh discipline. The old "driver" system, under which foremen and supervisors ruthlessly bossed men on the line, was abolished. And the old Henry Ford dictum against smoking in plants and offices was lifted—with one exception. Women were requested not to smoke during office hours.

The shift in labor policy had been signaled by young Henry, not long after he became president of Ford, in an important speech before the Society of Automotive Engineers. In that speech, which was prepared by Newsom, young Henry spoke of the social obligations of big business toward its workers. Calling for "industrial statesmanship—from both labor and management," young Ford added, "I assume . . . that all of us agree that labor unions are here to stay. Certainly we of the Ford Motor Company have no desire to 'break the unions.' . . . We want to strengthen their leadership by urging and helping them to assume the responsibilities they must assume if the public interest is to be served." A closer and more friendly relationship between management and labor, he argued, would increase efficiency and profits.

The speech, which made the front page of *The New York Times*, also caused quite a stir in Detroit. "It was the best speech I've heard in ten years," said George Addes, secretary-treasurer of the United Automobile Workers. And as *Fortune* then noted, "Most important to young Ford was to have his family's com-pany earn the reputation, which it did not have then, of being a good citizen in a changed social climate that the founder had never recognized." At the same time, Henry II's stature as a bold, innovative spokesman for industry was given another boost. He was receiving smart advice and had the wit to accept it.

Young Henry enjoyed every moment of his new-found ce-lebrity. Awards of all kinds were bestowed on him, among them the Christian Culture Award medal, presented annually by Assumption College of Windsor, Ontario, to "an outstanding lay exponent of Christian ideals." And he was chosen "Young Man of the Year" by the United States Chamber of Commerce. For public-relations reasons that now seemed important to him for the company, he began devoting a great deal of time to speaking on the "mashed-potato" circuit. In the beginning he spoke mainly on labor-management relations. But as time went on he expanded his horizons to include national and world affairs. And he had opinions on almost everything. Returning home on the *Queen Mary* from a trip to Europe with his family in April 1948, Ford declared that the Soviet Union was blocking the return of economic stabilization in Europe, emphasizing, "Somehow the Russians must be stood up to and told off." These sentiments, needless to say, were hardly in keeping with the pacifism of his grandfather, who had passed away only a year before.

And two years later, when North Korean troops poured into South Korea, Ford telegraphed President Truman, endorsing the administration's prompt action in intervening militarily. "I want you to know that all of us at Ford Motor Company stand ready to carry out any assignment the government may give us in view of the present situation," Henry wired. Six months later, in a speech in Dallas, he criticized the administration's handling of defense mobilization. "We cannot afford the luxury of business and politics as usual nor the jockeying for position by various economic groups," he said. Asked if his statement was an implied criticism of the Truman administration, he said, "It certainly is."

While in Rome in July 1951, Henry said he had no fears of an oil shortage in the United States despite the troubled situation in Iran. "We'll never have a gas shortage in America unless an all-out war comes," he told a news conference. "There are vast petroleum deposits in the United States, in South America and in Canada."

In 1952 Henry became more active politically. Describing himself as "an independent in political matters," he announced his support for Dwight D. Eisenhower in the presidential campaign. "I have become convinced that he and the Republican party—for the next four years, at least—offer America its best hope for forward movement and for national security." The following year Henry emerged in an entirely new role, that of an advocate of "free trade" in the automobile industry. In a speech he called for the abandonment of the high protective tariff, suggesting that a good beginning would be to abolish the 10 percent duty on foreign-car imports. "In order to buy from us," he contended, "they must be able to sell to us." With front-page stories appearing in *The New York Times* and *The Wall Street Journal,* Henry's views became the subject of considerable debate. The New York *Daily News* editorialized it was "inclined to go along with the general Ford thesis." And the liberal Americans for Democratic Action, in a letter to Ford signed by economist Robert Nathan, congratulated him for proposing "a lasting contribution to the unity of the free world."

Thus Henry Ford II, on the basis of numerous speeches, became a statesman. In July 1953 President Eisenhower named him a member of the United States delegation to the United Nations General Assembly, serving under Ambassador Henry Cabot Lodge, Jr. In his maiden speech Ford argued for increased aid to developing countries as "a sound investment in world stability for the future." And at a later session he tangled with a Soviet representative. But generally he got along with Moscow's emissaries.

"When I'd meet them in the morning," he said later, "they'd smile at me. I suppose somebody told them to do it."

"Did you smile back at them?" he was asked.

"Yes," Henry said.

"Did somebody tell you to do it?"

"Yes."

"Who?"

"My mother," he replied.

Henry's mother, Eleanor Clay Ford, a youthful and attractive woman, was the *grande dame* of the family, exerting considerable influence on her children and grandchildren. Though a major shareholder in Ford Motor, she rarely interfered directly in company affairs. This did not prevent her from talking personally with Henry on matters she felt important. Born in Detroit in 1896, she had been married to Edsel Ford in 1916 in a simple ceremony at the home of her uncle Joseph L. Hudson, the famous Detroit merchant. Among the guests was Thomas A. Edison. Following Edsel's death, she continued to live in the sixty-room mansion that she and her husband had built at Gaukler Pointe in Grosse Pointe Shores. Her four children, who were brought up in that big house with the stone shingles, lived close by and would come together for dinner or family parties. As grandchildren came along, the family get-togethers became bigger and more boisterous. When they grew older and went off to eastern schools, the grandchildren would see each other less frequently, but almost always at Thanksgiving or Christmas.

"Granny Ford was the kingpin, or should I say 'queenpin,'" says Benson Ford, Jr. "She ran the family until her death. She was a kind, loving woman, with great understanding. All my cousins liked her and talked to her. I confided in her a lot, and she liked me a lot. After she died, Uncle Henry took over. But it just wasn't the same; the parties and family spirit didn't seem the same."

To young Benson, Uncle Henry was an awe-inspiring figure. Big (two hundred pounds) and tall (six feet), he dominated the family by sheer personality. "I don't know why," says Benson, "but he just scared me. He was running the company and he was like 'wow' when you saw him. I observed him a lot, but I rarely talked to him because I was afraid of sticking my foot in my mouth and making a fool of myself. Of course I'd say hello to him, but usually I'd stay away from him conversationally."

Young Benson had no such trepidations about his father. Benson Sr., amiable and gregarious, tried to spend as much time as possible with his children, Benson Jr. and Lynn. And like his father, Benson Sr. became involved in many civic enterprises, among them the National Conference of Christians and Jews, of which he was a cochairman, and Detroit's United Foundation, which raised funds for the sick and needy, of which he wound up as board chairman. In the latter group he was aided by his socially skilled wife, Edith. At one "victory dinner" he called on her to deliver her report on the women's division.

"Mr. Chairman," she began, adding, "—and that's the last

time I'm calling you that, buster—"

When the laughter and applause subsided, she went on with her report.

Discharged from the army as a captain at the end of World War II, Benson Sr. returned to the company about the time his brother Henry was engaged in the power struggle with Harry Bennett. In January 1948, at the age of twenty-nine, he became vice-president of the Lincoln-Mercury division.

Meanwhile his brother William Clay Ford, six years younger, was named a director of the company and, following his graduation from Yale, began to work in the sales and advertising department. In 1947 he married Martha Parke Firestone, the daughter of Akron tire manufacturer Harvey S. Firestone, Jr. Henry II was his brother's best man at the ceremony, which took place in Akron's St. Paul's Episcopal Church. Among the guests were former New Jersey Governor Charles Edison, son of the inventor, and Laurence Rockefeller of the New York Rockefellers.

Perhaps the most popular of the Fords, William Clay most resembled his late father in physical appearance and manner. He was not as heavy-set as Henry and Benson and had a boyish charm that came across to the public. After four years of experience in the company William Clay, in 1953, was named a vice-president and manager of Special Product Operations. He was then twenty-eight years of age.

Not one of the three Ford brothers in the least resembled their famous grandfather. Not one was mechanically inclined. And not one followed old Henry's dictums about not smoking or drinking. All very quietly learned to enjoy the prerogatives of their enormous wealth, although at first they were not ostentatious about it. Though close, they had different sets of friends. And they enjoyed doing different things. Henry II was the golfer in the family. Benson liked to escape to the wheelhouse of his cruiser *Onika,* far more modest a vessel than his late father's sumptuous yacht. And Billy eventually bought his own professional football team, the Detroit Lions. "We brothers enjoy needling and kidding each other," Benson once told an interviewer. "Bill makes Henry cringe by calling him 'Hennie' and some other names I'd rather not mention. And he gets to me too at times. But we enjoy this and expect it when we get together."

In 1954 Benson and Billy attended the Indianapolis five-hundred-mile auto race. Afterward they and their guests returned to their suite in the Lincoln Hotel. A bartender was busily dispensing drinks from a well stocked bar. Down below, a pair of Hoosier policemen were rounding up some undesirables loitering near the entrance to the sedate hostelry. Suddenly they were hit by ice cubes hurtling from the Ford suite. Angry, the patrolmen went to the suite and started to admonish the occupants. But they calmed down when they learned the identities of the culprits, who had been indulging in some postrace playfulness. Mollified by Benson's diplomatic apologies, the officers each left with a pair of Ford autographs.

Henry, likewise, was given to exuberant behavior. A former associate recalled meeting him on the New York-bound *Detroiter* in 1949 or 1950. Henry was feeling no pain, he told *Newsweek*. In fact, the young industrialist managed to get himself thrown out of the bar car three times in one night. "He drank like hell then," the friend said. "The impression was what you'd expect: a spoiled-rotten kid. He was hollering that he was going to buy the train and fire the crew."

The "spoiled-rotten kid" wasn't doing too badly, however, as chief executive officer of the Ford Motor Company. All through the fifties the company prospered. Then came a celebrated disaster. This was the introduction of an entirely new model line that was supposed to be a monument to the late Edsel Ford. Fittingly, it was called the Edsel. Introduced in 1957 with great fanfare, the Edsel had sales of only 110,000 in three years. Innumerable defects plagued the early models and there were complaints about the styling. But despite all sorts of tinkering, the Edsel could not be saved. Production was discontinued. In all, over $300 million was expended on the Edsel, whose name quickly entered the language as a synonym for "dud." Years later Henry Ford II took full blame for the failure. "The timing was wrong—hell, we headed into 1958 and right into a recession, and everything went kaput," he said. Though it had been an expensive adventure, the Edsel did no lasting damage. The company recovered quickly.

Meanwhile, thanks to Ernie Breech, the company no longer resembled the one-man "country store" operation left by the founder, Henry Ford I. The new organization was frankly patterned after General Motors. Each division of the company was given as much autonomy as possible. Major moves affecting the whole company were generally group decisions, thrashed out in conferences of the top executives. Ostensibly Henry II shared the top responsibility with Breech, who was named chairman in 1954. Their offices adjoined each other. But the steady devolution of power that was revitalizing the company was also reducing Henry to just one more member of a management team. And apparently Henry didn't like it. "If I interpret this correctly," commented John Kenneth Galbraith, who had studied the company for years, "as Henry got older, he began to have some of the same reactions as his grandfather about the devolution of power which left him without power."

By the mid-fifties Henry began to assert more of his prerogatives. "My God," exclaimed an old-line auto executive whose company had been outmaneuvered by Ford, "young Henry's getting more like his grandfather every day." Said another, "With Henry you never know quite what he's going to do—and don't think that isn't an advantage in this industry."

Henry's penchant for doing the unexpected was dramatically demonstrated when he suddenly nudged Ernie Breech aside. What made the episode implausible was that Henry obviously had great affection for his dapper, mustached "cocaptain." In fact, in the spring of 1960 Henry appeared at a testimonial dinner for Breech at which he made an impromptu, near-tearful speech recounting all that Ernie had done for the company. And he had done quite a bit. The company had expanded sharply since he had joined Ford. Sales rose from $894,500,000 in 1946 to a record of $5,357,000,000 in 1957. Breech's tenure as chairman, to which position he was elected in 1954, also covered the conversion of Ford from a closely held family concern to a publicly owned corporation with more than 240,000 stockholders.

Only weeks after the testimonial dinner Henry turned to Breech and announced, "I've graduated, Ernie." Taking the hint, Breech moved over and eventually out. "Henry doesn't need me anymore," he said.

Another celebrated dismissal was that of Arjay Miller, who had started at Ford as one of the "Whiz Kids." In 1963 Miller was named president of the company. Five years later, returning one evening from a trip to Latin America, he was surprised to discover a message at the airport advising him to proceed immediately to Henry's office. It was then that Henry informed Miller that he too was being shunted aside—replaced by Semon E. (Bunkie) Knudsen, an executive vice-president of General Motors. Instead of being ousted, Miller was offered a face-saving job. He was to be "elevated" to vice-chairman. The move stunned the industry. Miller had long been considered "one of Henry's great favorites," as a Ford official recalls. Miller too was stunned, but, as he later said, "I was not going to get mad and I didn't. Henry was the boss." Miller soon left to become dean of the business school at Stanford.

As it turned out, Bunkie Knudsen's tenure was even shorter. One of the big names in the automobile business, Bunkie had grown up in the industry. His father had been president of General Motors. He himself had just been passed over for the presidency of G.M. And he had decided to resign as executive vice-president. Hearing this, Ford drove out to Knudsen's home in Bloomfield Hills, a plush Detroit suburb much favored by G.M. executives. Hoping not to be recognized, Ford drove out in an Oldsmobile. Would Knudsen come to Ford as president? Yes, said Knudsen, and a week later the deal was struck. Not only would Knudsen receive a yearly $600,000 in salary and bonuses—the same as Ford—but he was assured he would exercise strong leadership in running the company.

And exercise strong leadership he did. In so doing, however, he clashed with another executive, Lee Iacocca, the flamboyant onetime salesman responsible for the fabulously successful Mustang in the 1960s. Iacocca, tough and ambitious, had caught the eyes of both Mrs. Edsel Ford, still exercising influence in the company, and William Clay Ford, who had the ear of his brother. Just as important was the fact that Iacocca knew how to work with Henry Ford II. Which was a trait Knudsen did not possess. Bunkie, who felt he knew more about the automobile business than most people, refused to bend the knee.

Nineteen months after he had hired him Henry walked into Knudsen's office and said, "Bunkie, you'll be leaving." Henry gave no explanation to the astonished Bunkie, but later at a press conference he told the assembled newsmen, "Sometimes things just don't work out." Sitting at Ford's right was a smiling Iacocca, toying with an expensive black cigar. Asked how he felt about Knudsen's departure, Iacocca replied, "I've never said 'no comment' to the press yet, but I'll say 'no comment' now." In a sense history was repeating itself. Almost half a century before, Henry's grandfather had fired Knudsen's father, William S. (Big Bill) Knudsen, who had supervised the construction of the assembly line at River Rouge but had aroused the senior Ford's ire by proposing changes in the Model T. Big Bill then went on to General Motors, where he created the Chevrolet. Explaining the dismissal, Henry I had said, "This is my business. I built it, and as long as I live, I propose to run it the way I want it run. . . . I let him go, not because he wasn't good, but because he was too good—for me."

Like his fabled grandfather, Henry Ford II had made it clear he would brook no interference in running the company. That had become painfully obvious to Bunkie Knudsen. The night his dismissal was announced, Knudsen sat with a few friends. "I think," he said, nursing a drink, "Henry was afraid of losing his Tinker Toy."

6

JET-SETTER

At a Manhattan dinner party given by "Rocky" Cooper, the beautiful widow of actor Gary, there was a spirited argument about Vietnam and other cosmic subjects. The arguers were conservative columnist William F. Buckley, Jr., and liberal editor Emmet J. Hughes. Among those enthralled by the highly literate discussion was Anne McDonnell Ford, who could hardly wait to tell her husband about the "exciting evening" she had spent.

"That's the kind of evening I like to avoid," replied her husband.

Henry Ford II, the Chairman of the Ford Motor Company, the nation's second-largest auto maker and one of the world's best known business enterprises, never had much time for what he called "highfalutin" discussions. Intellectuals bored him. Whenever someone in the company used a word he considered

highbrow, he would ask for a definition. The malefactor, therefore, had ample warning never to pull that kind of stuff around
Henry again. Culture also bored him. He had little interest in
serious theater, ballet or classical music. Except for an occasional light tome while vacationing, Henry seldom read books.
As the years passed, Henry II became known as a "swinger,"
who wore his graying hair long in back and on the sides—and
who rarely averted his eyes from a pair of shapely ankles. Born
to the purple, every inch the child of inherited privilege, Henry
sought out the company of the "beautiful people," who fre-
quented such places as Southampton, the French Riviera and
the upper East Side of Manhattan. And he loved to gossip, not
so much about who was doing what to whom in the automobile
business but about who was sleeping with whom in international
society.

The "swinger" image developed over a period of time. At
first Henry and his young wife Anne indulged in pleasant,
relatively simple social activities, usually entertaining in their
home in Grosse Pointe. Following the birth of their son Edsel
Bryant Ford II on December 27, 1948, their social life became
more active. In the space of a few years they entertained Swe-
den's Prince Bertil, Belgium's King Baudouin and his brother,
Prince Albert, Prince Otto von Bismarck, grandson of Ger-
many's "Iron Chancellor," and his wife, Princess Anna Marie.
More mundane leaders also came to call. In 1951 Henry played
host to David Ben-Gurion after the Israeli prime minister was
honored at a civic reception on the steps of Detroit's City Hall.

In turn, the Fords were lionized wherever they went. In
Hollywood, Louis B. Mayer, the boss of Metro-Goldwyn-
Mayer, took them under his personal wing, supervising their
social life, and the attractive Fords dazzled the film capital.
Perhaps even more important, Henry managed to overcome
movieland's deepseated aversion to Ford's products. For decades, because of Henry I's anti-Semitism, the moguls had
refused to permit even the free use of Ford vehicles in film
scenes. The unofficial boycott was finally broken.

The Fords were also entertained at the White House and in
various European capitals. In Rome they were granted a special
audience by Pope Pius. And in London they attended a white-

tie dinner at the United States Embassy given by Ambassador Winthrop Aldrich. Among the fifty guests were Queen Elizabeth, Prince Philip, the Queen Mother and Princess Margaret. Henry and the princess danced a spirited Charleston later in the evening.

On their frequent trips to Europe the Fords shopped for treasures with which to furnish the home they planned to build. They were photographed at exciting auctions at Sotheby's in London and Parke-Bernet in New York, and their private collection became notable. Eventually they decided not to build their dream abode. Instead, they purchased the home they considered the most beautiful in Grosse Pointe. It was a huge, forty-odd-room red-brick Georgian mansion with five hundred feet fronting on Lake St. Clair. Formerly owned by Roy D. Chapin, late president of Hudson Motor Car Company, the mansion had been designed by John Russell Pope, who had also designed the Jefferson Memorial and the National Gallery of Art. Across the lake, in Ontario, Ford had a country lodge complete with duck marsh, which he humorously referred to as Mud Creek Lodge. There he would spend many a weekend, hunting ducks and birds. It was also a place where he could relax and "get away from everybody and everything." In the late fifties the Fords built a new home in Southampton. Resembling a French château, it was described as "gemlike, a miniature Versailles but with warmth." Furniture and art objects for the houses were transported across the Atlantic by ship, then hauled to both Grosse Pointe and Southampton by a caravan of vans, specially padded to protect the treasures.

It was a way of life that only the superwealthy could afford. And for the most part the Fords associated only with the superwealthy at the exclusive resort areas of the world—Palm Beach, Sun Valley, the French Riviera, St. Moritz, Jamaica and Nassau. Their companions were DuPonts, Drexels, Guests, Paleys, Wrightsmans, Morgans, Vanderbilts, Huttons, Whitneys, Vreelands, Rockefellers, Biddles, Belmonts and Astors. They particularly enjoyed being with the Gary Coopers (they flew to Los Angeles in 1961 for the actor's funeral), the Igor Cassinis (he was the society columnist for the Hearst newspapers), Italian designer Count Emilio Pucci and Countess Pucci, and Prince Aly Khan. Occasionally their paths crossed those of a young senator from Massachusetts and his dark-haired wife, the John Fitzgerald Kennedys.

Both Senator Kennedy and Aly Khan (who flew in from New York for the occasion) were at an elite Hollywood dinner party given by actress Merle Oberon and her husband, Bruno Pagliai, for Anne and Henry Ford, godparents of the Pagliais' adopted son. Among the filmland luminaries invited to the party was Zsa Zsa Gabor, who showed up with her ex-fiancé, Hal Hayes. When Miss Oberon told Zsa Zsa there was no place card at the table for her escort but that both could stay for cocktails, Hayes left, and so did Zsa Zsa. And thus a Hollywood feud was born, Zsa Zsa exclaiming to the press, "I'm deeply hurt." Anne Ford was embarrassed for her hostess. Henry thought the whole episode a big joke and, in his forthright manner, said so. And Anne thought her husband should have kept his mouth shut.

Nevertheless the Ford marriage seemed happy, secure and "till death do us part." No clouds appeared on the horizon. Henry II was deemed a great success in the business world. Anne Ford was busy with her charity works. Sometimes too busy. Once she was rushed to the hospital suffering from what was thought to be exhaustion. But the doctors diagnosed a mild attack of polio. She quickly recovered, and on her release Henry said, "We were very, very lucky."

They were also lucky in having three bright, handsome children. Charlotte, the eldest, and Edsel, the youngest, resembled their father; and Anne, the middle child, was almost a carbon copy of her mother. And in keeping with the Ford tradition, the children were constantly kept under surveillance. They couldn't ride their bicycles outside the Ford compound in Grosse Pointe. And they were chauffeured to and from school by armed men, usually off-duty police officers. The fear of kidnapping always hung heavily over the Ford household. At school, Charlotte recalled, she was not permitted to leave the grounds alone or form friendships with other girls. "It was a good twelve years of nuns," she added. "It was like a prison."

Henry II himself never had much time for the children. He was either traveling somewhere or he would get home late after a busy day at the plant. His daughters later recalled those days wistfully. "I just didn't see much of my father," Charlotte told an interviewer. "He was always away or coming in from work after we had gone to bed. We had a Christmas tree and presents, and birthday presents and all that, but looking back on it, I think I'd have been happy to have fewer presents and more parents." Her sister Anne had the same recollection. Sometimes, when their dad was home, the children would entertain their parents on a tiny stage in the living room. They would sing, dance, and tell riddles. And their father would laugh uproariously.

But while life was often lonely for the children, they never lacked material things. In fact, they had so many possessions that gifts lost any meaning. Charlotte has recalled that one snowy Christmas she and other junior members of the family were taken for a sleigh ride on the grounds of her great-grandfather, Henry Ford I. They were met at a playhouse, built just for the occasion, by a Santa Claus. Taken inside, the children found hundreds of dolls and toys. "It's all for you," Santa told them. "Help yourselves to whatever you want."

Ambitious for her children, Anne Ford placed them in the right schools, stressed deportment and prayed for "good" marriages for them. As the girls grew older they began to date, usually well-bred boys from the Grosse Pointe set. And they pleaded for an end to the constant surveillance. Relenting, their father withdrew the bodyguards who had always accompanied them. But the girls had to observe strict curfews. One of the boy friends, now a prominent Washington attorney, recalls that on dates Anne would be constantly checking her watch. On several occasions, when late, they would have to drive fast to get home by curfew. Otherwise Henry II was a genial father. Occasionally, when the girls entertained at home, he would call downstairs to ask whether he could join the party. And he would appear with a bottle of Dom Perignon in hand, pour drinks for everyone, and join in the conversation, often into the wee hours.

At first, largely because they traveled so much, the Fords made only rare appearances on the Detroit social scene. Then, in 1958, Mrs. Ford took over the cochairmanship of a Victor

Borge concert sponsored by the Friends of Modern Art, at last stepping into the role that had long awaited her—leadership of Detroit society. The following year she headed a committee of seven hundred women as general chairwoman of the Metropolitan Opera's season at Detroit's Masonic Auditorium. And she worked at it, making speeches, attending meetings, traveling through the state to assure the opera's tremendous success. In addition, she was a trustee of the Detroit Art Museum's Founders Society, a member of the fine arts committee of President Eisenhower's People-to-People program, a trustee of the Henry Ford Hospital in Detroit, and a member of the advisory board of the Catholic Social Services of Wayne County, Michigan.

Anne McDonnell Ford, however, was primarily interested in art. She had studied the masters as a young student at Grotanelli School in Siena, Italy, and had even interested her husband in collecting. In 1956 they made their first significant gift to the Detroit Institute of Arts, a fifteenth-century Italian wood sculpture of the Madonna. Within a short while they made other, more serious contributions—a Rembrandt, the museum's first Picasso, sculptures, bronzes, additions to the Meissen Swan service and Tiepolo's lost masterpiece, "Girl with Lute." In 1957 Anne was elected to the board of trustees of New York's prestigious Metropolitan Museum of Art. And during both the Eisenhower and Kennedy administrations she served on the White House Fine Arts Committee, helping to restore Blair House.

In December 1959 the Fords presented their oldest daughter at a debutante ball at the Country Club of Grosse Pointe. The Fords, not often given to public ostentation, spared no expense. It was The Party of the Year, not only for Detroit but for the nation. Many months in the planning, the party cost at least $150,000, an extraordinary sum in those preinflationary times. The Fords had imported designer Jacques Frank from Paris to transform the club into a replica of an eighteenth-century French court ballroom, replete with fake marble and bowers of fresh flowers. In newspaper interviews Frank was quoted as saying he had selected the eighteenth century because "parties had reached the top then." Europeans, he also noted, rarely held coming-out parties. But Anne Ford said Americans were more conscious of such social activities. "It's called child-pushing," she said, laughing.

Charlotte, who had turned eighteen, had flown in from Florence, Italy, where she was attending school. Earlier in the year she had graduated from the Convent of the Sacred Heart in Noroton, Connecticut. Her sister Anne, two years younger, who was attending Sacred Heart, informed her family she was "too excited to study." But the "most excited" in the family, according to his mother, was eleven-year-old Edsel Ford, "who is worried about having to dance with his sister."

On the big night a thousand guests gathered at the Country Club. Distinguished visitors from around the world flew in, including Gary Cooper and Lord Charles Spencer-Churchill, youngest son of the Duke of Marlborough, both suave in white tie and tails. From New York came the Igor Cassinis, the Winston Guests, the E. B. McLeans and the Charles Wrightmans. Also present to pay his respects to the daughter of one of his major competitors was John Gordon, president of General Motors, as was L. L. (Tex) Colbert, president of Chrysler Corporation. Invited, but unable to attend, were Frank Sinatra and Peter Lawford, both then making a film in Las Vegas. Ford had known Sinatra a long time. "He sang at my twenty-first birthday party," said Henry. "But he wasn't well-known then—he was just a singer in a band."

Before the ball Charlotte was given a dinner by her aunts and uncles, the Benson Fords, the William Clay Fords and the Walter Buhl Fords (her aunt Josephine and her non-Ford Ford husband). Then, escorted by her cousin Raymond Peter Sullivan III, of Glen Head, Long Island, she made her appearance wearing a strapless white satin Yves St. Laurent gown, embroidered with pink flowers, tourmalines and pearls. She also wore a diamond-studded gold bracelet with a butterfly motif, which her parents had given her for the occasion. As another surprise the Fords had engaged Nat "King" Cole to sing the popular songs she liked best including "You Made Me Love You." A New York society orchestra led by Meyer Davis began playing at 10:00 P.M. After breaking away from the receiving line, Charlotte danced with her proud father to a tune he had personally selected, "The Most Beautiful Girl in the World." Her brother Edsel, however, said he didn't want to dance. "It's a free country," he explained. But there were other, more eager males to dance with. Each one of her twenty-seven ushers—all sons of prominent Detroit families—whirled her around the floor.

At midnight, supper was served. But the booze flowed all evening and into the early-morning hours. So much so that, as one guest recalls, some of the more inebriated found it expedient to sober up by taking whiffs of oxygen from tanks conveniently spaced around the premises. Henry Ford II himself was never more relaxed. Resplendently attired in tails, he "helped" Meyer Davis conduct the Yale Bulldog and Whiffenpoof songs. And he stood next to Nat Cole as the "King" captivated his audience by singing a dozen or so songs from the ballroom floor. Henry could not be repressed. He danced with his wife, his mother and then with other eager ladies, commenting, "It's a good thing I don't have five daughters. I'd go broke."

The dancing continued until near dawn. Charlotte invited some of her young friends to her home for a postparty, which was finally broken up by a weary Papa Ford several hours later. Guests, who were still pulling into the circular drive, were turned away by a shivering guard who explained, "The party's over. They've all gone to bed." As the sun rose over the lake the Ford home was quiet at last.

A year and a half later the Ford home was the scene of another debut. Again Henry II spared no expense in assuring a spectacular party, this time for his youngest daughter, Anne. He invested at least $250,000 for an event that drew over one thousand guests. "And it's well worth it," he remarked as he watched his eighteen-year-old daughter, looking like a princess, float down the curved stairway of his magnificent Georgian mansion on Lake Shore Drive. Again under the direction of Jacques Frank, an eighteenth-century setting was prepared, with rose-trellised white summerhouses erected at each end of the garden. The only problem was that it began to rain heavily.

After news photographs of his family were taken, Ford strode to the bandstand, again presided over by Meyer Davis, who had flown in with "the boys" from New York. "Come on, Meyer, let's hear the music," he said, waving his arms in a brisk rhythmic beat that the society bandleader promptly picked up. And as the orchestra played a medley of rose songs— "Everything's Coming Up Roses," "La Vie en Rose," "Only a Rose" and "My Wild Irish Rose"—the reception line formed.

Finally Davis drummed for attention and asked that the dance floor be cleared so Anne could have her first dance with her father. The tune appropriately was "My Heart Belongs to Daddy." Young Edsel, who had refused to dance with his sister Charlotte at her debut, this time cut in on his dad for the second dance honors with Anne. He was then heard remarking to Benson Jr. and Alfie Ford that the garden fountain, spraying in the wind, would make a perfect giant shower bath. And his young cousins thought that the funniest thing they had ever heard. Then maestro Davis beat out and sang a composition of his own entitled "Man, That's *Anne*," which went in part:

> Flash! From coast to coast,
> The boys dig Anne.
> Man! She's the most
> Way out tennis fan,
> A love-set server,
> Man! That's Anne!

After a time Henry II took the microphone to announce the presence of "the best entertainer in the whole world" and Ella Fitzgerald, dressed in brown chiffon, took the spotlight. At first the crowd refused to quiet down. Finally Henry II bellowed, "Dammit, shut up!" Then he added, "Now I'm going to catch hell from my wife." After Fitzgerald finished her repertoire, ranging from "Night and Day" to "Mack the Knife," the dancing resumed. A lavish midnight supper was served in the summerhouses despite the torrential rain that kept at least a hundred retainers mopping through the night.

The publicity, however, was not so good in terms of public relations. Critics cited the expenditures for both coming-out parties as excessive and, in the words of one, "enough to feed hundreds of starving families a year." When asked about such criticism years later, Anne said, "Well, Daddy said it provided work for a lot of people. Actually, neither Charlotte nor I had any choice whatsoever about the debuts. They aren't any fun at all. First you have to get ready. Then all you do is just stand in line and receive people. Do you mean would I want my daughter to have one? No."

If her party hadn't been that much fun, young Anne certainly didn't show it that night. Though normally the quiet one in the family, Anne had been particularly effervescent. Which couldn't have been too easy for her, since the night before her dad had confided that he and her mother were about to break up their marriage. Only once at the party did Anne reveal the tension she was under. That was when, in front of news photographers, her father handed her a handwritten note. When she read the scrawled message she broke into tears. After hugging her father she kissed her mother. What the note contained remained a sentimental secret between the automobile titan and his heiress daughter.

The next night the Fords had a long talk with all three children about their forthcoming separation. "Everybody was in tears," said Charlotte. "It was crushing, especially since none of us was prepared for the news. I thought, 'What do I have to live for?'" And, she wondered, what had led to the impending breakup?

For some time it had been obvious that Henry II and Anne no longer had much rapport. Elegant and churchgoing, Anne cared little about the automobile business that consumed so much of her husband's time. And, as she was getting more and more involved in Detroit's never-ending round of charity affairs, her husband was getting more and more bored. Henry worked hard, and when evening came he liked to play hard. The last thing he wanted was to put on tails and accompany his well-coiffed wife to some ballroom downtown. But that was one of the penalties of being a social and civic leader. And whenever one of his pals would say what a "lovely lady" Anne Ford was, her husband would screw up his face and ask, "Did you ever get into the sack with a lady?"

Henry's idea of a good time was to unwind over copious quantities of Scotch and tell earthy stories. One place in which he liked to do his unwinding was P. J. Clarke's, a trendy Irish pub on Third Avenue in New York. At P. J.'s he would usually sit for hours with Patrick J. Doyle, a longtime police reporter for the *Daily News,* who would keep him amused with the latest gossip. Occasionally they would get into loud arguments. According to Doyle, Henry's use of expletives was "magnificent." Once, having nothing better to do, Henry and his newspaper chum wandered over to the *Daily News,* where they visited the city room. After spending a couple of hours talking to Doyle's colleagues, Henry said, "Gee, this is an exciting business."

Henry also loved to dance. Though he was on the large side, he moved nimbly as he performed the latest steps. And he loved to lead the orchestra. Once, at a Southampton party, Henry, fully clothed, led a Dixieland band in the playing of a favorite song, "When the Saints Go Marching In." Then, beckoning the band to follow him, he led its members, also fully clothed, into the swimming pool, all the time playing "The Saints." Another night Henry suddenly disappeared from a Southampton party he and Anne were hosting. Worried and embarrassed, Anne asked some guests to look for him. They soon found Henry racing his new car over the fairway at a nearby golf course. Somehow they convinced their host to return to his party.

By now Henry's ability to imbibe had become almost legendary. "I don't think he ever gets a headache," said his good friend Max Fisher, the Detroit financier. "He can mix wine and Scotch—and anything else." But another friend who had partied with Henry said, "Don't quote me, but he can get obnoxious." There was one hushed-up episode that occurred at a get-together at an exclusive club on Long Island. No one can precisely recall what set Henry II off. But the Chairman of the Ford Motor Company flung a cake at someone. Missing its target, the cake struck a portrait of the club founder. Though he did pay for restoration of the painting, Henry was banished from the club.

Said his brother William Clay Ford, "He has a *darn* good time when he has a good time." Which may well have been one of the problems that developed between Henry and Anne.

She constantly sought to restrain his uninhibited exuberance. At parties, for example, Anne always knew when it was time to go home. She had been brought up that way. But when Henry II was having a good time, he rarely wanted to leave. There were times when Anne would leave without him. On other occasions she would practically have to drag him home. All of which helped contribute to strains in their marriage. As a friend noted, "Nobody named Henry Ford likes to be pushed around."

When their separation was eventually announced, Nancy Randolph, the society editor of the New York *Daily News* recalled that, while vacationing at fashionable Round Hill in Jamaica, Anne and Henry had "noticeably different attitudes on what constituted a good time. Anne, elegantly dressed, self-contained, dignified, had a so-much-and-no-more attitude on dining, dancing and staying up late. Henry was plainly a bon vivant, a comfortably clad, hearty devotee of living it up. Some of their companions thought Anne restrained him too much. Or tried to."

That Henry was a "trifle prone to high jinks," particularly after downing a few, was also noted by another society columnist, Doris Lilly. "During a party at El Morocco, Henry took me to dance, and galloped me around for well over an hour. He held me tight and didn't talk much, for which I was grateful. I don't think I could have spoken, I was so out of breath."

But what most Grosse Pointers had believed to be an idyllic marriage ran into real trouble when Henry II met Maria Cristina Vettore Austin in Paris. Cristina, an Italian divorcée with "twinkly" turquoise eyes and natural tawny blond hair, was a close friend of Mrs. Rosemarie Ravelli Kanzler, whose fourth husband was none other than Henry's "Uncle Ernie." The first Mrs. Kanzler—Mrs. Edsel Ford's sister—had died in 1954 in a swimming-pool accident at Hobe Sound. The following year Kanzler married the spirited Swiss-born Rosmarie Ravelli, and ever since, as "Uncle Ernie" told Henry II, he had had his "batteries recharged." It was a new way of life for Kanzler. He was spending more time in Europe, "having fun." And he had added two European homes to the three he already had in the U.S., a magnificent new cottage in St. Moritz and a large mansion at Cap Ferrat on the French Riviera.

The new Mrs. Kanzler soon emerged as a luminary on the European social scene. But she seemed out of place in the more sedate setting of Grosse Pointe. Word had gotten around as to her humble beginnings, and it was even whispered that she had once been a manicurist. But what made Grosse Pointe particularly unbearable for Mrs. Kanzler was her feeling that the very proper Mrs. Henry Ford II had deliberately ignored her.

Perhaps inadvertently, Rosemarie Kanzler was to obtain her revenge. Along with her husband, in March 1960 she gave a dinner party at Maxim's in honor of Princess Grace of Monaco. Henry II, who was in Paris on business, was invited, as was the ravishing Cristina Austin, a fellow traveler with the European jet set (said to be a higher caste than the American variety). Cristina was in Capri at the time and at first she didn't want to come. She said she didn't have the proper clothes in Capri for such a party. But Rosemarie insisted that she come, saying not to worry about a gown, one would be awaiting her in Paris. At first it appeared to be just another fancy dinner party, and none of the guests could imagine the tremors that were about to be set off in the Ford dynasty.

Actually, Henry had met Cristina the night before. But, as she later recalled, it was only "How do you do?" At Maxim's, however, Henry asked the hostess if he could sit next to her. And that was when their romance began. As Cristina remembers that evening: "He told me within three hours of meeting me that he was going to marry me. I laughed. He had a wife. I told my sister that I'd met this amusing man who made some car—I couldn't remember which one—who said he was going to marry me. I said these American men are very impetuous." Later Cristina was to deny that she had set her cap for the married Henry. "It just happened," she said in her quaint accent. "I did not want to break up his marriage. Believe me, I did not break up his marriage. This marriage, it was already broke."

Which may well have been an accurate portrayal of the facts. As a mutual friend told columnist Liz Smith, Henry and Anne "had been married quite a long time; just long enough for him to begin to want to see a new vision of himself—in some other woman's eyes. He was always like a naughty kid around Anne and she was always putting him down."

Cristina was something else. Earthy and fun-loving, she liked naughty men—the naughtier the better. Henry, who was forty-three at the time, had never met anyone like her. And he was quickly smitten by her Mediterranean charms. Though at the time she claimed to be in her early thirties, Doris Lilly said she had evidence that Cristina was at least ten years older. Later an irate Cristina was to accuse Miss Lilly to her face of having "lied" about her age. And, indeed, reliable friends of Cristina definitely support her version of her age. Miss Lilly nevertheless admitted Cristina "looked better in a bikini than anyone I've ever seen," whatever her age.

Theirs necessarily was a secret courtship and Henry II was making more and more "business" trips to Europe. At first, Cristina told friends, she didn't think Henry was interested in much more than having a middle-age fling and would get over it pretty quickly. But at his urging Cristina moved to New York, obtaining a four-room apartment at 530 Park Avenue on the southwest corner of Sixty-first Street. What made it all most convenient was that Henry II maintained a suite at the Regency Hotel, which was located on the northwest corner. Needless to say, Henry was a frequent dinner guest across the street. Among her other manifest attributes, Cristina liked to cook. After dinner Henry would join in doing the dishes, something he had never done before in his entire life.

By late 1961 rumors of their friendship began showing up in so-called "blind" items in the gossip columns. It was then that Henry had a pang of conscience. He was worried about what a possible breakup of his twenty-year marriage would do to his children. And he was concerned about what a breath of scandal might do to his company, so dependent on the whims of a car-buying public. After a great deal of soul-searching, Henry Ford decided to break off the relationship. "He thought we had better not see each other again," said Cristina. And for a time they went their separate ways.

Henry sought to reestablish a relationship with his wife. But it didn't work. All through this period it was obvious that something was eating at Henry. What it was few of his associates knew. Some suspected, however, that his marriage was going to pot. And Henry made no effort to disabuse them of that notion. According to financier Max Fisher, who was close to Ford, "this was a period of excruciating torment to Henry . . . And I think I saw what a lot of other people did not see, and that was Henry's own insecurity with himself—a possible guilt complex. He wondered what he had done wrong, how had he contributed to the failure of a marriage . . . I tried to help him understand that a man must find his own happiness in his own inner emotional security, and that he could accomplish nothing by berating himself. A man deserves to have a mate."

Cristina, meanwhile, began playing the field. And that too troubled Henry. But what's a lady to do under the circumstances? Particularly a lady who felt their separation was not of her doing. "It was his idea," Cristina later said. "I never ask him to marry me. All I want is to be happy. As for his marriage, pfft! It was dead. I don't think a woman should let a husband know she is suspicious. Then the other woman becomes forbidden fruit. You know what I mean?"

Among Henry's rivals at the time was the cosmetics czar Charles Revson, whose womanizing was legendary. Cristina had met Revson in a most unusual way. Not long in New York, and stopping at the Pierre, she had gone to the hotel drugstore to purchase a lipstick. "My English wasn't very good and I didn't know what to ask for. I said I wanted a Revlon lipstick . . . that was all I knew. The drugstore didn't sell Revlon, but a man in the far corner of the store said if I liked Revlon he would send me some. The next day an enormous box of Revlon products came to the hotel for me. The man standing in the drugstore was Charles Revson."

Soon afterward Cristina moved to the Park Avenue apartment. And Revson, a bachelor at the time, could not trace her. He arranged for one of his artists to draw her picture from his memory. The drawing was circulated in Manhattan's better restaurants, where waiters were offered a thousand-dollar reward if they could help Revson find this woman from Italy. "In a restaurant where I was known, a waiter gave him the address," Cristina continued, "and for two weeks I would receive 300 roses each day. But there was no card." Finally a card came with a note from Revson asking Cristina to have lunch with him. "I telephoned and said it was no use . . . that I was in love with a man from Pittsburgh. I didn't want to tell him whom I really loved, but he found out." And that made Cristina even more desirable.

Not easily discouraged, Revson eventually persuaded Cristina to spend an occasional weekend with him at his country estate. The cosmetics king offered to put a million dollars in the bank as a guarantee of his intentions. If he didn't marry her, the million was hers.

Finally Henry couldn't stand it any longer. He telephoned Cristina and asked to see her again. They resumed their relationship. When Cristina told him of Revson's offer, he said, "Bambina, don't marry him."

Revson's pursuit of Cristina infuriated Henry. Years later, while sailing on his yacht in the Mediterranean, someone happened to refer to Revson as "Le Beau Charles." Irritated, Henry snapped, "Make that, 'Le Beau Kike.'"

Having given up Revson's million, Cristina in effect had settled for a part-time life with Henry without marriage. It was not the best of existences. At times she was lonely and depressed. Once, on a trip to California, she made the acquaintance of a European-born woman—a Washingtonian who was to become one of her best friends—at the swimming pool of the Beverly Hills Hotel. Over lunch she poured out her story. She was in love with a married man who had three children. She did not identify the man, but he was quite prominent on the American scene. And she didn't know what to do. She just had to talk to someone.

It wasn't the worst of existences either. By this time she had become a familiar figure in the better shops and in such gathering places as El Morocco, Le Pavillon, the Colony, La Caravelle and the "21" Club. And with a friend like Henry Ford II, her credit rating could not have been higher. Because of their friendship Cristina's photograph began to appear in newspapers and national magazines. Seldom, if ever, did Henry's name appear in connection with hers. *Harper's Bazaar*, for example, published a two-page spread, "Cristina Austin: a camera portrait by Richard Avedon," titled "The Eclectic Beauty." The photograph was of the left profile of Cristina; she wore no makeup or jewelry. Though it gave no reason for her prominence, it included a poem by Alice S. Morris, one line of which was, "Their beauty transcends locality, recognizes no frontiers."

Still, Henry II sought to keep up appearances. Once he and Cristina appeared at a fashionable restaurant, only to be told by the *maître d' hôtel* that no tables were available. When Henry insisted on being seated, the headwaiter was forced to whisper that his daughter Charlotte was dining inside.

One Saturday night Henry and Cristina drove to a Westchester restaurant in Ardsley. After dinner he asked the parking attendant for the car he had rented earlier in the day. The attendant brought him someone else's vehicle. But Henry, not knowing the difference, took off with Cristina for Manhattan. Meanwhile, back in Ardsley, the police were called in for what appeared to be a stolen car case. It was soon established that the car left in the lot had been rented by Henry Ford II. And the car Henry had rented was, of all things, a Chevrolet. Henry was called at the Carlyle. Yes, he had a Chevrolet in the hotel garage, explaining he occasionally rented competing cars to see how they ran. It was all a very funny story for the New York newspapers, which published every detail but one—the fact that Cristina had been with him.

And then one day it happened. While Henry and Cristina were dining, his wife entered the restaurant. She went directly to their table. "This was bound to happen some time," she said pleasantly. But always the well-mannered lady, Anne Ford quickly took her leave. For Henry it had not been the most happy of occasions.

Still Anne was hoping for a permanent reconciliation. And at times it looked as if Henry was indeed having second thoughts. For Christmas 1962 he presented Anne with a $65,000 necklace of pearls as big as marbles. And it was the talk of Detroit. Then he made several well publicized appearances with his wife at social events. Smiling, they both attended a performance of the Metropolitan Opera Company in Detroit. One of their last appearances together was in New York in June 1963, when they were among the "cover personalities" at a party for celebrities who had been featured on the cover of *Time* during the forty years of that magazine's existence. Their companions at the Waldorf were the John Hay Whitneys—he was publisher of the now defunct New York *Herald-Tribune*—who did not see anything amiss with the Fords that night.

Cristina did not know what to think. She spoke to some close friends, mostly Europeans, about her dilemma. One of them, Igor Cassini, the Hearst society columnist who wrote under the name "Cholly Knickerbocker," didn't think Henry intended to marry her. So he advised her to at least seek a prenuptial settlement from Ford. And according to Cassini, that's what Ford agreed to do. He made Cristina a cash offer, which Cassini reported as being a modest $37,000. Without mentioning names, Cassini published a "blind" item in the New York *Journal-American* of May 23, 1963, stating that a prominent industrialist and his beautiful wife (whom he did not name) were "happily together again—as we thought they would be after seeing them hand in hand at a recent dinner."

But within weeks Henry II was again seeing Cristina. And Anne Ford finally decided she had had enough. It had not been an easy decision. She had truly loved her husband. And her devotion to her religion precluded divorce. But she felt she had been humiliated enough. Rumors of discord in the Ford household began to sweep Detroit. But they were all denied by spokesmen for the Ford Motor Company. The rumors had gained particular currency when it was learned that Mrs. Ford had been spending a good deal of time in New York looking for an apartment. She finally chose a cooperative at 834 Fifth Avenue, a building in which such luminaries as Elizabeth Arden, Laurence Rockefeller and the Palm Beach Frank McMahons lived. The question being asked was why she needed such a layout when on her trips east she had at her disposal a big house in Southampton and an elegant apartment in the Carlyle Hotel.

The answer was not long in coming. On Saturday, August 3, 1963, their Detroit attorney, Pierre V. Heftler, announced that the Fords, after twenty-three years of marriage, had agreed to a legal separation—in effect, an agreement to live apart. The separation followed by four days the end of a seven-month centennial observance of the birth of the original Henry Ford. There was no mention in the curt three-line statement released by Heftler of divorce or any financial settlement.

The headlines were only hours old when reporters were chasing all over Europe to find "the other woman." And when they finally caught up with Cristina in Milan, where she kept an apartment, she insisted, "Mr. Ford and I are friends, very good friends. We've known each other more than three years and have met [in] different places, mostly in Paris. But that's not romance." Henry II, keeping quiet, was reported to have flown to the south of France. And Cristina said, "Our circles may cross." She then turned up at the office of a Milan newspaperman friend to see how his paper was playing the story. He jokingly wrote a fake headline quoting her as saying; I LOVE HENRY AND I WILL SOON MARRY HIM. Cristina turned white. "Oh, no!" she squealed. "That would ruin me!" She agreed to make it: MARIA CRISTINA DOES NOT DENY FRIENDSHIP WITH HENRY FORD.

The next day she disappeared from Milan amid rumors she was en route to a rendezvous with the elusive automobile magnate. Ford, meanwhile, was cruising along the Italian Riviera aboard his luxury yacht, the million-dollar *Santa Maria*. This was a 110-foot vessel that Henry II had had built to his specifications in the Netherlands. It contained air-conditioned suites for six passengers and quarters for a crew of seven. Henry's large stateroom was fitted out with gold-plated plumbing fixtures.

Among Henry's guests on this trip was Hollywood actors' agent Pat DiCicco, former husband of Gloria Vanderbilt. On arriving in the resort town of Portofino, Henry II was mobbed by at least a hundred reporters and photographers. At first he talked cordially with the newsmen about his craft, which had hit a storm leaving Monte Carlo. But when he was asked when he intented to join Cristina, Henry snapped back, "We won't talk about that." Then he stalked off, pursued by the *paparazzi*, as the photographers were called. Soon the *Santa Maria* left port for parts unknown—to newsmen.

Anne Ford, who had also slipped out of sight, eventually turned up in New York. She took over the Ford apartment at the Hotel Carlyle while she directed the decorating of her new Fifth Avenue suite. Her daughters Charlotte and Anne, meanwhile, were in New York. Her son Edsel was in boarding school. All were still upset over the split in the family. Charlotte, particularly, took it badly. But as she later said, she did not suffer as much mental anguish as had been widely reported. "I suppose we did feel rejected in a way," she said, "and I'll admit I was upset over it. But I didn't have any nervous breakdown."

On December 26, 1963, her mother turned up in Sun Valley, Idaho, for what was described as an indefinite period of skiing. She was accompanied by Charlotte and young Edsel, who broke his leg on the slopes a short time afterward and spent a brief period in Sun Valley Hospital. Daughter Anne arrived later.

Exactly six weeks after her arrival—the required period of residence for filing for divorce in Idaho—Anne McDonnell Ford appeared in a courtroom seventy miles away. After a twenty minute hearing she was granted an uncontested decree on grounds of mental cruelty. Whereupon Mrs. Ford slipped out of the courthouse and drove back to Sun Valley, where she went into seclusion. In Dearborn, where he was attending a board of directors meeting of his $5.5 billion company, Henry II declined comment. In all, the settlement, worked out at the time of the separation, cost Henry an estimated $16 million. Custody of their son Edsel was granted to Anne.

Later on returning to New York, she said, "I've had a hard year."

It had also been hard on Henry II's mother, Mrs. Edsel Ford, who was in her mid-sixties; she felt that the behavior of her eldest son was unforgivable. This, after all, was the first marital breakup in the proud history of the very proper Ford family. Moreover, Eleanor Clay Ford admired her elegant former daughter-in-law, who, she felt, had been embarrassed and wronged by a son who "had lost his senses." And she was particularly disturbed about reports that Henry was thinking of marrying a woman whose background was, to say the least, most exotic.

Not only was she disturbed but she was said at the time to have warned Henry against taking such a precipitous step. In fact, according to an undenied report in the New York *Daily News*, as a major Ford stockholder, she had even threatened to force her son out of his chairmanship. The accuracy of the report is difficult to ascertain. Recollections vary. Mrs. Ford herself passed away in 1976, and Henry II made it a practice not to discuss his private affairs. All that can be established is that he did not immediately marry the new woman in his life for whose sake, presumably, he had asked his longtime wife for a divorce.

Apparently Henry II managed to assuage his mother's feelings. For on the night of February 19, 1965, Henry took unto himself the very woman who had aroused such concern in family councils. But there were no members of the clan present when the auto magnate married Cristina Austin in a simple civil ceremony in a Ford suite in Washington's Shoreham Hotel. Henry II, dressed in a dark business suit, and Cristina, wearing a beige cocktail dress, exchanged vows before a District of Columbia judge, Milton S. Kronheim, Jr. A Ford public-relations man, James Newmyer, and Hildegarde Czerner, the proprietor of a chic Georgetown boutique, were the only other persons present.

Immediately after a wedding dinner at the Jockey Club the couple left for New York, where they hopped a plane for London. But it wasn't until the next day that the press was informed of the marriage. The announcement was made in Detroit by attorney Heftler, who had also announced the separation of Henry II from his wife a year and a half before. Another announcement came from the Roman Catholic Church. A spokesman for the chancery office of the archdiocese of Detroit said that, because of his remarriage, Henry II was automatically excommunicated from the church. This was also true of his Catholic bride, it was said. And since then Henry has refused to discuss his excommunication, for, as a spokesman said, he regards religion as "a personal matter."

So that they would not be surprised by newspaper publicity, Henry II telephoned his daughters to tell them he had just married Cristina. At the same time he suggested that they join him and his bride on his honeymoon in Switzerland. He said he would be staying at the Palace Hotel in St. Moritz and would reserve a suite for them. The girls were astonished at the invitation, to say the least. Neither of them had any intention of warming up to Cristina, because they were convinced she had broken up their parents' marriage. Their father, knowing this, suggested they they come and get to know his new wife better. Finally they relented. As it turned out, they couldn't have had a better time. They had expected to spend most of their time in their rooms, but instead their father made sure they were involved in his activities. In this way they did get to know their new stepmother, and, as Charlotte later said, "We found her enchanting."

It was at St. Moritz that Charlotte became involved with an old drinking buddy of her father's, the fabulously rich middle-aged Greek shipping magnate Stavros Niarchos. Niarchos had arranged a dinner party in honor of the newlywed Fords. And Cristina, who was most observant of such matters, asked Charlotte after dinner, "Did you notice how Stavros was looking at you?" Charlotte could hardly have *not* noticed. The next few weeks Charlotte and Stavros were inseparable. They went skiing together, and at night they would make the rounds together, sometimes with Henry II and Cristina.

Niarchos of course was married. His wife was the shipping heiress Eugenie Livanos. (Eugenie's sister, Tina, once married to that other Greek Midas, Aristotle Onassis, was then the Marchioness of Blandford.) Eugenie was Stavros' third spouse. And she had borne him four children, whom he adored. But marital fidelity meant very little in the jet-set capital that is St. Moritz in the winter. For, as Doris Lilly, the able chronicler of international society's doings, noted: "St. Moritz is just plain sexy and the Palace Hotel is a hotbed of passion. I don't know if it is all the fresh air, or the altitude. But I do know that I was there for two weeks before I even heard about the elevator. On the other hand, the carpets covering the staircase must be changed every month."

Ironically, Henry Ford II was the last to know what was really going on. After all, Charlotte was the serious-minded do-gooder in the Ford clan. She was not one for quickie romances. Not that she wasn't interested in boys. When she first moved to New York in 1962 she had met one whom she liked. He was a former Detroiter who was running an organization formed to combat juvenile delinquency in New York's ghetto areas. Charlotte became deeply involved in the organization's activities. And she became involved with the young man in question. Her father, however, was not too happy about all this, particularly after he learned that the organization was seeking a substantial grant from the Ford Foundation. Henry II quickly decided the young man was not for Charlotte, and he told her so.

His other daughter had also become interested in a man. And when she told her father about it, Henry wasn't too happy with him either. He told Anne he wasn't going to interfere with her marriage plans if she insisted on it, but he did want her to know of certain faults and weaknesses in the man. "And he enumerated them," said Anne. "He asked me to think about them before I went ahead and got married. I did think of them, and I stopped seeing him."

"Was your father right?" she was asked.

"One hundred percent," she replied.

In the summer of 1965 Niarchos continued his pursuit of Charlotte. The heiress was cruising the Mediterranean on the *Santa Maria*. Niarchos followed from port to port on his 190-foot *Creole*, the largest privately owned yacht afloat. But despite Stavros' reputation as a womanizer, few put two and two together. After all, it hardly made any sense. Stavros was an old jet-set friend of Henry II. And he was thirty-three years older than Charlotte. In fact, he was eight years older than Charlotte's father.

Charlotte was next seen with Stavros in London. They dined at Claridge's, attended cocktail parties and seemed to have eyes only for each other. Still, few of his friends thought of the affair as being serious. For it was felt that the "Golden Greek" was just having another of his perennial flings.

Except that this time the fling became serious. Not only was Charlotte deeply in love with Stavros but, as she learned on returning to New York, she was pregnant. After discussing her predicament with her sister, she decided to talk to her mother.

Needless to say, Anne Sr. was concerned. An abortion was out as far as she was concerned. And she advised her daughter to have the baby, whether in or out of wedlock. "I wasn't laying a Catholic trip on her," Anne Sr. said years later, "but I thought the baby would be the most meaningful thing in her life—which is the way it turned out."

Henry Ford was in Dearborn when he received a call from his daughters. They wanted to see him as soon as possible. "Is it important?" he asked. Yes, it was. So important, they added, that they would like to see him that very evening. Henry II grabbed a company plane and was in New York several hours later. Henry listened to Charlotte's story. As Anne recalled, she thought her father "was about to have a heart attack." Calming down, he asked some questions. And then he said, "Well, I guess we'd better go talk to Stavros."

Since Stavros was in London, they flew there the next morning. "Mother just happened to be there too, and so was Stavros' wife," Anne recalled. "Both of them were as understanding about it as they could be. Mrs. Niarchos agreed to get a divorce. But it was Daddy who handled everything. He was there when we needed him."

There were other problems in a possible Ford-Niarchos liaison. Some members of the family, most notably Henry's brothers, feared the passing of partial control of the Ford Motor Company into foreign hands. And then there was the matter of an ancient dispute Stavros had had with the U.S. government involving millions of dollars in taxes that he had avoided paying. As a consequence Stavros had been unable to enter the country lest he be arrested.

But Niarchos made it clear to his prospective father-in-law that he had no interest in the Ford Motor Company. Whether he signed any documents to that effect is not known. But Henry Ford was convinced the family would have no problem in that regard. As for Stavros' difficulties with Washington, Ford said he would see what he could do. After all, he had some pretty good friends in high places, among them Lyndon B. Johnson, whom he had supported for President in 1964. The relationship between the President and Ford was very close. In fact, there had been more than just talk for a time that LBJ might appoint Henry II as ambassador to France. The problem was the slight taint of scandal that was associated with Henry's marital difficulties.

Meanwhile Charlotte returned to New York with her mother and sister. The Ford women had been booked for a fashion layout in the New York *Herald-Tribune*. Eugenia Sheppard, then editor of the woman's page, was in charge of the project. The idea was to pose Anne Sr. and her daughters in her newly decorated duplex apartment on Fifth Avenue. Because Charlotte was obviously expecting, she stood behind a Louis XV chair to hide her expanding girth. Her mother obliged the photographer by swinging her coltish legs over the arms of the chair. "It's a historic picture," says Miss Sheppard. Whether historic or not, it certainly gave the willies to the sensitive souls at the public-relations department of the Ford Motor Company, particularly when it was reprinted in the national news magazines.

On December 14, 1965, Eugenie Niarchos appeared in a civil court in Juarez, Mexico, and requested that her marriage of eighteen years be terminated on the grounds of incompatibility of character. A decree was granted within five minutes. Two days later Charlotte Ford and her lawyer flew to Juarez from New York in a Ford plane. Soon afterward Niarchos arrived from Canada in another Ford plane. He presented Charlotte with a forty-carat diamond ring valued at $600,000, which became known in the Ford family as "the skating rink." Then they were married in a hotel room by a civil judge. The announcement of the marriage, made in New York in the name of Henry Ford II and his first wife, caught society napping. "Married!" exclaimed one of Charlotte's former escorts, "Charlotte Ford and Niarchos? I didn't even know they had been *introduced*."

The newlyweds then flew in another Ford plane to Nassau, where Niarchos had a house. To fly on to Europe they shifted to a chartered Boeing 707, complete with crew and over a hundred empty seats, at a cost of $40,000. They were accompanied by a valet and Niarchos's lawyer. Arriving in Zurich, they transferred to one of Stavros' private planes, which took them to St. Moritz. By then the press was hot on their trail.

Photographers grabbed pictures of the newlyweds, and newspapers around the world devoted considerable space to the May-December romance.

From the start it was a curious marriage. On arriving in St. Moritz they went to the Palace Hotel instead of to Niarchos' mountainside chalet, which happened to be occupied by his ex-wife Eugenie and their four children. Stavros kept seeing his ex-wife. Because of her pregnancy, Charlotte did not choose to ski. But Stavros and Eugenie went skiing almost every day. And the three of them lunched frequently before blazing fireplaces at the Corviglia Club. Even the most blasé of St. Moritz denizens were astonished at the spectacle of such unusual togetherness.

While Charlotte was on her honeymoon her sister Anne, who at the age of twenty-two was one of the youngest women ever to have been named to the best-dressed list, was married to thirty-one-year-old Giancarlo (Johnny) Uzielli. They had met the year before at a Christmas party. And as she told an interviewer some years later, she hadn't dated anyone else after meeting Uzielli. "He's the most gregarious man I've ever known, the most fun to be with," she added. "You know it's funny, thinking of my great grandfather's hatred of Jews, of international bankers, of Wall Street financiers. Now I'm married to one!"

Handsome Harvard-educated Uzielli, though of Jewish origin, had been born in Italy and raised a Catholic. He was a member of the New York Stock Exchange and a partner in his father's firm, Tucker, Anthony and R. L. Day. His brief first marriage was to Anne Marie Deschodt, a model, who later married Louis Malle, the French movie director. Uzielli was "absolutely terrified" of Henry Ford, he later recalled. "I'd only met him briefly, and here I had to go to his apartment and go through the formality of asking for his daughter's hand in marriage. I was scared to death. But the moment I walked in, Mr. Ford put me right at ease. He said, 'I know why you're here, and anything that my daughter wants is all right with me.'"

Charlotte of course couldn't be at her sister's wedding, although she was supposed to have been the maid of honor.

But she was most definitely on her father's mind the night before when, at a lavish reception in the Crystal Room at Delmonico's, Henry II stood up and announced how much everybody missed the honeymooners. Then, after champagne glasses were filled with Piper Heidsieck, Henry proposed a toast to "Anne and Gianni and Charlotte and Stavros."

Again it was a party in the Henry Ford II tradition. Mink, ermine, diamonds, emeralds—and security guards provided by the Ford Motor Company—were everywhere. The bride-to-be, her mother and her mother's constant escort, socialite Ted Bassett, arrived half an hour before the party was to begin. Almost simultaneously Henry II and Cristina drew up in another limousine. The five hundred guests, all carefully screened by the security guards, began arriving at the fashionably later hour of 11:00 P.M. They included young Winston Churchill and his wife, in from London; Winston's mother and stepfather, the Leland Haywards; Cee Zee and Winston Guest; Mary Lee and Douglas Fairbanks; Mary Lasker and Truman Capote. They were greeted in the receiving line by Henry II, his ex-wife Anne, and the romantic protagonists Anne and Giancarlo. Though she was prettily present, glittering in an attractive green gown, her long blond hair swept up, the new Mrs. Ford kept out of the spotlight. At midnight a lavish buffet was served. And all the while there was dancing to the music of the Wild Ones for frugging, and to Emory Davis, look-alike son of Meyer, for more traditional steps. Everyone appeared to be having a good time, Henry II most of all. He was on the dance floor without a letup, dancing with his former wife, among others. Finally, at about 3:00 A.M., the party ended.

The wedding took place the following evening at the Fifth Avenue apartment of Anne's mother. The bride was given in marriage by her father. A small reception for members of the family and a few friends followed the civil ceremony. Among the guests were the bride's uncles and aunts, the Benson Fords, the William Clay Fords and the Walter Buhl Fords. Also there was Edsel Ford, now seventeen and attending The Gunnery, a prep school, class of 1968. The reception was bubbly with champagne and gay with music and conversation. Under orders from Henry II, the Lester Lanin trio played "Italian" music in deference to the groom—"Arrivederci, Roma" and "Ciao, Ciao, Bambina." When the time came for the traditional group photograph, the first Mrs. Ford took her erstwhile rival by the hand and said, "Come on, Cristina, we're going to have our pictures taken together." Everything was terribly civilized.

Meanwhile, after three months of her St. Moritz honeymoon ("the only married life I had"), Charlotte Ford Niarchos returned to New York to await the arrival of her child. She settled down in a triplex owned by her husband at 25 Sutton Place, and, as she observed later, "You can't imagine how dreary the place was. The bedroom was done in junk. It's taken me two years to make the place livable." Shortly before the baby was due Stavros arrived in New York. It was his first visit to the U.S. in ten years. Somehow he had managed to settle his accounts with the U.S. government regarding his long-standing tax delinquency. But instead of forking over about $25 million, he settled for $1,468,000. The rest of the tax debt was written off as uncollectible. As the muckraking columnist Drew Pearson then noted of this deal, "It helps to have friends in high places."

In the final weeks of her pregnancy Charlotte moved over to the apartment of her mother. Her husband meanwhile was doing the town he hadn't seen for a decade. The night before Charlotte entered New York Hospital she accompanied Stavros to a gala exhibition of work by jeweler David Webb at French & Company. The next day she gave birth to a seven-pound girl whom she immediately named Elena. Little Elena had made Henry Ford II a grandfather for the first time.

After attending his daughter's christening, Stavros returned to Europe. When Charlotte and the baby were able to travel, they flew to Stavros' villa in Cap d'Antibes. There she received a telegram from him saying that he had flown off to an African safari with his youngest son. Next came an abrupt visit from a mutual friend who told her that Niarchos wanted a separation.

Charlotte returned to New York, where she made plans to divorce Niarchos. About ten days before she was to leave for Juarez to institute proceedings, Stavros turned up at the Sutton Place apartment. They then flew to his home in Nassau, where they spent five days. "It was really a honeymoon," Charlotte later told Henry Ehrlich of *Look* magazine. "You know, I think I am the only woman he ever really loved." Returning to New York they spent an apparently gay evening at El Morocco. The next morning, at 6:00 A.M., she flew with her mother to Mexico aboard a chartered plane. On March 17, 1967, she was granted a divorce on grounds of incompatibility. Asked why her marriage had broken up, she said bluntly, "He drove me nuts. My ex-husband is not a happy man. He can't relax. He has no office, his office is with him wherever he goes. I found out that he was married to his Telex machine. That was all that mattered to him. It's as simple as that."

To no one's great surprise, Niarchos reunited with Eugenie. They did not need to remarry, because in the eyes of the Greek Orthodox Church his fourth marriage, to Charlotte, had been null and void. It wasn't that the Church was opposed to divorce, but it allowed a man only three marriages.

But to everyone's great surprise, Stavros continued to see Charlotte. In fact, they were seeing more of each other after the divorce. They appeared together one night at El Morocco, causing Doris Lilly to observe that if the marriage hadn't worked, the divorce most certainly did. For months Stavros showered Charlotte with all sorts of expensive jewelry. And he called her almost every day. In August 1967 they toured Europe and North Africa together. While they were at the Mamounia Hotel in Marrakech, Charlotte fell ill and returned home. Her health was a problem. A year later Charlotte was stricken with Bell's palsy, a virus infection that paralyzed one side of her face. She has since recovered from it.

By this time Charlotte had had her fill of Stavros. He had sent her an expensive pin from Harry Winston, then had the bill delivered to her. She kept the pin but refused to pay the bill. Quarreling constantly, they would have loud shouting matches over the trans-Atlantic phone. And he would become angry over such things as her having said hello to the man he hated most in the world, his ex-brother-in-law and rival, Aristotle Onassis. "Greeks don't like to see you dead," she said. "They like to watch you die." She was referring not only to Stavros but to his assorted friends and relatives—particularly one relative, his mother, who lived one floor below her at

Sutton Place. Charlotte had never forgiven the senior Mrs. Niarchos for remarks she had made when Charlotte had married her son.

But as a result of her short marriage Charlotte drew closer to her father. She began to see more of him. "He's a lot more affectionate with my child than I think he was with me," she told author Booton Herndon, "and I love to see them playing together. And I'm so proud of him. He's aware of the change in our times. He knows he's Henry Ford. He believes that our form of government, our way of life is the best—it has certainly been good to us—and there is really nothing he can do but work hard to defend and protect it. I'm only sorry that he had to drive himself so hard all the time.

"At least if he works hard, he rests hard too," she continued. "I remember weekends after long periods when he'd sleep until two or three o'clock in the afternoon. I was in Nassau with him and he slept practically all the time. You don't hear about him when he's asleep. It annoys me when European friends tell me that Americans don't enjoy life. Well, Daddy is one American who does. He has the facility for really getting away from the office, for relaxing completely away from his work. And he deserves it."

7

PRESIDENTS

IF ANY DOUBTS REMAINED OVER WHO RAN THE FORD MOTOR Company, they ended with the ouster of "Bunkie" Knudsen in August 1969, after only nineteen months as president. This surprising development once again demonstrated that, like his grandfather, Henry Ford II was not a man to share power. As he often reminded his subordinates, "My name is on the building." And as long as his name was on the twelve-story headquarters in Dearborn—the Glass House—he was the top man, and make no mistake about it. Like his grandfather, too, he kept his distance from most of his underlings. Except for his brothers, Benson and William Clay, not even the top men of his company dared call him by his first name. No longer was it "call me Henry." His executives quickly learned that, because of his unpredictable moods, it was wiser not to become too chummy with the boss. As Lee Iacocca, the *Wunderkind* who then headed Ford's North American operations, explained, "I don't want to be fired for something I said to Mr. Ford over drinks at the 21 Club."

Henry's use of his ultimate power was often capricious. Thus, following Knudsen's abrupt departure, he appointed not one but three presidents to direct Ford Motor's day-to-day operations: Iacocca, Robert Stevenson, president of Ford's international operations, and Robert J. Hampson, president of the Philco-Ford and tractor operations. Philco was the Philadelphia-based electronics corporation that Ford had purchased in 1961. "Just about everyone on the board and at the top of management was against Philco," said a former Ford director. But since Henry wanted the company because it was involved in space and defense work, "we did it." Philco proved to be a disaster, losing millions of dollars a year. Eventually Henry was forced to admit that Philco was "a can of worms," but he would never concede that its acquisition, at his urging, had been a mistake.

Nor did he ever concede that his appointment of a troika of presidents was a mistake. Under his supervision, he insisted, the troika would work. The fact that Ford Motor had one of the highest executive turnover rates in American industry did not faze him either. "I think we've got good depth in management," he said. "I think we've got some very capable people."

The new management structure left Henry clearly in charge as Chairman, with three presidents all reporting directly to him and no intermediary or over-all company president. The result was an executive-suite atmosphere that knowing Detroiters likened to a Byzantine court. The rumor mill turned largely on which of the three executives—Iacocca, Stevenson or Hampson—seemed to be most in the Chairman's favor at the moment. Before long the betting was on Iacocca, who had earned his spurs by foaling the highly successful Mustang, the sporty car for Everyman. Iacocca was something unusual for a Ford executive. He was known to have occasionally told Henry he thought the Chairman was wrong. Even so, visitors to Iacocca's office would see him stiffen whenever Henry phoned. Iacocca's end of the conversation usually was "Yes, sir; yes, sir; yes, Mr. Ford."

Lido Anthony Iacocca was born in Allentown, Pennsylvania, on October 15, 1924, into what can be described as a Ford family. His father, Nicola, who had come from Italy at twelve years of age, launched one of the nation's first rent-a-car agencies, and most of his thirty cars were Fords. Nearly two decades after driving in America, Nicola, thirty-one, returned to San Marco, Italy, to choose a bride. She was sixteen-year-old Antoinette Perotto, and they honeymooned at the Lido in Venice, the source of their second-born's first name. Their first child was a girl, Delma.

Lido grew up in Allentown, a skinny middle-class Italian kid who early decided he wanted to enter the auto business, preferably with Ford. He graduated from Allentown High School, a member of the National Honor Society. "If knowledge is power, he is omnipotent," his class yearbook stated. "This, together with the ability he has developed in managing and directing school affairs, will prove a great asset in his career of engineering." After graduating from nearby Lehigh University with a mechanical engineering degree, he signed on with Ford as a trainee. But Lee—the nickname he assumed after leaving Allentown—wanted still more education. He obtained a leave of absence to earn a master's degree in engineering at Princeton University. Returning to Dearborn, he completed the eighteen-month trainee program in nine months. Offered a job in the company's engineering department, Lee Iacocca said he had other ideas. He wanted to be assigned to the sales staff "to get a feel of the industry." At the age of twenty-two he was transferred to Chester, Pennsylvania, as a salesman.

In ten years Iacocca sold so many cars that he attracted the attention of Robert S. McNamara, then vice-president of Ford. That led Iacocca to a job in Detroit as marketing director for Ford trucks. Within a year truck sales had jumped and Iacocca was promoted to car-marketing manager. And as McNamara moved up the corporate ladder, Iacocca followed. They were an anomalous pair—the senior man generally tight and well-disciplined, while his protégé was flashy and more outspoken. In November 1960, at the precocious age of thirty-six, Iacocca attained what was at one time his life's goal, a corporate vice-presidency (in charge of the Ford division, the heart of the company). It had not been a complete triumph—for Iacocca had planned to be there a year earlier. "He had a schedule for himself as to what amount of money he would like to be making," his wife Mary said. "It was on a little scrap of paper."

In taking over the Ford division, Iacocca succeeded McNamara, who was named president of the company. But McNamara did not hold his new position very long. John Kennedy had just been elected President. One Sunday night Henry Ford received a call at home advising him that McNamara was being considered for a Cabinet post by the newly elected Kennedy. "But if it's Secretary of the Treasury," McNamara told his boss the next morning, "I'm not going to take it." It turned out to be Secretary of Defense and McNamara took the job.

McNamara's departure did not affect Iacocca's rise. During the sixties he came up with a couple of winners, most notably the Mustang, followed by the Maverick—the first car aimed at competing with imported vehicles—as well as the luxury-laden Continental Mark III, which turned out to be even more profitable than the Mustang. Yet, unlike others who had risen from the sober, conformist ranks of the industry, Iacocca was perpetually outspoken and willing to swing away at fellow executives if he didn't think they were doing the job. At one meeting he outlined an ambitious plan for one of Ford's divisions, admitted it was risky, then looked at the division boss and added, "not that we've got much to lose."

But those who could meet Iacocca's exacting requirements liked working for him. "He moves," said one board member admiringly. And because of his ability to get things done, Iacocca was able to attract a group of loyal supporters within the inner circles of the company. They included both Mrs. Edsel Ford, an influential voice in family circles, and her quiet-spoken son William Clay Ford, who admired Iacocca's outspoken ways.

All of which gave Iacocca tremendous leverage as a corporate infighter—an attribute that, for a time, Henry II sought to use to his advantage. On the very first day "Bunkie" Knudsen was at Ford, Henry instructed Iacocca, "Keep an eye on him." Of course, as Iacocca later explained, this was Henry's basic technique in dealing with his top officials—playing each against the other and keeping them at odds.

Eventually Iacocca got what he wanted—the presidency of the Ford Motor Company. The troika concept, introduced after Knudsen's departure, just hadn't worked out. Henry II found himself enmeshed in too many of the day-to-day problems of his giant company, and, as he later conceded, they were "driving me up the wall."

Henry took particular interest in what the Ford Motor Company sponsored on television. On one occasion he personally called Leonard Goldenson, board chairman of the American Broadcasting Company, to complain about Howard Cosell. And the sportscaster's career was definitely on the line after the chairman of the Ford Motor Company—a major advertiser on ABC—took umbrage at the overly loquacious Cosell's first appearance on *Monday Night Football*. "Leonard, take that fellah Cosell off the air," Henry II advised. "It's impossible to watch the game." Concerned over the complaint, Goldenson called in Roone Arledge, president of ABC's sports division, to ask what he thought. Arledge asked that Cosell be given a five- or six-week trial. "If he tries to hog the mike, I'll pull the string on him," Goldenson later quoted Arledge as saying. Cosell was given the chance, and ten years later he was still being loquacious on *Monday Night Football*.

As the man in charge, Henry Ford sought to keep tabs on almost everything going on in the company. An electronic console next to his desk provided him with extensive records on over one thousand executives and other corporate data. And a desk calendar showed him where each of his thirty-six top officers would be every half day for the next week. "My problem is, I'm told, that I get too many details, and therefore I'm mucking up everybody else's water," Henry II said at the time.

What he needed was a tough, no-nonsense guy to relieve him of most of those details. And finally he decided that the "right guy" was Lee Iacocca. On December 10, 1970, in the auditorium of the Glass House, Henry personally introduced his new president to a large group of automobile reporters and editors. "It's a helluva Christmas present," Iacocca said, beaming.

Henry II was then fifty-three years old. Twenty-five years had passed since he had seized control of his grandfather's crumbling empire. He could look back and declare, as he did in an interview, that he had accomplished his most important goal—building Ford into a "viable company in the industry." That done, he went on, he still had no plans to retire. The job was too much fun. "I like it," he said. "I think there's a lot to be done and a lot of things to be accomplished. And I just like it. I'm probably standing in the way of a lot of people, but until I get thrown out, why, I don't particularly want to leave at this stage of the game. I think also that at the moment we're under such tremendous attack from all sides that it would be sort of an unfortunate time to walk out, even if I wanted to, which I don't."

The attacks, of course, were coming from critics who were arguing vociferously that the automobile industry had not done enough in the areas of safety and air pollution. Henry had strong views about the critics, particularly Ralph Nader, whom he described as being "full of crap." As for Nader's pet project of installing air bags in cars, Henry said the idea was "a bunch of baloney." And he accused the government of "crying wolf" on the subject of auto emissions. What also annoyed Ford now was "the power of labor unions." He suggested "we . . . should seriously look at . . . whether it should be controlled." Such acerbic observations frequently caused headaches for those of his underlings who had to deal with Washington, labor representatives, or consumer groups after the Chairman had spoken.

The irony was that, despite these outbursts, Henry Ford had come to be regarded as one of industry's leading liberals. *The New York Times,* for example, in a profile describing him as "a complex industrialist," noted that he was a "man aware of today's social problems and wanting to do something about them—fast—business style."

Henry's politics were unpredictable. In 1952 he strongly supported Dwight D. Eisenhower for President, to such an extent that he was later accused of having pressured Ford dealers across the country into contributing to the Republican campaign. Testifying before a Senate subcommittee, Henry conceded that he had asked his dealers to contribute, but he claimed not to have exerted improper pressure. Committee Chairman A. S. Mike Monroney suggested that while Ford may not himself have used such pressure, "I am afraid you don't realize the importance of the great Ford name." At any rate, the hearing got nowhere as Republicans heatedly tangled with Democrats in partisan fashion. But during the 1956 presidential race, Ford assured the Senate Elections Subcommittee that "no system has been organized to solicit political contributions" from his dealers for the Eisenhower reelection effort.

Henry played a less conspicuous role in the 1960 presidential contest between John F. Kennedy and Richard M. Nixon. In fact, though he publicly endorsed the Republican nominee, he contributed an equal amount to each candidate. Following JFK's razor-edge victory, Henry sought to cotton up to his old drinking buddy. In a speech before the United States Chamber of Commerce, Ford said he was impressed by the President-elect's cabinet appointments, adding, "There is no evidence as yet to support the fear that we are in for careless or radical economic surgery "

Still, Henry's support of Nixon later haunted him. He sought to exorcise that ghost by claiming it was all largely a misunderstanding, occasioned by the fact that his wife, Anne, had been a gung-ho Nixon supporter. Thus, in a conversation with Paul B. ("Red") Fay, Jr., as Kennedy's Secretary of the Navy later recalled, Ford said:

Listen, Red, I'm sure the President must think, because of all the noise Anne made up in Connecticut, that I was a Nixon man all the way. I was not. She just got so wound up and involved it looked as though I was just as committed. That wasn't the case. To support her, I gave five thousand dollars to the Nixon campaign. But more important, I'm a patriotic American. I want to help and I think I can make a contribution. I'd like to serve in some sort of a role if I could . . . in some capacity.

Informed of Ford's remarks, President Kennedy said, "Well, we'll see if we can't find a spot for good old Henry."

Fay never did find out whether "good old Henry" had been offered anything. But a year later, at his annual stockholder meeting, Ford hit out at the President. Referring to JFK's anti-inflation policy, he said, "I fear that the enormous power that can be mustered by a determined and resourceful President might be used increasingly to impose informal but nonetheless direct controls of business and, possibly, of labor.... Politically, it has dangerous implications."

Despite this, relations between the Kennedy administration and the Ford Motor Company remained on an even keel. Whenever the President traveled anywhere, the White House would request the loan of Ford automobiles. "Good old Henry" had given orders to his regional representatives to honor all such requests. One representative, Patrick J. Hillings, recalled that one time he had to round up two hundred new cars for a presidential party's visit to the Los Angeles area. As always, Pierre Salinger, JFK's press secretary, obtained a red T-bird for his personal use. "The problems arose after Kennedy returned to Washington," says Hillings. "Many of the cars were never properly returned. We had to hunt everywhere for them. So we would hire people to pick them up. We'd usually find a car outside Angie Dickinson's place. Salinger's red T-bird was always at some different house or apartment. But everybody seemed to have had a good time. And that's all that Henry Ford was interested in."

According to Hillings, the same arrangements were provided the Johnson White House, "though Lyndon's boys never overdid their requests." President Johnson had made it clear that he did not want his friendship with Henry Ford to be abused, at least not by his underlings. Johnson was forever calling Henry, seeking his advice, and the motor magnate was gratified. So gratified, in fact, that he was among the first to announce he intended to support and vote for LBJ in the 1964 presidential contest. The endorsement came about in a peculiar way. Henry had given no inkling of what he was about to do when he, as a leader of the Detroit community, had driven out to the airport to greet the President. After chatting with Johnson aboard Air Force I, Henry found it necessary to go to the men's room in the terminal building, where he ran into a reporter.

Asked what he thought of the President, Ford said without hesitation, "I think he's terrific." News of Henry's remark flashed across the country, and in an editorial *The New York Times* commented that it "provides dramatic new evidence of the breadth of Mr. Johnson's political appeal."

Along with other business and financial leaders—most of them Republicans disaffected by their party's nomination of Barry Goldwater—Ford met in the White House with the President to form the National Committee for Lyndon Johnson.

Also working for the Democratic cause was Henry's daughter Charlotte, who among other things raised a large sum of money for the Johnson campaign at a Texas-style barbecue at her mother's Long Island home. Charlotte had grown close to Lynda Bird Johnson, to whom she introduced George Hamilton, the movie star. Subsequently, the President's daughter and the actor became a well-publicized "item" in the gossip columns. "Charlotte only likes people with names," her father said. And she appeared to date only people with names, among them Cary Grant and Rod McKuen, the pop poet. She was particularly fond of Jean-Claude Killy, the French skier, whose picture she kept on her living room table. For a time she also dated Frank Sinatra, who took her to the opening game of the 1969 World Series in St. Louis. But Sinatra, who was between marriages, was not for her. For one thing, he didn't like to dance, she said, "and I do." Besides, said Charlotte, Sinatra was "basically a woman hater," like her former husband, Niarchos, "but more human and considerate. He has a heart as big as New York City."

Charlotte, however, disputed her father's characterization of her as a celebrity hound. "I only like people who've done something with their lives," she said. And she herself tried to do something about her life. But it wasn't all that easy. For a while she considered taking a job with New York City's antipollution agency, until someone noted that much of the problem was caused by automobiles. Then "the poor little rich girl," as she sardonically referred to herself, thought of working for the Ford Foundation, but she was talked out of it by her father, who suggested that she might be regarded as a family spy. Finally she was talked into doing some work for the National

Urban League, which was headed by Whitney Young, Jr. It was Young who convinced Charlotte to find out for herself what was taking place on the streets of Harlem. But when she drove into the black community in her limousine, she discovered she was not entirely welcome. "They get their backs up when we try to help them," she reported.

Whitney Young and Henry Ford had become good friends. They had met on an industrialists' tour of Eastern Europe sponsored by Time-Life Incorporated. Communist officials were amazed that a black man, one of America's "oppressed minorities" in their book, was traveling with a group of fat-cat, bloodsucking capitalists. One particularly obnoxious border guard in Hungary was shocked when Henry Ford II, whose name he knew well, got off the tour bus carrying Whitney Young's bag. "Man," Young said later, "you ought to have seen that fellow's face. . . . He must have figured I was Henry's valet, and I'd probably get off the bus dragging my ball and chain."

It was on this trip that Young sought to persuade Ford that he should take more of a leadership role in the area of social problems. "Listen," Young told him, "I'm going to make you the white Moses. You're going to be known in history as the businessman who turned this critical period of black and white relationships around."

Later that year the "white Moses" sent a check for $100,000 to Young, saying, "You are a wonderful guy and run a wonderful organization." Then he invited Young to come to Dearborn to address his top executives, some of whom were opposed to giving preferential treatment to blacks when considering job applicants. "I told them what I told all businessmen," Young said later, "to give Negroes a chance to prove themselves. Don't expect us to produce all Lena Hornes and Ralph Bunches. Just remember there are some dumb white people too." As a result of his trip, Young estimated, at least 50,000 more jobs were provided. Another result was that Henry agreed to address the National Urban League convention. "It was one of the most moving addresses I've ever heard," said Young.

What Ford had described as "the anguish and despair that come with being poor, being black, and living in the ghetto" exploded with a vengeance in Detroit in the summer of 1967. One of the most costly racial riots of the century nearly leveled entire sections of the city. As a result Henry helped create the New Detroit Committee, which was aimed at cleaning up the city after the riots. Then he helped launch the National Urban Coalition, which was formed in Washington to back urban programs. In January 1968 Ford received a call from the White House asking him to meet with President Johnson. At LBJ's urging he organized a group of industrialists into the National Alliance of Businessmen in order to find jobs in private industry for the hard-core unemployed. As chairman, Henry worked hard. He even canceled a long-planned African safari with Cristina to make sure the NAB was properly launched.

Though Henry disliked being labeled politically, he did not cavil when an article in *Look* magazine described him as a "Johnsonian Republican." He made no bones about how much he admired Lyndon Johnson. "I consider him one of the greatest leaders we ever had," he said. And Lyndon considered Henry a prize example of what an American industrialist should be. In one of his last offical acts as President, LBJ awarded Ford the Medal of Freedom, the highest honor the Chief Executive can bestow on any civilian. Previously he had asked Ford to return to the United Nations as a member of the U.S. delegation. "But," as Henry said, "I had been there once and I didn't want to go back again."

The Fords were frequent guests at the White House. The first time Cristina went there was in November 1965 for a dinner party given by the Johnsons in honor of Princess Margaret and Lord Snowdon. The Fords had been married less than a year, and naturally everyone wanted to take a look at the mysterious lady Henry had married. The well-tanned Cristina dressed appropriately in a glamorous white dress and emeralds and wore a fall with curls cascading down the back of her neck. "People noticed me when I walked in," she said later. "I was very embarrassed." She was even more embarrassed when, dancing with the President in her perilously low-cut gown, she suddenly found too much of herself exposed on one side. The accident caused momentary confusion, but Cristina covered up quickly. Nevertheless the episode was duly reported by a couple of society columnists. But as Cristina later reminisced, it was an evening she would never forget. "I had never had a coming-out party, so to me, privately, that was my coming-out party."

Henry was absolutely shaken when on March 31, 1968, President Johnson announced to a surprised nation that he did not intend to seek his party's nomination for reelection. The reason, obviously, was the war in Vietnam, which had been going badly. Though Henry later claimed he had had his doubts about the war, he had privately assured the President of his full support. And the President had assured him that, despite the growing number of antiwar protests, he intended to carry on.

Still, there were rumors that LBJ was about to pack it in. In fact, Ford's West Coast representative, Pat Hillings, told him at an executives' lunch one day that he had heard on the Washington grapevine that the President might soon be making an announcement to that effect.

"You're nuts," Ford told Hillings. "I'll bet you a hundred bucks you're wrong."

Hillings, a former Republican congressman from California, decided it would be the better part of valor not to argue or bet with the boss. "Well, we'll see," he said.

Henry never brought the subject up again. Following LBJ's surprise announcement, Henry wired the President: "I deeply regret your decision not to seek re-election."

Henry wound up supporting Hubert Humphrey against Richard Nixon for the presidency in 1968. He had never liked Nixon, and the feeling was reciprocated. For one thing, he had publicly described Nixon's rival for the GOP nomination, Nelson A. Rockefeller, as "the best qualified Republican for the presidency." Henry's brothers did not follow his lead. Benson, for example, supported Nixon and chaired a large fund-raising dinner in his behalf. William Clay turned up as chairman of Michigan Businessmen for Eugene McCarthy, who had unsuccessfully sought the Democratic nomination.

On the eve of Nixon's inauguration Henry gave a party in Washington for the outgoing President, Lyndon Johnson. Held at the stately old F Street Club, several blocks from the White House, the party was in the best Ford tradition, with numerous bouquets of fresh flowers, drinks in cut-glass tumblers, musicans with stringed instruments and scores of elegantly dressed guests. A large number of students from nearby George Washington University were outside to greet the more recognizable political celebrities. And, surprisingly, they even cheered the arrival of President Johnson, whom so many had undoubtedly been reviling because of Vietnam. They shouted long and hard for Vice President Humphrey and Senator Edward M. Kennedy. And they went bonkers when Henry sent out trays of caviar-topped canapés, petits fours and several bottles of champagne.

Finally Henry himself appeared to introduce departing guests. Throwing his arms around Kennedy, he shouted, "And here's out next President." The students went wild. "Kennedy and Ford in seventy-two," they chanted. And Henry went up and down the line, shaking hands like any politician and delivering himself of a bit of moralizing. "Kids, you're great," he told them. "You've got a great future ahead of you. I want you to have a good life. Be good citizens..."

None of this sat too well with some stockholders, who felt that Henry's political views were doing damage to the company. At the May 1969 annual meeting the issue surfaced when Evelyn Y. Davis, a perennial critic of management, accused Ford of spending too much time on political matters. "Perhaps now that the Democrats are out," she said, "you'll give more time to the company." Henry snapped back, "I give my time to the country; I don't give it to a party."

But word had gotten back to Dearborn that President Nixon was none too happy with Henry's freewheeling remarks, particularly those uttered outside the F Street Club. On sober reflection Henry realized he had probably overstepped himself in his relations with the President. And that might not augur too well for his company's relations with the new administration. Henry decided to make amends.

"I got a clarion call that Mr. Ford wanted to make his peace with President Nixon," recalls Pat Hillings, the former congressman who represented Ford's West Coast interests. "And my assignment was to get them together."

Hillings, who had long been associated with Nixon in political battles, flew to Washington, where he met with the President. "Was Henry sober when you talked to him?" asked Nixon. Hillings assured the President he was. Nixon thought for a few seconds. "Okay, then," he said, "we'll set it up."

Some weeks later the Fords were invited to the White House. The occasion was a large state dinner for the Turkish premier. Later there was a smaller affair attended by only eight people. On the first anniversary of the National Alliance of Businessmen, Nixon presented a silver platter to Ford as an award for his services. Engraved on the platter were the signatures of both Presidents Nixon and Johnson. When asked how he thought the new President was doing, Henry said, "I think he's doing a great job."

Still, there was none of the camaraderie that had existed between Henry and Lyndon Johnson. Nixon and Ford never were comfortable with each other. And at a time when the President felt he needed all the support he could get from molders of public opinion, Henry surprised his underlings by calling for an end to U.S. participation in the Vietnam war. This was shortly after the Kent State affair of May 1970, in which four antiwar protestors were killed by Ohio National Guardsmen. "I do not think we can get our economy back on an even keel or find the resources to solve our domestic problems, or regain the confidence of young people, as long as there is any doubt about ending the war," Ford told his stockholders. Nixon, who had undertaken a program of Vietnamization presumably aimed at getting the U.S. out of the Southeast Asian quagmire, was incensed. He noted to associates that Ford had never gone public with such views about the war during the Johnson administration.

A month earlier Henry had turned up in Moscow with his wife and daughter Charlotte for a nine-day visit. Along with two company officials, they were greeted and feted in a way that would have pleased the czar. They were put up in a mansion in the fashionable Lenin Hills and flown privately around the Soviet Union in an eighty-passenger jet. In Moscow they were driven around in the Soviet equivalent of an American luxury limousine. And while the fashionably dressed Cristina and Charlotte turned Russian heads on sight-seeing tours, Henry was closeted with top Soviet officials, including Premier Aleksei N. Kosygin for talks ostensibly "to discuss East-West trade."

But the air of mystery was dispelled when Henry, at a Moscow press conference, disclosed that the Soviets had asked the Ford Motor Company to help build a large truck-manufacturing complex. Though Ford declined to say whether his company would do so, he did say he was interested in doing business with the Soviet Union. After all, his company's subsidiaries were already selling cars and trucks to Czechoslovakia, Yugoslavia, Poland, Romania and Bulgaria. And the U.S.S.R. could provide an even greater market for Ford products. Even his grandfather had not been averse to dealing with the Bolsheviks, as Henry noted. In fact, in Stalin's day, Henry Ford I was regarded not as a capitalist exploiter but as a kind of industrial messiah who had brought the miraculous Tin Lizzie within reach of the American working class.

There was a problem, however. After considerable internal discussion, the Nixon administration concluded that the truck project was not one of Ford's better ideas. For one thing, the Soviets, despite a chronic shortage of trucks, were sending all they could spare to Hanoi. And American pilots, shot down while attacking these vehicles, were now being held in prison in North Vietnam. All of which was pointed out in a magazine interview by Secretary of Defense Melvin Laird. "Before giving away the technology to construct trucks in the Soviet Union, and establishing plants for them," said Laird, "there should be some indication on the part of the Soviet Union that they're not going to continue sending trucks to North Vietnam by shiploads for use on the Ho Chi Minh trail."

Henry replied sharply in a written statement, describing Laird's remarks as "highly misleading" and appearing "to be a gratuitous attack on my common sense and patriotism." At a stockholders' meeting, however, he announced that he had "advised the Soviet Government" that it was "not feasible for us to give further consideration to their proposal."

Though generally angry at the questioning of his patriotism, Henry decided it would be best not to continue taking potshots at the Nixon administration. In fact, in early 1972 he secretly contributed $50,000 to the President's reelection effort, a per-

sonal contribution that, though legal, was later to prove an ___
embarrassment when it was disclosed during the unfolding of
the Watergate scandal. In publicly announcing for Nixon against
George McGovern, Henry said, "He's the best qualified." The
declaration didn't constitute an act of courage. If ever there
was a sure thing, it was Nixon's reelection.

Henry had a change of heart after Watergate. In May 1974,
when Nixon was on the ropes, Ford took a public swing at the
beleaguered President. Characterizing the Watergate affair and
its aftermath as "awful" and "terrible," he said he felt "let
down" by the events of the past year in Washington. Stopping
short of demanding the President's resignation, he called instead for impeachment proceedings to settle the matter. His
remarks made him the first high-ranking automobile executive
to publicly take a critical stance toward the President.

But even before Watergate unfolded, Henry Ford was faced
with a scandal that was to prove a greater humiliation than that
of the Edsel catastrophe. Except that Henry, unlike Nixon, was
not forced to resign. Instead, the company was fined $7 million
for cheating on the emission-control test required by the Environmental Protection Agency. The cheating involved falsi-
fication of records supplied the EPA. Though no one blamed
Henry personally for the fiasco, he nevertheless felt it was the
low point of his business career. He conceded that he may have
misled those responsible for the cheating because of his tough
remarks condemning the stringent requirements of the 1970
Clean Air Act. "I still don't like the law," he said, "and I think
it ought to be changed. But you have to play by the rules. You
don't cheat."

These were words that would return later to haunt Henry
Ford when he himself became the target of numerous allegations of breaking the rules.

8

ENJOYING LIFE

AWAY FROM THE JOB, HENRY FORD II APPEARED TO BE TOTALLY unconcerned about his public image. Well aware of his reputation as a jet-setter, he would tell interviewers how much he deplored having his private life reported in the world's newspapers and magazines. But there was very little he could do about it, he insisted, "so I might as well relax and enjoy it." And enjoy it he did; so much so that at times he appeared to be saying; "This is the way I am and I don't give a damn what anyone thinks."

Henry could get boisterous, particularly after a few belts. And he would usually say whatever came to mind. "Not only did he drink like a stevedore, but he would talk like one," says a former associate. "His language around Charlotte would have curled your hair." When under the influence, Henry would often disregard the conventions. One night in the early seventies he turned up with three old buddies at the Bronze Door restaurant in Grosse Pointe. Henry didn't like what a pianist was playing. To attract his attention Henry pulled out a pocket whistle and blew a piercing blast. The other diners, though far from amused, said nothing. In Grosse Pointe, Henry was king. And the king could do no wrong.

Then there was the time when Charlotte Curtis of *The New York Times* looked on with amazement as the Chairman of the Ford Motor Company squirted Perrier water at an Italian count perched in a tree. The episode occurred at a wild party in a fancy outdoor restaurant on the Riviera in August 1969. After the steak and baked potatoes stuffed with caviar were out of the way, the guests—mainly titled Italians and rich Americans—joined the guitarists in singing Spanish songs and at least one rollicking lyric in faint praise of the late Benito Mussolini. By the time the dessert and liqueurs arrived, the guests were throwing champagne glasses at the hearth, roses at the guitarists, and unshelled almonds at each other.

But the height of the action came when Count Giovanni Volpi climbed a tree carrying a plate of vanilla ice cream and raspberries. From that vantage point the handsome Roman millionaire began lobbing blobs of dessert at his friends, including Henry's daughters Charlotte and Anne, both of whom fled to safety, and Cristina, who squealed and threw her arms up over her face. Roaring with laughter, Henry shouted, "Come on down, Foxy. You're going to get hurt."

The count responded by aiming some ice cream at Henry. He missed. Henry, who had nicknamed the count "Foxy" because *volpi* is the Italian word for foxes, picked up a bottle of Perrier, shook it vigorously and squirted it upward. "You got him," his daughter Anne squealed with joy. Just when it looked as if there might be a lull, the owner of the restaurant fired a cap pistol and threw another chair on the roaring fire.

Henry's antics abroad were not greeted with amusement by his brothers, concerned about the family image. "We led our separate lives," said William Clay. As for Henry's well-publicized associates on the Riviera, Billy added, "It's not my cup of tea. I've got no use for that group. I don't particularly enjoy the foreigners he's apt to get associated with." Benson Sr., by then spending much of his time at his home in Hobe Sound or on his 78-foot yacht, the *Onika*, echoed his brother, adding, "The trouble with Henry is he doesn't know when to stop."

Nevertheless Henry had his defenders. "All of his faults," said Sir Patrick Hennessey, who represented Ford interests in the British Isles, "are very human ones. He works hard, and when he relaxes he wants to have a good time." Sir Patrick spoke as an expert. Over the years the old Fusilier had done a lot of barhopping with Henry.

Not all of his hosts were as sanguine about Henry's conduct as was Sir Patrick. Henry's legendary drinking habits had led to too many uncomfortable situations. One such incident led to the breakup of a relationship between the Ford Motor Company and an Italian-operated company headed by Alejandro DeTomaso. In 1969 DeTomaso had designed the Pantera, a two-seat sports car powered by a Ford engine. Lee Iacocca liked it so much that Ford bought it. Soon afterward Ford Motor purchased 80 percent of three companies—Ghia, Vignale, and DeTomaso Automobili—all three controlled by DeTomaso. Ford then put them under the umbrella of a newly formed Delaware company, DeTomaso Inc., and employed DeTomaso to run the three subsidiaries in Europe, reporting directly to Iacocca.

Alejandro DeTomaso was born in Buenos Aires in 1928. The son of wealthy parents, he had gone to school with Ernesto ("Che") Guevara, who later became one of Fidel Castro's principal revolutionary leaders. In 1954, because of Juan Peron's repression, DeTomaso fled Argentina "for political reasons." Since one of his grandfathers was Italian, he went to Italy, where he became a racing-car mechanic for the Maserati brothers. After a fling as a racing driver he took savings of $11,000 and two racing-car engines and set up in the custom-car business under the name DeTomaso Automobili. His wife, another noted sports-car racing driver, went to work with him. The former Isabel Haskell, Mrs. DeTomaso was a granddaughter of one of the founders of General Motors. They were married in 1957 at her father's home in Palm Beach.

DeTomaso and his American wife cut quite a social swathe. They were in the upper reaches of Italian society and were invited everywhere. In August 1972 the DeTomasos were in

Sardinia. On their way to an elegant party to which the Fords had also been invited they had stopped off at a piazza for a leisurely aperitif when Henry came rolling by with Cristina and some friends. According to DeTomaso, the Chairman had already been drinking heavily. And he was wearing jeans with an American flag sewed on the seat. DeTomaso was shocked. Turning to his wife, he said "We're not going to the party."

Another example of Henry's "grossness" was an incident in St. Moritz. DeTomaso was scheduled to dine with Count Volpi at the Palace Hotel. When the count finally arrived he was accompanied by Henry Ford, "super drunk, as usual." But what made matters even worse, according to DeTomaso, was Henry's behavior on the dance floor, selecting girls to dance with at will and then grabbing them "by their bosoms and private parts." The king, again, could do no wrong.

The next morning Henry called DeTomaso and said, "I guess I was a bad boy last night." Which, in a way, was "Henry's manner of apologizing." There were other incidents, mostly brought on by Henry's excessive drinking. "He could drink anything and everything," says DeTomaso. "He could mix wine, cognac, Scotch—all in one evening. At the same time, he gorged food and smoked heavily. The amazing thing to me was that by nine the next morning he invariably was in good shape."

In time it became obvious to DeTomaso that Henry was not pleased to have one of his employees moving in the same social circles as he—among the Volpis and the Bulgaris. Besides, Henry had never encountered anyone like the DeTomasos. Unlike his other, more obsequious underlings, they refused to bow the knee in his august presence. And this infuriated him. So much so that he sent a memo to Iacocca demanding that he "get rid" of DeTomaso. The memo was unusual in that Henry had never before put such demands in writing. Usually when he wanted to get rid of someone, he would personally instruct Iacocca: "I want him fired by five o'clock or you're fired. I don't want any f—— excuses."

And even though in most cases he hated to do it, Lee Iacocca would play the hatchet man. "I did what I was told," he now says. In DeTomaso's case Iacocca arranged for a buyout of the industrialist's 20 percent share of the Italian subsidiaries, thus severing his links with the Ford company. DeTomaso understood Iacocca's impossible position and they remained good friends, a fact that did not sit too well with Henry. But DeTomaso made it clear he would never forgive Henry Ford.

Iacocca was finding it increasingly difficult to reason with Henry. There was no dealing with the Chairman when he was in one of his chameleonlike moods. There was no arguing with him when, for example, he handed down the surprising edict for the company's annual executives party: "No wives!" When asked why not, Henry said, "Women are no damn good." Which, in retrospect, may have reflected the tensions that were beginning to erupt between Henry and Cristina.

At first their marriage seemed to have satisfied Henry. As his friend Max Fisher then said, "He's very happily married. I think there's been quite a difference in him since his second marriage"—meaning that life had become fun for Henry. And less inhibited too.

Henry's nephew Benson, while paying a visit to his uncle, found Henry and Cristina swimming naked in the pool. "You've got to remember that to his nephews and nieces, Uncle Henry was way up there on a pedestal," says Benson. "Which may explain my astonishment on finding Uncle Henry and Aunt Cristina cavorting in the buff. It was all so unexpected."

Benson had wanted to discuss some business with his uncle, who was then spending Christmas at LaCosta, a posh Southern California resort. Benson had called in advance and his uncle had suggested he drive down from his home in Whittier. He took along a college buddy, Elliott Kaplan. Clearing security, they arrived at Henry's private cottage, where they found Henry and Cristina in the pool. Henry immediately got out, saying he wanted to put on some clothes. Cristina then sat at the edge of the pool, talking to the boys. "It was quite a sight," recalls Benson. "We made small talk until Uncle Henry emerged. And then Cristina resumed swimming."

As Benson now recalls, there was no indication at the time that there was anything amiss with the Fords. Their marriage appeared to be made for the women's magazines. And sure enough *Harper's Bazaar* and *Ladies' Home Journal* ran spreads on what the latter journal described as "The Fabulous Life of Mrs. Henry Ford." It was a fabulous life indeed, one most women could only dream about. Generally, at her Grosse Pointe mansion, she slept late, getting up in time for a daily massage at 10:30 A.M. Though she loved to eat a lot, usually pasta, Cristina remained stylishly thin—too thin in the opinion of Sophia Loren, who once told her, "Remember, your husband married you because you are an Italian." She kept thin by exercising for about an hour a day, riding bicycles while visiting in the neighborhood, and (as a frustrated ballerina) taking private ballet lessons.

At one time Cristina had as many as a dozen dogs; one was named Dickie after Lord Mountbatten, who had sent the frisky black Labrador retriever to the Fords as a gift. Otherwise her time was spent shopping, taking the two-hour treatment at the Kitty Wagner Facial Salon or going to her hairdresser, who was quoted as saying Cristina selected her coiffeurs with her husband in mind. "He's a man who likes her soft . . . he doesn't go for anything plastified."

There were times when it was not easy to be the wife of the Chairman of the Ford Motor Company. Shortly after their marriage, in fact, it was common knowledge among the international set that Cristina was somewhat less than completely enchanted about living in a suburban retreat. "It is sometimes lonely in Detroit," she told a New York interviewer. "I walk the dogs and go to bed early." But, she added, after reflecting, she really wasn't much for the mad social whirl. "I really do like to go to bed at ten." Nevertheless she would make frequent visits alone to New York, occupying a penthouse suite leased by the Ford company at the Regency Hotel. One night she returned from dining with a friend to discover that the hotel apartment—consisting of a living room, three bedrooms, three baths, and a kitchen—had been entered and that at least $50,000 of her jewelry had been stolen. "Somebody must have been following me," she said, adding that no one, "not even the hotel," knew of her planned three-day visit. Henry, who joined her the following day, complained of the theft: "In a hotel like this, you don't expect that sort of thing."

Security was much tighter at the Ford's Grosse Pointe home.

Guards provided by the Ford Motor Company police force constantly patrolled the grounds, keeping close tabs on the elegant Georgian mansion, a treasure trove of works by some of the world's greatest artists—Van Gogh, Matisse and Degas. Guards frequently accompanied Ford to and from work. Generally he returned home fairly late, and he would relax by watching television while dining with Cristina from lap trays. "When he comes home," she once said, "I try to amuse him— not to be heavy, not to say, 'What you been doing? How long you stay out? What time is now? You five minutes late!' Nothing. He can come home at nine o'clock. I smile and say, 'You have a good time?' He feel that he's free. He's always tied up in the office. He has to be there every hour, every minute, so at home I make him to feel free."

Only later was Cristina to learn that her busy husband was not always tied up at the office, as he claimed.

While Cristina spent much of her time keeping in trim, she found it almost impossible to persuade her overweight husband to exercise. Occasionally, however, she did get him to bicycle with her or play a game of paddle tennis. "Exercise bores me," he told her. "Why should I be bored?" As a consequence, Henry would frequently go on a diet. His most common meal was a hamburger, which he would usually order in his executive dining room. Once when he was conferring with two aides, one of them mentioned casually he was on a salad diet. A side benefit, the aide claimed, was that it bolstered his sexual prowess. In his penthouse dining room a little later the waiter asked Mr. Ford what he wanted for lunch. Peering over his half glasses, Henry said, "The salad."

That Henry was having fun on the side was well known to a few associates who were forced to listen to the Chairman's tales of sexual conquests. At times it got embarrassing, particularly when Henry boasted of having "made it" with the wives of certain executives. Once, the Chairman claimed, he had completed a seduction on a diving board. And he couldn't understand how, with "all the stuff available," some of his executives could remain faithful to their wives. He would also rib Iacocca about going to church and "believing in God." Iacocca, a devout Catholic and good family man, would say nothing, though inwardly seething. As he later told friends, "One can take all sorts of crap in pursuit of the almighty buck." And yet, in retrospect, Iacocca has wondered whether his former boss's putdowns of women and derogation of family values were not in themselves a reflection of the bitterness Ford felt because of his own marital failures.

At first Cristina did not have the slightest inkling of what was going on. She had grown accustomed to spending long hours by herself in the Grosse Pointe mansion. She read long historical novels and grew orchids in a tiny hothouse. And she took up sculpting. She even tried to do Henry's head, but he insisted he had no time to pose. For a woman who enjoyed parties, Cristina did remarkably little entertaining at home. It wasn't that she didn't want to entertain. Henry just wasn't up to it. "My husband is really what I call a Sicilian," she once explained. "He wants his wife home; he doesn't want big entertainment. He says, 'I am tired when I come home. I want to enjoy you, and we don't need a lot of people around.' I agree and tease him, 'You are right. I am the wife. You are the star.'"

It hadn't been that way at the beginning of their marriage. Cristina was the star, and Henry seemed delighted with the attention given his new bride. Photographers jostled for position whenever they arrived at social events. The Fords made quite a splash when they reached the Plaza Hotel in New York to attend what their host Truman Capote called his "little masked ball for Kay Graham and all my friends." All Truman's friends included over five hundred diplomats, politicans, scientists, painters, writers, composers, actors, producers, dress designers, social figures, tycoons and what the host called "international types, lots of beautiful women and ravishing little things." Also invited to the masked ball in honor of the president of the *Washington Post* were Anne McDonnell Ford and the Ford daughters, Charlotte Niarchos, who sat with Lynda Bird Johnson, and Anne Uzielli, who danced with her husband, Giancarlo. But nobody seemed to have more fun than Cristina Ford, who wore an angel mask, without the halo. Newly established on the social scene, she was the object of considerable curiosity on the part of most of the guests.

At first it was party time most of the time, a constant round of entertaining and being entertained. And it was travel time much of the time. There were trips to near and far places. There were fleets of limousines and aircraft at their disposal. They had millions of dollars and felt no guilt about spending it. Money of course meant very little to Henry. He had always had it. Cristina's pleasure in having money was unalloyed. "I take pleasure in it because I didn't have it before," she explained. "Money is to make people happy . . . I hate people who keep their money, who don't spend it or give it to anyone . . . they are the most selfish people."

Being the wife of Henry Ford did present some problems. As she explained to a *Life* reporter in 1971, "I wanted to believe in my heart that people were my friends because they liked me, just me, not because I was Mrs. Henry Ford II. At the same time, I knew it was not always true. I had a blind spot about it because I was an optimist. I wanted to think nobody would take advantage of me. But many, many times they did— that's life. I don't get so wounded anymore. It is up to me to intuitively separate the genuine friends from the phonies. I am quite aware of who is who." One person who was definitely not phony was Patricia Nixon. "I think Mrs. Nixon epitomizes the American simplicity and niceness," she said. On one occasion Cristina sat near the First Lady during dinner. "Before that she showed me all around the White House. She was so simple, so herself. There was no phony about her."

Henry was making the Washington scene more frequently. Not because he liked it particularly, but rather because he personally sought to counter the "excesses" of those government bureaucrats who were imposing their "anti-car biases" on an industry whose health, he argued, was so vital to the nation's economic future. Also of increasing concern were the inroads into the American market made by imported cars. "We've only seen the beginning," he said of the influx of imported cars on the West Coast. "Wait until those Japs get hold of the central part of the United States."

And while Henry became a familiar figure in Washington, roaming the corridors of power, Cristina occasionally made the social rounds with her good friend Hildegarde Czerner. In 1968,

Hildegarde opened a boutique in Georgetown which she named La Strega—the witch—after Cristina, who was delighted. "I love Washington," Cristina said on visiting the boutique. "I'd love to live here." Unlike Detroit, Washington "is very international," she went on, "and it needs a new hostess, no?"

Cristina had her opportunity to play Washington hostess at her husband's traditional inaugural reception in January 1973. Richard Nixon had been overwhelmingly reelected to the presidency, but he and Pat were unable to attend the reception, which, as usual, was held at the F Street Club. A subdued Henry was on his best behavior as he and Cristina greeted a long line of Nixon luminaries and other movers and shakers, including Henry Kissinger and Martha Mitchell. "Martha," Cristina cried as she kissed the ebullient wife of the former Attorney General on both cheeks. The Mitchells and Kissinger, having paid their respects, left early to attend other inaugural events.

But the vacuum they left among the three hundred guests was quickly filled with the arrival of Imelda Marcos, wife of the president of the Philippines, accompanied by her personal physician and several secret service agents. Because she had recently been stabbed by a would-be assassin in Manila, Mrs. Marcos was busy explaining the state of her health. "I'm better," she said, "but it will be a long time before I'm healed." Her right hand, done up in splints, was resting on a gold chain that served as a sling, and there were nasty scars on her arm. "Don't worry about me," she said to Cristina, trying to soothe her. "No, please don't cry." Cristina, who looked as if she were about to, didn't. Instead, she patted Mrs. Marcos and went on to such other guests as Mrs. Jacob K. Javits, wife of the then New York senator. "Bombola," they called each other, an affectionate diminutive they considered more fun than "Bambina." Drinking it all in was one of Nixon's speech writers, William L. Safire, who in a future incarnation as a *New York Times* columnist was to write, as we'll see, about a certain mysterious manila envelope allegedly handed to Henry Ford by Imelda Marcos.

Imelda Marcos and Cristina Ford first met in early 1971 when the Fords were visiting the Philippines. It was on that occasion that President Ferdinand Marcos initiated discussions about the possibility of Ford building an automobile stamping plant in his country. The Chairman said he might be interested. Meanwhile Imelda and Cristina became the closest of friends. In late 1971 Cristina was Imelda's guest in her tent at the Shah of Iran's $100 million celebration of the twenty-five hundredth anniversary of the founding of the Persian Empire at Persepolis. Cristina would often arrange her schedule to meet the Philippines' First Lady either in Manila or in some European capital.

In 1974 Imelda became the target of considerable domestic criticism for flying Cristina and other jet-setting luminaries, supposedly at government expense, into the Philippines for a birthday party. On one such trip Imelda presented her with a ring made of diamonds and pearls, as well as an indigenous dress made of banana leaves. "It took one year to make that dress," Cristina exulted on returning to Grosse Pointe. "It is off-white and all hand-embroidery. It is so beautiful."

Cristina was also exultant about a trip she had made to England in the summer of 1970. After all, how often do you get chauffeured around by the Queen of England? Which is what happened when Elizabeth II drove Cristina in her Jaguar to a polo field near Windsor Castle to watch a match. The players included the queen's husband, Prince Philip, and her son, Prince Charles. Earlier Cristina had dined at the castle with the queen and her family. Others at the luncheon included the Duchess of Gloucester and Lord Mountbatten, whom Cristina was visiting. Cristina was also on hand when Antenor Patino, the Bolivian tin heir, gave a lavish ball at his palace outside Lisbon. And she flew to Madrid to witness the marriage of the late Francisco Franco's granddaughter.

Cristina was doing more and more traveling on her own, and her good friend Hildegarde Czerner suggested that perhaps that was not too wise. "Leaving Henry all alone might not be too smart an idea," she told Cristina. But Cristina argued that Henry was so busy that most of the time he hardly knew she was gone. And, anyway, Henry was always off on some business trip of his own, to which he claimed "no wives" were invited. And hanging around Grosse Pointe by herself was not exactly Cristina's idea of a good time.

Besides, Cristina had no concern about her marriage. It was a marriage, she told a *New York Times* reporter in March 1973, based on friendship, understanding and communication. "They are the most important things for two people living together . . . we have that," she said. "If you are happily married, no one can break it up. I would put my husband near the most glamorous, beautiful woman in the world and I would not worry, because of the relationship we have."

The relationship looked solid from the outside. There was no hint of discord in May 1973 when the Fords led a glittering array of celebrities into New York's Metropolitan Opera House for the International Diamond Jubilee Gala saluting the legendary Sol Hurok, who was marking his sixtieth year as an arts impresario. Cristina, who was program chairman, swept into the scarlet and gold theater in a Givenchy gown she had bought in Paris. And what a program it was; with Isaac Stern, Mary Costa, Van Cliburn, Roberta Peters, Jerome Hines, and members of the Royal Ballet, Stuttgart Ballet and the Metropolitan Opera. Seated in the Ford box were General Franco's granddaughter and her husband, the Prince and Princess Alfonso de Borbon, Truman Capote, Merle Oberon, New York socialite Mrs. Joseph Meehan, and Guilford Dudley, former ambassador to Denmark, and Mrs. Dudley. Following the concert, Cristina and Hurok led a polonaise at the Pierre Hotel, opening the ball. After making a brief appearance Henry left for the airport to board a private jet for Detroit, where the next morning he was scheduled to appear at groundbreaking ceremonies for the gigantic Renaissance Center project that he had helped put together in downtown Detroit.

In September 1973 the Fords turned up in Boston to celebrate Henry's son's graduation from Babson College. For Edsel Bryant Ford II it had been quite an achievement. It had taken the twenty-four-year-old scion five and a half years to complete the required business administration courses at the easygoing Boston institution. But he finally managed to do it, and that was excuse enough for his friends and assorted Fords to gather for a celebration. What was billed as "the graduation party of the century" took place on a midnight cruise around Boston Harbor aboard an excursion boat. It was a "black tie and sneakers" affair, and Edsel's father, in black tie and navy blue sneakers, was dressed appropriately. Accompanied by his wife and his daughter Anne Ford Uzielli, Henry carried a properly chilled magnum of champagne. Anne's husband, Giancarlo, brought his own white wine. And also a speech of sorts. Uzielli said that under such circumstances some colleges might expect "a library or a dormitory," but that Edsel had gone to "forty-seven schools, which comes to six dormitories, five football fields and a library."

"We don't need a football field," said Dr. Henry A. Kriebel, Babson's president. "But we do need a library." Kriebel presented Edsel with a plaque commemorating his work on three Babson seminars. Edsel had somehow prevailed on his father to speak on the subject "Detroit Retools for Tomorrow." The movie industry's Jack Valenti and director William Friedkin had showed up as the speakers on the subject "Who'll Save Hollywood?" And Howard Cosell and Edsel's uncle, William Clay Ford, had accepted Edsel's invitation to speak on "The Game Makers."

Edsel thanked Dr. Kriebel, the professors who had worked with him on the seminars, and his roommate, Douglas Reed, for staging the party. "And I want to thank my father for having me," he went on. "I wouldn't have been here without him. And my mother. And I want to thank my stepmother."

Cristina beamed and Henry waved. Asked how he felt about his son's graduation, Henry said quietly, "I am very pleased. Very, very pleased."

Edsel said he planned to join the company, beginning in the product-planning area. "I'm not really very mechanically minded," he said. "I could change the spark plugs or the oil, but I'm not much of an engineer." Eventually he hoped to work his way into the marketing and advertising side of the business. "Unfortunately, it isn't like it was in the days when a Ford just walked into the company. I'll have to go out and prove myself, which I really want to do. I hope some day to run the company, but if I can't, I can't."

Needless to say, Edsel had no trouble landing a job in the vast Ford empire. He was assigned to a middle-management post at a Ford marketing office in Los Angeles. And in September 1974 he took unto himself a bride, the former Cynthia Layne Neskow, who was working for the Kenyon & Eckhardt advertising agency in Boston, where they had met. The wedding, a traditional one, was held at the First United Presbyterian Church in Tequesta, Florida, where the bride's father, a retired navy captain, was an oral surgeon. Serving as bridal attendants were Edsel's two sisters, Charlotte and Anne. Charlotte's daughter, Elena Niarchos, then eight, was flower girl, and Allesandro Uzielli, a year younger, was ring bearer.

Charlotte, who gradually dropped Niarchos from her name following her 1967 divorce, was now Mrs. J. Anthony Forstmann. She had married the New York investment banker in May 1973 at her sister's Park Avenue apartment. Forstmann, also previously divorced and the father of three children, was a Yale man. A golfer by avocation, he had met Charlotte not on the links but in Southampton some years before.

Among those attending Charlotte's civil ceremony were Henry and Cristina Ford; the bride's mother, now Mrs. Deane F. Johnson, who flew in with her husband from their home in Bel Air, California; Mrs. Edsel Ford and Mrs. James McDonnell, the bride's grandmothers; and the bride's brother, Edsel. At Charlotte's request, there were few prenuptial events. The most festive was a wedding-eve party given by the bride's parents. About seventy men and women received invitations for the black tie dinner-dance at the Carlyle Hotel, and, as usual at such Ford parties, there was an equal number of security guards. Toasting his "firstborn" was Henry Ford. "Hurray, hurray, the first of May," he intoned, "Charlotte and Tony are getting married today." He was followed by his former wife, Anne Johnson, who said she couldn't follow such competition. Her son, Edsel, toasted the two people "paying for the party"—his parents. Forstmann's contribution was a poem he wrote for his bride-to-be.

Most of the guests, including former New York Mayor Robert F. Wagner and the recently widowed Mrs. Bennett Cerf, were delighted to see Henry's first wife and to meet her new husband, Deane Johnson. For several years, following her 1964 divorce from Henry, Anne McDonnell Ford had played the field. She had been seen in the company of such assorted worthies as television producer Mark Goodson, socialite Serge Obolensky, singer Gordon MacRae, but most often with the twice-married sportsman Ted Bassett. After a skiing trip to Gstaad with Bassett in early 1966, Anne returned to New York, where she told friends she had decided to break off the relationship. Within days Bassett married a Palm Beach socialite thirty years his junior. Nevertheless the story ended happily when Anne met Deane Johnson, a Beverly Hills attorney. Following Johnson's own divorce, they were married in Charlotte's New York apartment, with only a few close friends in attendance. Anne then moved west with her husband, where she began leading an active social life among the landed Angeleno gentry and showbiz royalty. (William Holden, Norman Lear and Dinah Shore were among her husband's clients and friends.)

Not as happy a denouement was the breakup of Anne Ford Uzielli's marriage to her stockbroker husband, Giancarlo. The couple, whose marriage was the most glittering ornament of the 1965 Christmas season, separated late in 1973. A little more than a year later they were divorced in Manhattan Supreme Court, following hearings held after normal hours. Anne, then thirty-two, was granted custody of the couple's two children and the right to resume her maiden name.

But within months Anne Ford Uzielli—she continued to use her married name—had found herself a new beau. He was Governor Hugh Carey of New York. It was a May-December romance. Then fifty-six, Carey was only a few years younger than Anne's father. Carey, whose wife, Helen, had died of cancer the previous year, had been avoiding the social circuit, devoting most of his personal time to his twelve children. Carey met Anne at a dinner party for Frank Sinatra. The party, at Patsy's Italian restaurant, was given by former Mayor Wagner and his new bride, the former Phyllis Cerf. Carey, who found Anne to be "a person with a very fine sense of humor, a person with a very gifted intellect, a sense of *joie de vivre*," began seeing her regularly. And soon there was talk of a possible marriage. The talk continued for some years, but by early 1981 the romance was over.

There was also talk of trouble in Henry Ford's household.

Henry and Cristina seemed to be going their separate ways. Cristina was spending more and more time away from Grosse Pointe, returning to the Lake Shore mansion just long enough to change clothes. But it was her continuing trips to see Imelda Marcos, the still-stunning (at forty-six) "Iron Butterfly" of the Philippines, that led to all sorts of rumors.

Later, after the marriage was on the rocks, Rosemarie Kanzler Marcie-Riviere was quoted in the *Detroit Free Press* as saying of Cristina: "She fooled him, she fooled me. She was never a wife to him. She was always off to New York every chance she had or visiting Imelda Marcos in the Philippines."

Whatever the truth of these rumors, Henry began to drink more heavily than usual. But he soon found solace in the arms of a thirty-five-year-old woman named Kathleen DuRoss.

Events began coming to a head in February 1975 when Cristina flew to Manila, where she was Imelda's house guest at the Malacanang Palace. Then she and Mrs. Marcos flew to Nepal to attend the coronation in Katmandu of the twenty-eight-year-old King Birendra. Accompanying them to the mountain kingdom were the Christiaan N. Barnards, who had been in the Philippines for the opening of a hospital for heart surgery. Getting a hotel room proved to be no problem for Cristina. Imelda ordered a member of the Philippine entourage to move from the Soaltee Oberoi, where the VIPs were quartered, to make room for the Italian-born socialite. "I was in Manila and Mrs. Marcos told me to come along," Cristina told a correspondent. "So I came." But she was soon exhausted from all the receptions and parties that kept her up until the early hours of the morning. Still, she intended to see some temples. Lord Mountbatten, who was there with the British delegation headed by Prince Charles, had insisted she break away and do some sight-seeing. "The trouble is these parties," Cristina went on. "And I've never been to this part of the world."

Cristina's sight-seeing was interrupted, however, when she learned that her husband had been arrested on a drunk-driving charge in California. Even more upsetting were news reports that Henry had been in the company of a comely former model from Grosse Pointe identified as Kathleen DuRoss. Cristina vaguely remembered her. She recalled having met the woman in Detroit at a ceremony honoring Cristina for her work raising funds for Italian flood relief. DuRoss had been there as the guest of the Italian consul. And apparently that was the first time Henry had met her. But DuRoss was never part of the Grosse Pointe set and Cristina had quickly forgotten her. Until now in, of all places, Katmandu. Dismayed and embarrassed, Cristina cut short her trip and rushed back to Grosse Pointe.

Cristina, needless to say, had not had the slightest inkling that her husband had been seeing another woman. Henry had been the soul of discretion in carrying on his latest liaison. In fact, even though Cristina was out of the country, Henry had arranged for separate flights to California for himself and his newest paramour. Henry wasn't looking for trouble. But trouble came anyway. He and Kathleen had dined in a small French restaurant in Goleta, a suburb of Santa Barbara. Henry later claimed he hadn't had too much to drink—a Dubonnet on the rocks and a local wine, Pinot Noir.

But that's not what the California Highway Patrol said after one of its officers on Saturday night patrol arrested Henry shortly before midnight. The officer, Gene Hunt, had pulled him over after noticing that his red and white 1975 Ford sedan was going the wrong way on a one-way street, not far from the University of California at Santa Barbara. Officer Hunt, who said Henry appeared intoxicated, gave him a roadside sobriety test on the Breathalyzer, and the industrialist flunked. Henry was handcuffed and taken to the Santa Barbara Hospital for a blood test.

He was then booked for "driving under the influence of an intoxicating beverage" and held for four hours in the slammer until he posted $375 bail. According to one report, Henry "pulled a lot of strings" seeking "to hush up" his arrest, including one early-morning call to the Federal Bureau of Investigation. But it was all too late. Though he was ordered to appear in municipal court, Henry flew back to Detroit. In court his lawyer entered a plea of no-contest to a drunken-driving charge. Whereupon the judge fined him $375 and placed him on probation for two years, stipulating that if the Chairman of the Ford Motor Company was convicted of the same offense in California within two years, he would draw an automatic sentence of six months in jail and a $500 fine. It was noted by a *New York Times* correspondent that out-of-state residents usually received only the fine if convicted on a first offense. And that wasn't all. After receiving official notice from California of his no-contest plea, Michigan authorities announced that the driving license of Henry Ford II, the grandson of the developer of the Model T, had been suspended for ninety days.

Shortly after his return to Detroit, Henry attended a dinner given by the Society of Automotive Engineers in honor of his old friend Vice-President Nelson A. Rockefeller. Before entering the ballroom Henry was asked what he had been doing in California on the night of his arrest. "All I have to say," Henry said, smiling, "is 'Never complain, never explain.'"

9

CRISIS

SOME YEARS LATER CHARLOTTE FORD, SEEKING TO EXPLAIN her father's erratic conduct, said that he "finds it very hard to handle his emotional life." He has, she went on, "a weak side when it comes to women," and he always falls for "strong, tough cookies."

Kathleen DuRoss certainly filled the bill. Thirty-five years of age ("I couldn't be any younger and have a nineteen-year-old daughter"), she was strong, tough and street-wise. Detroit-born, she was an alumna of Cass Technical High School. Widowed at the age of nineteen, when her equally youthful husband David was killed in an automobile accident, she was left with two daughters, whom she supported, she said, "with Social Security, renting from my family, modeling and jobs like bookkeeping for a blood bank." But it was as a $45-an-hour model that she made her reputation. She was frequently seen at social events on the arm of some prominent gentleman. For a time she had dated Jerome P. Cavanagh, the former mayor of Detroit.

On returning from Santa Barbara, Henry instructed the raven-haired Kathy to hole up in her Grosse Pointe terrace apartment and say nothing to anyone about their ill-fated California rendezvous. Emerging from seclusion one morning, however, she encountered Pete Waldmeir, columnist for the *Detroit News,* who wanted to know what had happened. According to Waldmeir, "She answered questions directly, but said that if I printed it then, she'd really be in a jam."

"I'm no Fanne Fox," she told Waldmeir. "And he's no Wilbur Mills."

The reference was to the chairman of the House Ways and Means Committee, whose illustrious career had come a cropper the previous fall when his excessive drinking and affair with an exotic dancer were accidentally disclosed. Wilbur Mills had, in fact, been one of Henry's more powerful friends on the Hill, one whom Henry would visit from time to time. Now Wilbur was through, having lost his job. Which was something that, despite a similar misadventure, didn't happen to Henry. One reason was that, unlike Mills, Henry generally had a good press. Newsmen, for example, were not as anxious to follow up on Santa Barbara as they had been on the Tidal Basin story.

Another reason perhaps lay in the fact that the episode did not appear to have resulted in problems at home. Cristina, on returning from Nepal, had decided not to play the role of the wife betrayed. Thus there were no fireworks. Cristina had accepted her husband's explanation that there was less to Santa Barbara than could be deduced from news reports. Yes, he conceded, he had been with another woman. She was one of the many models employed for Ford promotions at automobile shows. Having run into her in California, he had invited her to dinner. And, anyway, it was all very "platonic."

Though not entirely convinced, Cristina felt she had no alternative but to accept Henry's story. According to a close friend, she was willing to let bygones be bygones. After all, as a sophisticated European, she was well aware of Henry's frailties. Still, she resolved to do everything possible to make her marriage work. Now seemingly chastened, Henry vowed he would never see the DuRoss woman again. And as Cristina told her friend, he seemed genuinely sorry he had caused his wife embarrassment.

But the gossips really had a field day when Kathy DuRoss announced she intended to open a discothèque in downtown Detroit. Kathy said she wanted the new establishment, which was to be called L'Esprit, to resemble the kind of "in" place Regine had established in Paris. "Detroit is not the most exciting city in the world," she said, "and it's time we did something about it." The official word was that while Kathy was the idea person for L'Esprit, her financial backer was a Detroit lawyer who owned the building. The unofficial word was that Henry Ford II had at least a piece of the action.

L'Esprit opened on a Thursday night, May 22, 1975, and correspondents for such national publications as *People* and *Women's Wear Daily* turned up for the event. Kathy, who was the center of attraction, conceded she was suspicious of all the attention she was getting. "I'm still naive," she said. "I hope it's not just because I was the girl caught with Henry Ford in California." And she was indignant that some detractors had accused her of using that publicity to further her business venture. "I would never base anything I do in the future on that," she added. "There have been a lot of modeling offers since then which I refused." All she wanted, she went on, was to provide Detroit with a place where people could go to dance in glamorous surroundings and where they could sip French coffee spiked with almond liqueur.

Though Henry conspicuously did not show up on opening night, his son did. Edsel was glad to be there, he said. After all, he had known Kathy for some time. In fact, prior to his own marriage, he had occasionally dated her. Along with his wife, Cynthia, Edsel happily posed for pictures at L'Esprit. Published the next day, the photographs fueled even more gossip about Henry's relationship with Kathy DuRoss. And Kathy didn't seem to mind. "What will be will be," she said. All she was really interested in, she insisted, was the success of her new discothèque. She had the feeling that operating L'Esprit would prove to be more satisfying than modeling. "This is a fulfillment," she added. "It's a feeling of personal accomplishment."

Another personal accomplishment, but one she rarely mentioned, was her continuing relationship with Henry Ford. Though Henry never put in an appearance at L'Esprit, he was seeing Kathy fairly regularly. His excuse to Cristina was that he had important business that kept him at the office. Nevertheless Henry sought to be discreet. He would dine with Kathy at out-of-the-way places or at the homes of his financial pal Max Fisher and his son Edsel, who was working for the company in Detroit. And when Henry visited his lady friend at her home, he would wear a red wig as a disguise. But neighbors recognized him and he became known as the "E. Howard Hunt of Grosse Pointe." Even more ludicrous were the times he arranged for an ambulance to pick him up after an evening at Kathy's apartment. Again to no avail. Word of Henry's conduct soon spread at cocktail parties and at Grosse Pointe hairdressers.

By now too the word had gotten back to Cristina. The time had come for a showdown. This time Henry was only too willing to admit he was seeing Kathy. From then on, the arguments in the Ford household became hot and heavy. The servants at their Georgian mansion could hardly believe their ears when they heard some of the things that were said. For Henry, particularly when he was in his cups—which was becoming more frequent—could get extremely vulgar. Once in a fit of anger he called a guard and ordered him to bring in a large male dog. Then he demanded that Cristina permit the hound to mount her. Cristina, who fled in tears to her bedroom, later said, "It was all so sickening." Even then, however, she was willing to forgive her husband. "I thought he would come to his senses," she explained. "I knew he was having great problems at the office."

And indeed he was. For by then Henry was also in emotional turmoil over Lee Iacocca, who, in his estimation, had become too big for his britches. How to get rid of the "wop," as the chairman was now so inelegantly referring to the president of the Ford Motor Company, had become a major preoccupation. Ousting Iacocca would not be easy. But Henry was determined to do so.

He was equally determined to resolve his dilemma at home. Shortly before Christmas 1975 he made his move. And for Cristina it was, in spite of everything, unexpected. She had agreed to fly with her husband to England to spend the holiday with Lord Mountbatten shooting pheasant. In fact, she was packing her bags when Henry suddenly announced he wasn't taking her. "I've got other plans," he said. "And they don't include you." Cristina demanded an explanation. And Henry gave it to her with the bark off. He was "fed up," he said. He had had "enough" of her. Besides, she couldn't handle one man, he went on. Now he had a girl who could handle twenty. With that Henry Ford walked out of Cristina's life. He then flew to England with Kathleen DuRoss.

Several weeks later his personal lawyer in Detroit officially confirmed that Henry and his second wife, Cristina, after ten years of marriage, had "separated and are now living apart." And a Ford company spokesman said that the board Chairman had decided to make the announcement because "Suzy" in the New York *Daily News* had broken the story that morning. "That the Fords had separated was getting to be so well known even the gas attendants in Grosse Pointe were talking about it," the spokesman added. Henry, who was still in England with Kathleen, was unavailable for further comment. Also unavailable was Cristina, who, after spending ten days alone in Sun Valley, was reported to be in seclusion at the Ford mansion in Grosse Pointe.

The announcement dismayed Henry's family, none more so than his mother, Eleanor Clay Ford. Now nearly eighty and ailing, the strong-willed matriarch thought that her eldest son had once again taken leave of his senses. Not that she had been particularly fond of Cristina. As for most members of the family, Cristina had been too exotic for her midwestern tastes. What concerned her, however, was all the unsavory publicity. But she didn't live to see most of it. On October 19, 1976, Eleanor Clay Ford, who had become one of the wealthiest women in the world through her marriage to Edsel Ford, passed away at Henry Ford Hospital after what was described as a lengthy illness.

For Lee Iacocca the death of Eleanor Clay Ford was a particular misfortune. Long an admirer of his blunt-talking, hard-driving ways, she had been one of Iacocca's most important allies. Once, in Henry's presence, she had stated that the family owed Iacocca a great debt. "You have made my sons look good," she told him. Which was probably the last thing Henry Ford II wanted to hear. After all, as he had often reminded his top executives including Iacocca, it was his name that was on the front of the Glass House. Also, Henry had long resented his subordinate's high visibility. Iacocca was the first auto man ever to make the covers of *Time* and *Newsweek* in the same week. That was when the Mustang was introduced in 1964. And ever since, Iacocca had been a favorite of the automotive media. For, as William Serrin wrote in *The New York Times Magazine,* he is "brutally honest and has great style."

Apparently his mother's remark kept eating at Henry. So much so that Iacocca came to feel that the Chairman was jealous of him. Whenever Iacocca felt he was being pressed unfairly by Henry, he would turn to *"The* Mrs. Ford"—as she was called to distinguish her from the other Mrs. Fords—and she would seek to moderate her son's pressure at informal family meetings. Usually she would be supported by her other sons, both of whom also admired Iacocca. But Benson Sr. and William Clay had their own problems, the former mainly alcoholic, and Henry seemed to resent their counsel. At one point, in fact, Henry grew so irritated with Benson that he suggested that his brother stay home and not report for work. Henry said he would mail him his checks. As for Billy, who now drank only soft drinks, he was beginning to spend more time with the Detroit Lions than he did at the Glass House.

But Billy did tell Iacocca that his brother had been sounding off about him more than usual in family circles. A more specific warning came, however, from former actors' agent Pat Di-Cicco, who had done so much carousing in years past with Henry. DiCicco, who was dying of throat cancer, asked Iacocca to come visit him at his Sutton Place apartment. Speaking in Italian, DiCicco said, "Don't trust Henry. He wants to destroy you. Keep on fighting." The reason, according to DiCicco, was Henry's increasing concern about perpetuating his family's control of the company. Henry was making no bones about wanting his son Edsel to take over eventually. Standing in the way of his dream was Iacocca, who had emerged as one of the more powerful presidents in Ford history. Under his stewardship the company had attained record profits and sales. All of which endeared Iacocca to the board of directors, most of his fellow executives and, of course, Ford dealers across the country.

DiCicco's warning did not come as a big surprise. As far back as 1972 Iacocca had known that Henry was seeking to keep him in his place. That was when the Chairman torpedoed Iacocca's plan to appoint Harold K. Sperlich, an outstanding new-car designer, as head of Ford's operations in Europe. Sperlich, who had helped in the design of the original Mustang in the early 1960s, was known as one of Lee's protégés. Henry told Iacocca he had someone else in mind. That someone else was Philip Caldwell, a Harvard business school graduate, who was named chief executive officer of Ford of Europe Inc. As Caldwell's president Henry named William O. Bourke, who had been in charge of Australian operations. Their chief virtue in Henry's eyes was that they weren't "Iacocca's men."

As relations between them became more strained, Iacocca finally confided to intimates that "hard feelings" had developed between Ford and him. "Nobody can get along with Mr. Ford," he said at one point. It was always "Mr. Ford," not "Henry," even when Henry urged Iacocca to call him by his first name. "You don't get close to the king," said Iacocca. As a result, Iacocca rarely socialized with Henry. Only once, Iacocca's wife Mary told a Detroit interviewer, did they invite the Fords—Henry and Cristina—to their Bloomfield Hills home for dinner. Lee's parents were present, and after eating, the group watched film slides of a gathering of Ford Motor Company executives and their wives.

In the summer of 1975 Iacocca knew for certain that Henry was seeking to goad him into quitting. Much to his horror, he learned that the Chairman had authorized an exhaustive and far-ranging probe into his personal life and business ethics. This was no mere audit of his travel and expense accounts, as he had first been led to believe. The investigation, which ultimately cost the Ford company some $1.5 million and went far beyond anything anyone could recall in Dearborn, was headed by Theodore Souris, a former Michigan Supreme Court justice and a senior partner in Bodman, Longley, Bogle and Armstrong, the prestigious Detroit law firm which had long represented the Ford family. The financial aspects of the probe were handled by Norman A. Bolz, partner in the accounting firm of Coopers & Lybrand.

Before the investigation ended, there were to be allegations of wiretaps, buggings, burglaries, stolen documents and strong-arm tactics by some of the hired investigators. As a former friend of Iacocca, himself the alleged victim of these tactics, commented, "It was far worse than anything that was supposed to have taken place during Watergate." Initially the probe concentrated on a convention of Ford dealers in Las Vegas which Iacocca and several other Ford executives attended. "They had the rooms bugged," a dealer friend said. "They were even bribing the girls to find out if we were dating anyone." Private detectives roamed the hotels, asking showgirls whether any of them were dating any of the Ford executives. "The irony of all this," the friend continued, "was the fact that Henry was always supplied with hookers whenever he came to Las Vegas. And he could get pretty rough with the girls. Yes, he was that kind of guy. But, Henry being Henry, such episodes were usually hushed up."

Soon the investigation of Iacocca was widened to include interrogating employees of a number of Ford Motor suppliers, including the United States Steel Corporation, the Budd Company, the Kenyon & Eckhardt and J. Walter Thompson advertising agencies. The probers demanded to see the books and records of these companies, which generally complied. The companies were not willing to get into a hassle with such a valued customer as Henry Ford. As for Iacocca, the mere fact that he was the subject of the wide-ranging probe proved damaging to his image in the industry. The very questions asked about him were pernicious, in that they were generally of a leading and accusatory nature. The probers sought information about Iacocca's relationships with suppliers, his investments, his purchases, his friends, and how he entertained.

Iacocca learned of the dimensions of the probe only from

friends and business associates who had been interrogated. Over five hundred interviews were conducted across the country and at least fifty Ford executives, considered close to Iacocca, were intensively grilled. At Henry's insistence a good part of the investigation focused on a travel agency headed by William Fugazy, Sr., a close friend of Iacocca's. The Fugazy company had been doing a large amount of business with Ford Motor, handling the company's routine travel arrangements as well as running incentive contests designed to boost dealers' sales. And Henry was absolutely convinced that suppliers like Fugazy were giving kickbacks to top Ford executives. Moreover, he had gotten it into his mind that Fugazy was somehow associated with the underworld.

This of course was nonsense. Fugazy, who comes from one of New York's leading and better known families, dating back to 1870, presides over a $60 million, family-owned conglomerate that encompasses fleets of buses and limousines, a variety of corporate transportation services and a nationwide network of franchised travel services. He operates out of a small but comfortable Madison Avenue office, its walls covered with photographs showing Fugazy playing golf or attending social events with celebrities such as Jackie Gleason, Gerald Ford, Richard Nixon, Frank Sinatra, Bob Hope, New York Yankees owner George Steinbrenner and Terence Cardinal Cooke. In 1973, Cardinal Cooke presented him with the Man of the Year Award in New York. Previously, he had been knighted by Francis Cardinal Spellman. Everywhere one looks, however, there are mementos of Fugazy's friendship with Iacocca. Behind his desk, for example, there is a picture of Lee hugging Fugazy's father, Nicola. And on a nearby ledge there's a photograph of Iacocca standing in front of a Mark V. The handwritten inscription reads: "Al mio carissimo amico Bill con i migliori augori. Lido" ("To my dearest friend Bill with the most sincere wishes").

At the time of the investigation, Fugazy had been a partner in the J. Walter Thompson Agency. By coincidence, J. Walter Thompson was also doing a lot of advertising work for the Ford Motor Company. At first J. Walter Thompson was hesitant about permitting Ford's investigators to examine Fugazy's files.

Until a call came from Henry personally. According to Fugazy, the Chairman threatened to cancel the advertising agency's lucrative account with the Ford company unless the Fugazy files were immediately produced. "While I was away in Florida," says Fugazy, "the investigators were given the keys to my office and they illegally took all my files including my income tax returns—which they didn't return for many months." Fugazy also claims that he was kept under surveillance and that his phones were tapped. "Talk about Watergate!" Fugazy says.

Finally, after months of probing into every aspect of Lee Iacocca's life, both personal and public, the investigation was abruptly terminated. And it proved to be an all-time bust. Not one shred of evidence of any wrongdoing had been uncovered. A full report was provided Franklin Murphy, an outside director who was chairman of the Ford board's audit committee. Murphy, who had not authorized the investigation in the first place, was outraged. As he told Iacocca, "Henry came in with a cannon and went out with a pea shooter."

Iacocca was informed of the findings (or lack of them) by none other than Henry himself. The Chairman did not apologize. Instead, he indicated that the probe had been little more than a customary "audit." Though enraged, Iacocca said nothing. That evening he met with some friends. "Now the trouble really starts," he told them. "What Henry wanted more than anything else was something to use against me, a hold to keep me in my place. But he's discovered there's no skeleton in my closet. And he's pissed."

So "pissed," in fact, that Henry ordered Iacocca to cancel Fugazy's contract with the Ford Motor Company. "Anyone who is in the limousine business has to be in the Mafia," he insisted. Iacocca could hardly believe his ears. He reminded Henry of how the contract had come about in the first place. Back in 1963, Carey, a major transportation company, had turned down a proposal from Ford Motor to use its Lincoln Continental in New York City. Carey claimed the luxury car was too awkward for city traffic and used too much gas. At Henry's suggestion, Iacocca called Fugazy, who said yes.

Iacocca also reminded Henry that it was Fugazy who had arranged for Pope Paul to ride in a Lincoln instead of a Chrysler when the Holy Father was visiting New York. Fugazy had been in Rome with Iacocca and Cardinal Spellman when Henry called from Dearborn. The Chairman was all excited. He had heard that a Chrysler was to be used in the papal procession. Could anything be done about replacing it with a Lincoln? It was Fugazy who arranged the switch—a masterful publicity break for the Ford Motor Company.

But the Chairman wasn't interested in what he called "ancient history."

"Get rid of him," he barked.

An embarrassed Iacocca dutifully called one of his best friends to tell him he was through. It was a call that, aside from wounding his pride, cost Fugazy at least two and a half million dollars. But Fugazy understood the impossible situation Iacocca had found himself in. "I felt more sorry for Lee than I did for myself," he says.

In the midst of all this turmoil Henry Ford encountered a problem he hadn't expected. Shortly after returning from England with Kathy DuRoss he began to suffer severe chest pains. Rushed to St. Joseph Mercy Hospital in Ann Arbor, he was told that he had angina pectoris, the result of a chronic and degenerative heart condition. After eleven days of hospitalization he was released to begin what turned out to be six weeks of convalescence. And though he continued to have occasional heart pains, he rejected his doctors' advice that he get a bypass operation. Yes, he told an interviewer, he had considered that option but wasn't going ahead "because I don't want to have it."

Still wearing the beard he had grown in the hospital, Henry appeared affable and in good spirits. He explained to Robert W. Irvin, automotive writer for the *Detroit News,* why he believed there should always be a Ford in the future of the world's second-largest automobile company:

> The family owns thirteen percent of the equity and has forty percent of the votes. That forty percent has already passed on to the generation below me. So, we have a very important stake in the future of this company. This is a big company. It has a lot of stockholders, a lot

of employees, a lot of dealers and a lot of responsibility to the consuming public.

It has got to be run as a public company, regardless of how much ownership we have. But because of our huge investment we cannot abdicate our ownership position in any way, shape or form. I think the public really wants, after I go, to see somebody called Ford somewhere right at the top of the company in some kind of position.

I have never said that before but I'm saying it now because I don't give a darn and the diamonds can fall where they may. . . . I am just making a comment on something I feel strongly about.

Ford conceded he had "not thought this out in detail. There should be a Ford at the top of the company somewhere but how this is to be accomplished is still to be defined."

One thing was certain from Henry's remarks: though Iacocca technically was next in line as his successor, there was little likelihood of this occurring. But when asked about rumors circulating around Detroit that Iacocca might be leaving, Henry said: "I don't know why; I never heard that. That must be just another one of those lovely rumors you people hear."

Lovely or not, there was substance to the rumors. Holding onto his increasingly unpleasant job had become humiliating for Iacocca. As he then told intimates, he planned to quit in October 1979—after his fifty-fifth birthday—so as to qualify for his pension. Meanwhile he was prepared "to take all of Henry's crap" for three years.

But Henry Ford II had other ideas.

10

REAL ESTATE

FOR SOME YEARS LEE IACOCCA HAD SOUGHT TO CONVINCE Henry Ford of the necessity of switching quickly to the manufacture of fuel-efficient, small cars. What with Arab oil embargoes and the inevitable rise in gas prices, he could see the handwriting on the wall. He believed the era of big, gas-guzzling vehicles would soon be over. And to remain competitive, Iacocca wanted Ford Motor to begin planning a front-wheel-drive "minicar" patterned after new Japanese models.

Iacocca and his chief ally in the company, Hal Sperlich, the brilliant new-car planner, felt a sense of urgency about pushing their "small is beautiful" concept. They were aware that in the wake of the 1973 oil embargo, General Motors had quietly begun pouring billions into the creation of its own small front-wheel-drive car. Chrysler too was thinking in those terms. Only lack of ready cash kept Chrysler from an early start on a prototype. Working closely with Sperlich, Iacocca came up with the numbers needed to turn his dream of small Fords with little engines into a reality. In all, about $3 billion would have to be raised for the switchover.

No way, said Henry Ford II.

Iacocca continued arguing his case. But the man whose name was on the front of the building refused to budge. At a final review of Iacocca's proposal in 1975 the Chairman said, "We're just not going to spend that kind of money. I've turned conservative and that's it."

Sperlich, however, was unwilling to take no for an answer, even from the Chairman. He argued that Henry's decision made no sense. Which was too much for the Chairman, who cornered Iacocca one day and, referring to Sperlich, said, "Get rid of that guy. I don't want him around." In October 1976 Sperlich was assigned to a relatively obscure post in the company. Soon afterward he quit to become a top executive at Chrysler.

Years later Lee Iacocca was still seething over Henry Ford's refusal to institute a down-sizing program. Though he had become top man of another auto company, he could not contain his anger over the dire consequences that had befallen Ford Motor as a result of Henry's shortsightedness. "That was the greatest strategic error in fifty years at the company," Iacocca maintained. "It was not like making a mistake in a small battle. The *whole damn war* was based on that arbitrary decision."

Because of that decision Ford Motor paid a heavy price. The losses of its North American automotive division in 1979 and 1980 were enormous. And Henry publicly acknowledged he had goofed in not pushing a small car in the United States. But Iacocca, still seething, didn't buy Henry's candor: "When you own a big piece of the company, you can always fall back and say, 'Well, I feel bad, but I'll take the responsibility,' (as if he were) suffering along with the widows and orphans."

Stabbing a thick Imperial cigar in the air, Lee Iacocca added, "I'd give Henry Ford an *F* for management."

Ford officials have contended that the main reason for Henry's refusal to fund smaller cars was the fact that the company was being buffeted by recession. Which Iacocca does not deny. But Iacocca also notes that while profits were indeed being severely pressed, Henry was diverting company funds into the construction of the Renaissance Center, a futuristic complex of four 39-story office buildings, restaurants, stores, bars, shops and nightclubs, all topped by a 73-story hotel on the edge of the Detroit River. And this was done largely on Henry's say-so. Exactly how much Ford Motor money was finally invested in RenCen, as it is popularly called, is in dispute. At a meeting of Ford directors in the spring of 1975, when stockholder dividends were cut, the board approved the expenditure of $20 million. Iacocca, however, claims that Henry arranged for an investment of $80 million, and that for a time the figure was kept from the board. But a complaint in a stockholders' suit maintained the investment was closer to $150 million. Whatever the figure, says Iacocca, the money should have been invested in planning for fuel-efficient cars.

Henry first became interested in real estate because of Max Fisher. A self-styled "diversified-company executive," Fisher has dabbled in many business ventures—and has done well in most of them. But he is perhaps best known as a leader of the Jewish community with extensive ties in Republican circles. He is also well known as a friend, confidant and occasional business partner of Henry Ford II. From time to time Fisher and his wife Marjorie traveled with Henry and Cristina. On a trip to Israel in 1972, while their wives remained in Jerusalem, Fisher and Ford went down in a disabled Israeli air force helicopter in the desolate Sinai Desert. Neither was injured, and they were rescued half an hour later by another helicopter, which took them to their original destination, an Israeli army base on the Suez Canal. Looking through high-powered binoculars across the small stretch of water, they could see Egyptian troops, who were looking back at them with their own binoculars.

The Ford-Fisher relationship has been more than social, however. Fisher has constantly advised the motor magnate on tax-sheltered investments. These deals were usually put together with A. Alfred Taubman, a Detroit builder who became famous in the real estate business as a developer of shopping centers across the country. One of his projects was the highly successful Fairlane Town Center in Dearborn, which Taubman owns jointly with the Ford Motor Land Development Corporation.

Because of tax shelters, Henry Ford II was able to escape paying most federal taxes for some years. Thus he made many nontaxable millions in addition to his nearly million-a-year taxable salary from Ford Motor. And he often would brag about "screwing" the government. On several occasions he told Iacocca, "You've got to be a fool to pay income taxes." Thus Henry was constantly looking for lucrative investment opportunities. One such was a casino on the French side of the Caribbean island of St. Martin. Henry invested $300,000 in the gambling emporium, and he convinced Iacocca to put up $100,000. Eventually the deal fell through. Henry, however, managed to get his money back. Iacocca, not as lucky, dropped his $100,000.

Henry Ford's involvement in the building of the Renaissance Center won him many kudos as a civic-minded citizen anxious to rescue Detroit from years of blight and racial problems. For years the troubled city had become more drab and empty, while the surrounding suburbs attracted most new office, industrial and apartment construction. The race riot of 1967 spurred the move to the suburbs. From 1960 to 1970 the city lost 160,000 residents. Major retailers such as Saks Fifth Avenue and F.A.O. Schwartz began building stores in suburban shopping centers. And a major effort to build a domed sports stadium in the city was threatened by the determination of the Detroit Lions, the professional football team owned by Henry's brother William Clay, to move to Pontiac, twenty-five miles to the northwest.

In Henry's words, the Renaissance Center was planned as ʔ "catalyst" to lure business and people back to the city. RenCen, nowever, was not actually Henry's brainchild. It came about as a result of the concern felt by Dwight Havens, then president of the local chamber of commerce, that the city's businessmen were demonstrating "a sorry lack of spirit towards saving Detroit." And he wanted to do something almost bigger than life. Exactly what, he did not know. All he knew was that it had to be a project that would shake Detroit out of its doldrums. And he also knew that the only man who could spearhead any such major endeavor was Henry Ford II.

Havens decided the only way to get Henry interested was through his longtime business associate Max Fisher, then spending considerable time in Washington as an unofficial adviser to the Nixon administration. Fisher was amenable. He agreed to broach the subject to Henry. Finally, in the winter of 1970, Havens chaired a meeting at his Michigan Avenue headquarters attended by many of Detroit's movers and shakers. Besides Ford and Fisher, there were the mayor, the governor, top people from General Motors, Chrysler and American Motors, utility company executives, bankers and financiers, major local businessmen such as Joseph L. Hudson, Jr., and big-name national executives such as K-Mart chairman Harry B. Cunningham.

"All of us agreed we had to do something," recalled Fisher.

By prearrangement, Henry nominated Fisher as chairman of a coalition that would be named Detroit Renaissance. Fisher said he would accept only if Henry agreed to serve as cochairman. Also as scripted, Henry agreed. Out of this and future meetings grew the concept of the spectacular riverfront building project that eventually would be called Renaissance Center. Henry was enthusiastic, more enthusiastic than he had ever been before about anything having to do with Detroit. He assigned a top executive, Wayne Doran, president of his company's Land Development Corporation, to work on the technical real estate details. Ford himself agreed to raise the money.

Henry was less enthusiastic about a proposal that the new coalition build or finance a football stadium on the riverfront. His brother, William Clay, had made it clear that he wanted to move his football organization to a stadium in Pontiac if that city could afford to build one. "When it comes to a stadium," Henry said at one meeting, "I'm going with my brother Bill." Nevertheless there was sentiment within the coalition for a downtown stadium. But Henry said, "If Renaissance is going to get into the stadium business, I'm getting off Renaissance." And, as usual, Henry's views prevailed.

As did his views on what would be built on 28.5 acres of choice land in downtown Detroit. It would be a spectacular complex of buildings along the riverfront, to be designed by architect John Portman, who had created the famed Peachtree

Center in downtown Atlanta. Henry had visited Peachtree and had been impressed with the way Portman had used aerial walkways to link a series of buildings, including a giant merchandising mart, a Regency Hyatt Hotel and three office buildings.

On November 24, 1971, Henry Ford unveiled his plan for Detroit. Sitting next to him was Mayor Roman S. Gribbs, who said that the riverfront project was "magnificent." Gribbs, who had been desperately seeking to keep major companies from moving out of Detroit, added, "Henry Ford is synonymous with Detroit. I think Henry Ford II will become synonymous with the rebirth of Detroit."

"For Henry, it was like having a new toy," one friend recalls. He began devoting much of his energy to raising funds for the riverfront venture. But, as he quickly discovered, it wasn't easy. Detroit's money people weren't overly anxious to invest in what most of them had come to believe was a hopeless, no-win white elephant. General Motors, for example, wasn't too interested. And its chairman, Richard C. Gerstenberg, told Henry so.

But then Henry did an unheard of thing: he walked into the G.M. headquarters on Grand Boulevard to have lunch with Gerstenberg. Even before he left the building, rumors spread on Wall Street that a G.M.-Ford merger was in the offing. Which of course was not the case. Henry had put in a strong pitch for G.M. to get involved in the riverfront project. Again Gerstenberg demurred. "I told him it was a little difficult to visualize how we could cooperate jointly with Ford," he said later. But Henry persisted. At the annual Christmas party Gerstenberg announced that General Motors had indeed agreed to cooperate with its archrival. "Detroit needs this project," Gerstenberg said, "and I want to commend my great friend Henry Ford for taking the initiative in launching it." In the end G.M. wound up investing $12 million.

G.M.'s decision to join with Ford made it less difficult to sell the project to others. "If Ford Motor Company had been the only investor," said Wayne Doran, "many of our competitors and others would have said, 'This is some crazy venture that Wayne Doran talked Henry Ford into. We want no part of that—it'll never fly.'"

Not all those who eventually invested thought the project would fly. Still, they invested. And for different reasons. As then K-Mart chairman Harry B. Cunningham recalled, "To be candid, I thought the project looked very ambitious. I hoped it was going to be feasible, but frankly I doubted it. Henry came out to my office and we chatted." Cunningham's office was in suburban Troy, where K-Mart had moved its world headquarters after pulling out of postriot Detroit. And some K-Mart executives felt a sense of guilt about having precipitously moved out of the city.

After his chat with Cunningham, Henry left with a commitment that eventually became a $2 million investment. "We looked on it not so much as a good business investment as we did an investment in Detroit's future," recalled Cunningham. "Henry doesn't have any clout with the K-Mart Corporation. But he does in the automotive world. And once General Motors and Ford are committed to this kind of project, it isn't too difficult to get commitments from the many auto supplier firms."

According to a survey published by the *Detroit News,* fifty-one corporations ultimately invested in Renaissance Center. Of this number, thirty-eight gained all or a substantial portion of their business from the auto industry. Six investors were banks, financial institutions or insurance companies that had substantial deposits from or did significant amounts of business with the auto makers—primarily Ford and G.M. The remaining seven partners had more limited connections with the industry. They included Amoco Oil, the Automobile Club of Michigan, Parke Davis, a Detroit-based company that sells pharmaceuticals to clinics and hospitals supported by the auto companies, and Western International Hotels, which operates the Plaza Hotel inside RenCen. Also investing were the publishers of the *Detroit News* and the *Detroit Free Press,* who viewed the project as a possible boost for their declining city. Then, of course, there was K-Mart.

Not all the corporate participants were overjoyed about being forced to invest. One, in fact, told the *Detroit News,* "The logo of Renaissance Center should have been a twisted arm." Another put it this way: "It was little more than a sophisticated protection racket . . . I got the distinct impression—although nobody ever said it in so many words—that if we didn't kick in

X number of dollars, our contracts with Ford and G.M. might be revaluated and we might not end up with as much business as we have now. What does that sound like to you?"

Still another company official said, "I made the decision on my own because, frankly, none of our other executives thought it was wise to invest in the project. For the record, I said that 'it was something to prove our concern for the city where the bulk of our business comes from.' We actually did it because Henry Ford asked us to. Ford and G.M. are two of our largest customers. What can you do when they ask? You have to come up with the money."

Ford's man Wayne Doran took umbrage at allegations of arm-twisting. Maintaining that such talk was "ridiculous and untrue," he added that he had "concluded that all it amounts to is people who want to stroke themselves and say, 'See Henry and I are like this—real close. He cares enough about me to twist my arm.'"

The problem with this analysis is that all those doing the complaining insisted on anonymity. As one executive put it, "The only reason we invested was to preserve our business with the auto industry. If we go on the record with this, we'll cut our throats the same—maybe worse—than if we had said 'no' to Ford."

Three years after Henry first unveiled his plan, and after construction had begun, the RenCen project ran into difficulties. Because of soaring expenses and general inflation, the estimated construction costs rose from $237.5 million to $337.5 million, and Henry found it necessary to search hard for the extra $100 million. Beginning in late 1974, Henry traveled to New York, Los Angeles, Chicago and London, talking to industrialists and bankers in search of more financing. In London, Henry asked about the possibility of getting Mid-eastern oil money for the project. He personally met with representatives of Arab sheiks who were seeking to put to use billions of excess dollars earned since the oil boycott and price increases. But as Henry later reported, he "struck out" with the Arabs because Ford Motor did business with the Israelis. "One of the problems is that the Ford Motor Company is on their boycott list," he said, "and while we are just one of the many partners in the

Renaissance Center development, nonetheless we (Ford) are the managing partners."

The financial problems seemed insurmountable. And there was only limited time before Henry would have to make the decision on whether to stop work on the project. The decision "to fish or cut bait"—as Henry so originally put it—was not an easy one. But he was determined to fish. He decided to use some muscle to convince Ford suppliers to make investments. He dispatched J. Paul Bergmoser, executive vice-president and now president of Chrysler to fly around the country to tell people at Firestone, U.S. Steel, the Budd Company, General Tire and dozens of others that Henry wanted more dough. At least $40 million was raised in this fashion. Back he went to General Motors and other original partners, getting them to increase their investments. But the bulk of the additional funding eventually came from the Ford Motor Company, thus assuring the first phase of the Renaissance Center. The appropriation of these funds meant that the retooling of Ford production for smaller, fuel-efficient vehicles—for which Lee Iacocca had been pleading—would definitely be placed on the back burner.

In April 1977 the formal dedication of Renaissance Center took place. The occasion was marked by a lavish charity ball, attended by 650 of Detroit's leading socialites and businessmen, in the ballroom of the Detroit Plaza, centerpiece hotel, said to be the world's tallest. At the last minute, Mrs. R. Jamison Williams, cochairperson of the gala, received word that Henry would not be there. Only moments before, Mrs. Williams had been on the phone with Henry's estranged wife, Cristina, who also canceled her table.

Henry's absence was particularly noticeable. After all, he had been primarily responsible for the creation of what everyone agreed was the most spectacular addition to Detroit's skyline in its history. Only Bob Hope made mention of the missing man. After the guests had finished a meal consisting of melon, tournedos Lorenzo de Medici and an ice cream bombe, the comedian took the spotlight. Waving his arm about the cavernous ballroom, Hope cracked, "How do you like Henry Ford's rumpus room?"

Needless to say, rumors swept the ballroom as to why Henry had stayed away. Lee Iacocca, who was there with his wife, told reporters he had no idea. Only later was it learned that Henry had been playing stepfather in Dearborn, walking Deborah Anne DuRoss—the twenty-one-year-old daughter of Kathy DuRoss—down the aisle of Martha Mary Chapel.

The next day Henry turned up to greet Vice-President Walter Mondale and take him on a tour of Renaissance Center. Accompanying them was the black mayor of Detroit, Coleman A. Young, who had come into office in 1974. Henry took advantage of the occasion to ask Mondale whether President Carter planned to impose a stiff federal excise tax on full-size cars. Henry said he was troubled over reports that the President might seek an additional $500 tax on "larger, less gas-efficient cars" to discourage fuel consumption. "I'm quite concerned about the potential for increased unemployment here," he added.

If Mondale knew the answer to Henry's question, he wasn't telling. The Vice-President suggested that Henry would have to wait until Carter spelled out his energy program.

Henry could hardly contain his annoyance. He felt, as he said privately, that the Carter administration did not know "its ass from its elbow" about auto industry problems. All he would say publicly, however, was that he had a "few disagreements" with the President over government interference with the industry. As a result of uncertainties over regulations of auto pollution, fuel economy and safety, "we're just in a mess," he added. Still, Henry insisted, he was "not sorry" about having supported Carter's election the previous year.

Henry's endorsement of the Georgian had come as a surprise. After all, Carter's opponent, Gerald R. Ford, was from Michigan and had long been known as a friend of the auto industry. The reason, according to those who saw a good deal of Henry in this period, was even more surprising. Henry, it was said, was just plain annoyed that another Michigander named Ford had become more famous than he.

Henry's support of Carter had included the cosponsorship of a fancy luncheon at New York's "21" Club at which the Democratic candidate addressed fifty blue-chip corporate and financial leaders. Carter, who spoke as a former businessman rather than in the populist tones that had characterized his acceptance speech at the Democratic convention, came out strongly in favor of free enterprise and multinational corporations. All of which was "music to my ears," said Henry. Only later, two years after the event took place, was it to prove slightly embarrassing. The Federal Election Commission ordered Carter's campaign committee to repay the U.S. Treasury a sum of over $3,000 after ruling that the luncheon constituted an illegal contribution. Also fined were Ford's cosponsors. But Henry was not fined, because, having been warned that his $1,510 contribution might be illegal, he had asked the Democratic National Committee for the return of his money.

Politics now were no longer as important to Henry Ford as they had been in years past. For one thing, he could find little rapport with the Georgian crowd occupying the White House. And he was incensed at the "strange-looking characters" whom Jimmy Carter had moved into federal agencies dealing with the auto business. Once, in fact, he had confronted "this bearded guy" who had been giving him a hard time, saying, "Bet you drive a Volkswagen."

"And you know what?" Henry went on, "The creep said he did!"

Meanwhile the Renaissance Center, to which Henry had devoted so much effort, was not proving an unqualified financial success. Even Henry was forced to concede, "It's a mixed bag, you might say." There were recurring complaints that the towering river complex had "stolen" tenants from other downtown buildings. In other words, RenCen had merely rearranged what downtown activity had already existed. Critics also contended that RenCen had not, as it was intended to do, reattracted businesses that had earlier fled to the suburbs.

Some of the criticism was savage indeed. Henry was particularly annoyed with the appearance of an underground newspaper calling itself the *Fifth Estate*. RenCen security forces were alerted to pick up and destroy copies of the ten-page periodical, which had been slyly planted in the lobbies of the hotel and office buildings. Each page portrayed a very unflattering picture of what the editors termed "that big fort on the river." There were fabricated quotes attributed to the city fathers and Henry Ford. Henry was quoted as saying, "It's not our money and we didn't lift a finger to actually build it, but we'll take the credit. Besides, the whole sterile thing can fall into the river tomorrow and, frankly, I wouldn't give a damn. It'd be a helluva tax break, which isn't such a bad idea, now that I mention it."

Much more troubling was the filing of a stockholders' suit (later settled out of court) alleging that "the defendant Ford" had imparted advance information of his company's investments in Renaissance Center as well as the Fairlane development "to close personal and business associates," including Max Fisher and Alfred Taubman, "who then used said information to make advantageous land purchases in the proximity of and in the aforementioned projects." As a consequence, the complaint alleged, Henry Ford II was "unjustly enriched," since "Fisher and Taubman made available to the defendant Ford tax sheltered investment and such other financially beneficial investments."

Unlike Renaissance Center, however, the Fairlane Town Center, in suburban Dearborn, proved to be an immediate success. Built by Al Taubman in partnership with the Ford Motor Land Development Corporation, Fairlane consists of an 800-room Hyatt Regency Hotel, a shopping center with 150 stores, twin office towers, an apartment and condominium complex and several smaller office buildings. A futuristic, Ford-produced people-mover system, an automated train, links the hotel with the shopping center. And all of this was developed on land that had once been farms and the great Fairlane estate owned by the original Henry Ford.

In all, 2,360 acres of Henry I's prized land was involved in his grandson's deal with Taubman. And though only a small portion of the acreage was used to create the Fairlane Town Center, even such limited use of the land was too much for some Ford shareholders, who, at the 1976 annual meeting, beefed to Henry about possible damage to the environment. There were even complaints about the decision to tear down a building that had once been the gatehouse of his grandfather's estate.

"I thought the gatehouse was an eyesore and I told them to

tear it down myself," said Henry. He also said the firm had no plans to build on a 130-acre wooded area of the Ford property that was involved in a lawsuit by environmentalists.

One shareholder aroused Henry's anger when he contended the firm had "blatantly lied" in denying that the Fairlane development would hurt the environment, because "that forest is going to be destroyed, lost forever."

"I resent the fact that you say we lied," Henry replied. "That 130 acres is a junk heap. We are not liars. We may not agree with you, but that doesn't mean we are lying."

Still other critics noted the incongruous position of Henry Ford in promoting both RenCen and Fairlane at the same time. RenCen, obviously, was supposed to bring business back to Detroit. But Fairlane was taking business away from the city. United Airlines, for example, had vacated its downtown facilities to set up shop in its own building in Fairlane. The Auto Club of Michigan also vacated much of its downtown office space to relocate in Fairlane. Even J. Walter Thompson Company, the advertising agency that handled the Ford account, moved its operations from Detroit into its own Fairlane building.

Because considerable shopping traffic was now being diverted to Fairlane, the once mighty department stores downtown took a beating. But the scapegoat proved to be not Henry but his partner Al Taubman. The very mention of Taubman's name in Detroit was apt to evoke an angry reaction. "Taubman has raped the downtown," said a local writer on land use. "Why build huge shopping centers in the suburbs when there is nothing downtown?"

Known as the "High Priest of Shopping Centers," Taubman has rarely responded to criticism. When his name surprisingly popped up on John Dean's enemies list during the Watergate days, he refused to comment. For one thing, he has a distinct dislike for the press and a love of privacy. A sleekly dressed, barrel-chested wheeler-dealer, he operates from a small office in the Detroit suburb of Southfield. From there he masterminded the battle for control of one of the richest pieces of underdeveloped land in the nation, the Irvine ranch in California's booming Orange County. Forty miles south of Los

Angeles, and consisting of nearly 80,000 acres of fertile land bordering the Pacific, the ranch has been the most fought-over piece of western real estate since the Little Big Horn. And Taubman emerged the victor over giant Mobil Oil.

Owned by the James Irvine Foundation, the ranch was being developed according to a master plan that called for slow growth and strict environmental protection. As a result of the 1969 Tax Reform Act, the foundation was required to sell most of its stock. Mobil put in a $200 million bid for the land, promising to continue the foundation's conservative development policies. Mobil was well on the way to winning the land when a group of millionaires, headed by Al Taubman, banded together to submit a new bid. Among the millionaires were Henry Ford II; Joan Irvine Smith, a descendant of the ranch founder; Charles Allen, Jr., the New York financier; and Max Fisher. Eventually, after a bitter battle, the Taubman group won out over the oil company. But the $337 million the group paid for the ranch— one-sixth of all of Orange County—saddled them with a five-year $240 million debt, which many observers felt could not be repaid short of wholesale land sell-offs.

Thanks to a booming real estate market and aggressive sales tactics, Irvine's new owners managed to rid themselves of their $240 million purchase debt in record time. And the Taubman group was assured of enormous profits on their original investment. As far as Henry was concerned, he was doing better in real estate than he was in the automobile business.

But he had begun to worry. Word had been leaking out that because of tax-sheltered deals he had been reaping huge profits while paying low federal taxes. And that kind of publicity was the last thing he needed at a time when the Ford Motor Company was plunging into economic troubles.

"This publicity is starting to concern me," he told Lee Iacocca.

11

THE
FORD FOUNDATION

LITTLE WAS GOING WELL FOR HANK THE DEUCE—AS DETROIT-ers had begun to call Henry Ford II—in the mid-seventies. His erstwhile "bambina," unwilling to fade away, remained luxuriously ensconced in the Ford mansion in Grosse Pointe. As far as Cristina was concerned, her estranged husband would have to make the next move. And Henry was at wit's end trying to decide what to do. Divorce seemed out of the question. For one thing, it would be extremely costly. And then, as a close friend told *Newsweek,* Henry would "have to declare himself in public, with family details he'd rather keep quiet." Better to remain in limbo than to have all those painful details— already the subject of considerable gossip—publicly aired in a courtroom.

One thing that could not remain in limbo was the Iacocca problem. Henry had long before decided to get rid of his tough-talking number-two man. But he did not know quite how to go about it. For unlike the other top executives whom he had so abruptly dismissed, almost without a second thought, Iacocca was extremely popular, not only with his board of directors but with Ford dealers around the country. At sales meetings, for example, while the dealers were always happy to shake Henry's hand, they would invariably get off in a corner with Iacocca for "the real skinny," as one of them put it. It was almost as if Lee, not Henry, were the boss of the company. And Henry didn't like it a bit. Of course, as a friend once told *Esquire,* Iacocca had "spent ten years learning to talk 'dese, dem and dose' in order to speak the language of the toughest car dealer." And he was willing to spend considerable time with them, learning their problems and generally keeping them happy. Which was something Hank the Deuce rarely did. Socializing with dealers was not his idea of a good time.

Besides, he had serious personal problems. The roof seemed to have fallen in on Henry, emotionally, following his mother's death. His health, the fallout from his drunk-driving arrest, and his problems with Cristina and Iacocca, all seemed to have a traumatic effect on the Chairman. So much so that Henry began drinking very heavily. And under the influence he became more uninhibited than ever. One media type recalls that he had observed a "well-soused" Henry urinating into a potted palm outside a fancy Grosse Pointe restaurant. Then there was the occasion when the Chairman, feeling no pain, rolled into a Christmas party and, addressing the women guests, asked loudly, "Anybody here want to hump?" There were scattered titters, but no one said a word. For, as usual, in Detroit the king could do no wrong.

After a private meeting with his brother, William Clay Ford confided to a then top executive that Henry looked like a "worried, beaten" man. "I'm beginning to think he's on cocaine," Billy said.

Billy by now had resolved his own personal problems. He had had a successful bypass operation on his heart. Also, he had conquered his own drinking problem by joining Alcoholics Anonymous, and was now given to drinking Cokes. Mainly he was preoccupied with the fortunes of his lackluster football team. His office routine at the Glass House rarely varied. He would show up late, answer the mail for several hours, then return to his Grosse Pointe home. Unlike Henry, he wasn't one for parties. Watching television into all hours of the night was his main relaxation. His name rarely appeared in the social columns. In 1976, however, he received a modicum of attention when he supported the independent candidacy of Eugene McCarthy for President.

His brother's heart ailment propelled Billy momentarily into the spotlight. For Henry had made it clear that, no matter what happened to him, there should always be "somebody called Ford" in the driver's seat of the huge auto company founded by his grandfather three quarters of a century before. That, naturally, focused attention on his brothers, Benson, fifty-six, and William Clay, fifty-one, who were both directors and vice-presidents of the company.

Benson immediately took himself out of competition. "I'm afraid I'm not available because of my health," he said, explaining that he also had suffered from angina and other cardiac problems. Besides, he said, his wife Edith had been seriously ill. Only recently she had undergone an operation for cancer of the throat. All of which had convinced Benson that he should take early retirement.

"That sort of leaves it up to Bill, and I think he would be receptive," said Benson.

There had been family discussions, of course, about a possible succession. But nothing had really been decided. "It's just something to think about with the view to having someone from the family at the top of the company," said Benson.

He also noted that his own son, Benson Jr., and Henry's son, Edsel, were "both coming along." Edsel, in his mid-twenties, was just beginning to show interest in the family business. Benson Jr., almost the same age, lived in Southern California, where he was attending Whittier College. "As soon as he finishes school back there," said his father, "he wants to come back here and work for the company. I think he would start in some training program like Edsel has been doing."

Neither Henry nor Benson Sr. ever encouraged their daughters to have anything to do with the family business. Henry, in fact, was dead set against having any women at all involved in the top echelons of the company. "All they can do is screw things up," he frequently told Ford executives, citing several Fortune 500 companies as horrible examples. Henry never hid his anti-feminist sentiments. In a 1978 interview with Lally Weymouth, published in *The New York Times Magazine,* he conceded that "we were not very much for women in the automobile business until recently." Asked whether he would like his daughters to be interested, he said, "Well, you know, I never thought about it to any great extent. I know Anne wouldn't be interested. I don't know if Charlotte would be or not—now she's doing that dress business, so she has her own thing to work at."

Needless to say, Henry had never asked Charlotte, who, in fact, would most definitely have been interested. She made no secret of the fact that her father's "antediluvian" attitude had annoyed her no end. "I begged him a long time ago to put me on the Ford Foundation board but he said no," she noted. "If he'd had his way, there would not be a woman on his [Ford Motor] board." But he didn't have his way. Bowing to the pressures of the times, he finally agreed to the presence of a woman on the board. She was Marian Sulzberger Heiskell, of *The New York Times* publishing family. And Henry thought that was one way to keep in the good graces of what to him was the most important newspaper in the world.

At the time that Henry's health was first seriously in question, William Clay Ford told Bob Irvin of the *Detroit News* that he would be willing to succeed his brother as chairman. "I'm not campaigning for the job but I wouldn't try to avoid the responsibility if that seemed to be what others wanted," he said. However, he made it clear that he didn't want the full-time job of running the company, adding: "If that meant simply serving as chairman, chairing the company and shareholders' meetings, OK. But as for actually running the company—no. I wouldn't want the job on an everyday basis."

Of course, almost everyone knew who he wanted to run the company on a full-time basis. For William Clay had never made any secret of his friendship with and admiration for Lee Iacocca. It was this fact more than anything else that convinced his brother Henry that he would have to move quickly on the

Iacocca problem. Adding to his sense of urgency were the occasional twinges of chest pain from his heart disease. Now more than ever was he aware of the fact of his mortality. And should the inevitable come sooner than later, there would be only one man who was immediately prepared to take command of the company—Lee Iacocca. And as far as Henry was concerned, his second-in-command was already too strong, too independent and too popular with board memebers and the all-important ranks of the dealers. But perhaps Iacocca's major sin was the fact that he wasn't a Ford. Iacocca's accession to the throne, Henry believed, would threaten the family's control of the company.

Henry grew almost paranoid on the subject. He began thinking in terms of an Italian plot against him. The plotters, of course, were Iacocca, Fugazy, DeTomaso, Uzielli and Cristina. He had seen *The Godfather* and he was actually convinced that the film accurately portrayed the Italian capacity for vengeance. Which, needless to say, was nonsense. (Some years before, following his trip to Israel, Henry had become convinced that he was the target of an assassination plot by the Black September band of Arab terrorists. As a consequence he took security precautions that for a time curbed his personal freedom.)

For a non-Italian, Henry was a pretty good plotter himself. Slowly but surely he had begun cutting Iacocca down to size. In 1972 he had signaled his intentions by rebuffing his second-in-command in assigning Phil Caldwell and Bill Bourke to the company's European operations. Four years later he recalled Bourke to Dearborn, appointed him head of the embattled North American automotive division and said, "I want to see Iacocca's blood all over the floor." And he had other plans for Caldwell.

Those plans became known in April 1977 when Henry announced the creation of a three-man Office of the Chief Executive to operate the company. Under the new arrangement Henry would continue to serve as Chairman and chief executive officer for at least three more years. But then, to most everyone's surprise, he bypassed Iacocca and designated Phil Caldwell, who was virtually unknown outside the company, as a new vice-chairman and number-two man. And he made it clear that when he was not in his office, Caldwell, not Iacocca, would run things.

At a forty-minute news conference at the Glass House, Ford was asked whether the new management structure was a way of allowing Edsel more time to prepare himself to take the helm of the company. Henry replied the he hoped that his son, then in his late twenties, would head the company some day, but that at present he was "a good ten years away" from even a vice-presidency. Reminded that he himself was twenty-eight when he took over Ford Motor in 1945, Henry grinned and observed, "Times have changed."

As for the new trimotor arrangement, Henry put it bluntly: "I am first among equals. If something happens and for some reason or other there is no way to work it out on a consensus basis, then I've got, uh, an extra vote." Henry smiled and the reporters laughed. Not smiling or laughing was Iacocca. As *The New York Times* reported, he "was restless at times and appeared a bit uneasy while Mr. Caldwell sat calmly, occasionally breaking into a grin." Caldwell had reason to grin. Some weeks before, in London, Henry had informed him he was slated for even bigger things.

Biting his lip publicly, Iacocca handled what might have been a difficult situation with style. At a staff briefing a Ford executive reported, "Lee said, in effect, 'Hey, we're a team.' He's one tough cookie. He simply closed the door on any infighting."

Inwardly, however, Iacocca seethed. Only among close friends and at home did he give vent to his true feelings. Finally, in exasperation, his wife asked, "Why don't you quit?" And he should have, he now says. The main reason he didn't was the $970,000 compensation (salary plus bonuses) he was drawing each year. This was equal to what Henry himself was getting and $20,000 more than the amount paid G.M. chairman Thomas A. Murphy. "Frankly," says Iacocca, "I was greedy."

But that wasn't the entire story. Despite Henry and his infuriating antics, Lee Iacocca loved the Ford Motor Company. After all, it had been his home for nearly three decades. And during most of his adult life he had hoped one day to take full command. Now that possibility appeared less and less likely.

Still, he was going to say what he had to say. Courageously he argued that the Office of the Chief Executive—no matter how good it looked on paper—made no sense in the real world. It was, Lee insisted, a three-headed monster incapable of making the big decisions. But Henry was only half-listening. In his imperious manner, he dismissed Iacocca's objections out of hand. "It will all work out in the end," he declared. From then on Iacocca began to play a smaller day-to-day role in running the company, and the flow of decision-making often bypassed him as lower executives reported to Phil Caldwell. By then Iacocca knew that he had had it. He began making very secret soundings about a possible top job in another industry.

Fully resolved, however, was another problem that had long been agitating the Chairman. And that had to do with the Ford Foundation, set up originally to protect the family assets. To avoid payment in taxes by the family of over $300 million when Henry Ford I died, company lawyers, in the thirties, had devised a scheme to split the company stock into voting and nonvoting shares. The voting stock would remain in family hands. The nonvoting stock would be assigned to a Ford Foundation. The Foundation was incorporated without fanfare in January 1936. Making out a check for $25,000 as an initial contribution, Edsel Ford declared, "It will be on a small scale and I have no intention of making it larger."

And when Henry Ford II inherited his father's seat on the Foundation's board in 1943, it was still little more than an inhouse charity, supporting such Detroit institutions as the Ford Hospital, the Ford Museum and the Detroit Symphony Orchestra. Thanks to the growth of the Ford Motor Company, however, it became the world's largest philanthropy—"a large body of money completely surrounded by people who want some," in the oft-quoted words of Dwight MacDonald. And it also became one of the more controversial organizations devoted to the public good.

In 1951 Paul Hoffman, former head of the Studebaker Corporation and administrator of the Marshall Plan, was named the Foundation's first president. His first step was to move the Foundation's headquarters from Dearborn to Pasadena, California. Then, as associate directors, he hired Robert Hutchins, former chancellor of the University of Chicago, Milton Katz, professor of law at Harvard, and Chester C. Davis, a former New Deal agricultural specialist.

Before long the Foundation was immersed in controversy. A headline in the *Chicago Tribune,* then more conservative than it is today, read: "Leftist Slant Begins to Show in Ford Trust." And columnist George Sokolsky also went after the Foundation: "Henry Ford . . . made nearly all his money in this country, but Paul Hoffman, who is spending that money, seems to prefer to put that money into remote bottomless pits and to expend it for meaningless purposes." And a news magazine, sneering at the "projectitis" of the Foundation, wrote of its "big and expensive staff of busy people who think up and sort out innumerable projects, to be bestowed with plenty of money upon specially created agencies or upon professors hard pressed to live on their academic salaries." Since huge amounts of tax-exempt funds were involved, congressional committees became interested. And Henry Ford II began to feel the heat.

In 1952 Henry spent several weeks at "Itching Palms," as the Pasadena headquarters was jocularly called. And he didn't like what he saw. What with top staff, including the president, constantly quarreling, Henry found what he later described as "utter chaos." Besides, he felt that Hoffman and Hutchins were too capricious in the dispensing of large chunks of money for what often seemed to some to be esoteric projects. In a jovial moment Hutchins himself had tossed off a verse beginning:

How firm a Foundation we saints of the Lord
Have built on the faith of our excellent Ford.

The joviality did not last long. Henry made known he wanted Hoffman's head. As one of Hoffman's friends put it, "Paul was far more liberal than Henry. Henry Ford was really ultra-conservative then." Henry, however, told Lally Weymouth that he and Hoffman had "got into some kind of squabble. He brought in some reasonably radical fellows but that didn't have anything to do with it. We just didn't think he was doing the kind of job we thought should be done."

In February 1953 Hoffman's "resignation" became official. And with him went Hutchins, Katz and Davis. That was what Henry wanted and that was what he got. For he was still in firm control of his family's Foundation. Succeeding Hoffman was a president more to Henry's liking—H. Rowan Gaither, Jr., a San Francisco lawyer who had also headed the Rand Corporation. Henry thought that things finally were under control.

As a "sort of goodbye present to give Paul Hoffman something to do," in Henry's words, the eight Foundation trustees voted a $15 million grant to set up the Fund for the Republic. And, as Henry later said, it wasn't his "favorite organization." For it was to cause him aggravation, almost without letup. Besides Hoffman as chairman, the Fund wound up with Robert Hutchins as president. The Hutchins appointment was not exactly greeted with joy by either Henry or his fellow trustees at the Foundation, one of whom said, "This means trouble."

And trouble was not long in coming. There was an uproar over the very first grant approved by the Fund—$25,000 given to the American Bar Assocation to determine whether congressional committees were abusing their investigatory power. Such columnists as George Sokolsky and Fulton Lewis, Jr., saw in the Fund for the Republic a leftist threat to the republic. And some congressmen took up the cry. A congressional investigation focusing on the Ford Foundation was authorized. Its chairman, Representative Carroll Reece of Tennessee, asserted, "There is important and extensive evidence concerning subversive and unAmerican propaganda activities of the Ford Foundation. . . . Here is the last of the great American industrial fortunes . . . being used to undermine and subvert our institutions."

Liberals rallied to the defense of the Foundation. They pointed to its many good works, particularly in the arts, in education and in civil rights as more than justifying its vast expenditures. "Whatever its shortcomings," *The New York Times* was to say, the Foundation "stands as a proud monument to capitalism." The attacks also angered Henry. Waldemar Nielsen, who went to work for the Foundation in 1952, recalled that when the executive committee "gathered in a mood of great concern" at the Links Club in New York, Henry said, "Goddammit, it just makes me sick, this whole attitude that we've got somehow to shape ourselves to the wishes of these people. We're good Americans and we've got a right to our position."

Henry soon changed his tune. Dealers across the country were complaining. There were boycotts of Ford products. The boycotters contended that the Ford Motor Company was, in effect, bankrolling the "subversive" activities of the Fund for the Republic. The American Legion leaped into the fray. Its national commander, Seaborn P. Collins, denounced the Fund for assertedly seeking to depict communism as hardly a serious threat. And the House Committee on Un-American Activities announced it might hold public hearings on Fund activities.

Henry meanwhile was receiving hundreds of letters from outraged citizens protesting the Fund's activities. Perhaps typical was one by William F. Buckley, Jr., then best known as publisher of the *National Review*. Published in the magazine, the letter said, "a number of persons . . . have begun to boycott Ford products" because they believe the Fund and the Ford Foundation have a "moral and personal if not legal connection." Buckley then asked Ford to comment on seven Fund activities. Among these were a $5,000 grant to a group employing a librarian who had refused to answer congressional (HUAC) questions; omission of certain anti-Communist works from a Fund-subsidized bibliography on American communism; and distribution of 35,000 copies of a defense of the Fifth Amendment, but only one thousand copies of a reply.

In response to these critics, Henry sent out a form letter over his signature. In it he argued that the Ford Motor Company had no control over either the Ford Foundation or the Fund for the Republic. But as board chairman of the Ford Foundation, he naturally felt "a deep sense of concern for any action that reflects discredit on either the company or the Foundation." And though he had "no legal right to intervene in the affairs of the Fund for the Republic," he went on, he nevertheless had exercised his right "as a private citizen" to question how the Fund sought to achieve its aims. "Some of its actions, I feel, have been dubious in character and inevitably have led to charges of poor judgment. What effect my comments may have remains to be seen. I am satisfied, however, that no public trust can expect to fulfill its responsibilities if it does not respond to intelligent and constructive public criticism."

Then, in an exquisite piece of timing, the Ford Foundation announced that it would channel $500 million—the largest sum of gifts in the history of philanthropy—to privately supported colleges, universities and voluntary nonprofit hospitals. In all, 4,157 American institutions were to be aided. And across the nation there were huzzahs in praise of the Foundation—even from right-wing critics. One of them, John O'Donnell of the New York *Daily News,* put it this way in his column:

> Let's be practical about this. Ford is carrying on a terrific competitive fight with General Motors and Chrysler. There is no doubt that the actions of Hutchins and his free-wheeling Fund for the Republic started actual but unorganized boycotts against Ford products by veterans and foes of the Communist pinko fringe. The announcement of the half-billion award was intelligent timing, perhaps necessary timing, but that doesn't change the fact that it was one of the greatest gestures to aid our national welfare ever made by private corporate wealth.

In November 1955 the Ford Foundation announced that it would begin selling off its Ford Motor Company stock. This meant that the world's largest family-owned industrial empire would become a publicly owned company. The reason was the desire of the Foundation trustees to diversify their investment portfolio. It was also disclosed that the Ford family shared the trustees' belief that it was unsound for the Foundation to put all its eggs in one basket. The announcement, which was made after a year of negotiations between representatives of the Foundation and the Ford family, was front-page news across the nation. *The New York Times,* in fact, devoted over two full pages to the story.

Ten million shares of Ford stock went on sale to the public in January 1956. The single biggest issue in the history of Wall Street, it netted over $640 million. The company acquired 350,000 new stockholders, each entitled to one vote a share.

As far as Henry was concerned, the sale had his full approval. "We could have stopped it," he said later, "[but] I thought it was a good idea to get out on the market. If you don't have shareholders, you might take some risks and not think of profits first. I think it's better to have it open than have it seem closed."

In May 1956 Henry Ford II stepped down as board chairman of the Foundation. But he remained a member of the board. At one board meeting the proposal was made for a huge grant to the Urban League, the organization devoted to black problems. This was before Henry had become friendly with Whitney Young, Jr., and a personal contributor to the League. The idea of a major foundation supporting civil rights organizations, even a group as moderate as the Urban League, then seemed daring. Consequently there was tension as the trustees discussed the proposal. One of the participants recalled that Henry remained silent during the meeting. Finally someone asked him what he thought. "I think it's okay," Henry responded, "but let me know if you ever get ready to make a grant to Martin Luther King."

As the Foundation kept on selling off its Ford stock over the years, diversifying its holdings, it became more and more independent of the Ford Motor Company. But, more significantly, Henry Ford II was finding that his influence, which had been "first among equals" on the Foundation, had diminished considerably.

In March 1966 McGeorge Bundy became president of the Foundation. He had served as national security adviser to Presidents Kennedy and Johnson. As such, he was involved in controversy, particularly over his role in promoting the Vietnam war. As president of the Foundation he found himself in new controversy. In June 1967 the Foundation had subsidized the registration of black voters in Cleveland during the mayoralty contest. The victor, Carl Stokes, a black man, won by a tiny margin. The cry went up that the Ford Foundation, by financing black registration, had contributed importantly to Stokes's election. Which led Representative Wright Patman, the Democrat from Texas, to ask: "Have the giant foundations made, or do they plan to make grants that will aid certain candidates for national, state and local office? Does the Ford Foundation have a grandiose design to bring vast political, economic and social changes to the nation in the 1970s?" Coming not from a right-wing yahoo but from a self-styled populist, the question caused concern in the magnificent glass palace that now housed Foundation headquarters on New York's East Side.

Then, following the assassination of Robert F. Kennedy, Bundy approved travel and study grants amounting to $131,000 for eight members of the New York senator's staff. It was, to say the least, an impolitic decision. Nevertheless Bundy sought to defend it in an appearance before the House Ways and Means Committee investigating foundation abuses. He insisted that the grants were "educational," within the meaning of the Foundation's charter and the laws granting tax-exempt status to the group.

"If you ask me if the money was well spent, I will say, 'Ask me several years from now.'"

"That isn't the question I asked," replied the ranking Republican on the committee, John W. Byrnes of Wisconsin. "I asked where this grant comes within the 'charitable, educational or scientific' language of your charter. It looks like severance pay."

Bundy said the grants were "fully justified in educational terms" for the "development of the individuals" who received them. And he added that no decision had yet been made as to whether any of the recipients of the grants would be required to publish anything on the results of their travels.

It also turned out that the Foundation had a policy of paying for certain trips overseas by members of Congress. Bundy, denying any intention to influence votes, said the trips were undertaken "in the public interest as educational activities."

The House committee did not buy his story. The Tax Reform Act of 1969 prohibited "any attempt to influence any legislation through an attempt to affect the opinion of the general public." Seeking to rein in other excesses, the bill levied a tax on what it termed improper grants, placed restrictions on grants to individuals, and slapped a 4 percent tax on the annual income of foundations generally. Bundy's appearance before Congress had been disastrous indeed.

None of this sat well with Henry Ford II. Again his company, which by now had no formal relationship with the Foundation, was hearing from outraged citizens concerning its doings. After all, it was the *Ford* Foundation, wasn't it? And the Foundation, considering itself on the edge of social change, was funding civil-rights, environmental, women's-liberation and public-interest groups. While undeniably experimental, its programs had not been uniformly successful—at least in the eyes of its critics. Its support of decentralization in the New York City school system had, in fact, proved disastrous. Its funding of the community-controlled schools in the Ocean Hill-Brownsville section of Brooklyn in 1968 was said to have contributed to racial upheaval.

"We've had a lot of disagreements," Henry later said of Bundy, adding, "I think he had a very shortsighted attitude on things my grandfather was interested in such as the Henry Ford Hospital." When Henry first proposed that a large grant be provided the Detroit hospital, founded by his grandfather, Bundy balked, arguing that the money could be better used elsewhere. But Henry put on the pressure. So much so that finally Bundy gave in. In October 1973 he announced a $100 million grant to the Henry Ford Hospital in connection with its ten-year expansion program in research, education and medical treatment. In making the announcement, however, Bundy emphasized that it was a "one-time-only" grant, because the Foundation did not ordinarily fund such programs.

Relations between Henry Ford and "Mac" Bundy worsened. There was a personal factor. They just didn't like each other. Bundy, after all, was an Eastern intellectual who had taught at Harvard. And Henry disliked intellectuals, particularly uppity ones who didn't bow the knee. What also separated the two men, one trustee told Lally Weymouth, were "general philosophical differences. I think the board was much more liberal than Henry and more willing to move into unconventional fields. Henry is really quite a conventional man in many ways and the Foundation has been doing quite unconventional things."

Henry, for example, protested when he heard that David Freeman, a Foundation executive, had been selected to conduct a study of the nation's energy problems. "I told them Freeman was not the fellow to do the study, but they picked him," Henry said. The result, Henry claims, was a fiasco. The 1974 Freeman Report, which was well publicized, called for stricter government controls on energy. And according to one trustee, "Henry got a lot of static from his oil friends and the industrial establishment." Corporate America had also protested the huge funding the Foundation was providing for public-interest law firms and environmental groups. These firms and groups frequently engaged in litigation on such matters as equal employment opportunities, consumer rights, pollution, tax reform and greater federal regulation of business. And Henry agreed with industry that what was proposed was either too idealistic or too costly or both.

But no one at the Foundation was really paying much attention to Henry. By January 1974, when the Foundation had disposed of its last share of Ford stock, Henry had become just another member of the board of trustees. He was no longer "the first among equals [with] a veto over everything," according to Fred Friendly, the Foundation's top communications expert. "By 1975-76 this Foundation was a free-standing product of Henry Ford II but it was not any longer Henry Ford's Foundation," he added. Which, as it turned out, was more than Henry could abide.

None of the trustees had any inkling of how deeply Henry felt when they gathered for their regular meeting in New York in December 1976. Henry, in fact, had joined in paying a tribute to a departing trustee, Judge Charles Wyzanski of Boston. The next morning, however, each of the trustees found under his door a letter from Henry disclosing he was resigning from the board of the Ford Foundation. The letter, which was not made public for a month, indicated that Henry's interest in the Foundation had waned. "After 33 years I have come to the point where I have pretty much done all there is to do as a trustee and have said all there is to say," he wrote.

Not quite. In his sometimes testy four-page communication, Henry said that while he took "pride in the Foundation, it has also been a cause of frustration and sometimes plain irritation." In particular, he complained that the Foundation was spreading itself too thin, had developed a "fortress mentality" that rejected outside ideas, and had failed to devote enough attention to strengthening the capitalist system that made its philanthropy possible. "I'm not playing the role of the hardheaded tycoon who thinks all philanthropoids are Socialists and all university professors are Communists. I'm just suggesting to the trustees and the staff that the system that makes the Foundation possible very probably is worth preserving."

McGeorge Bundy, taking a soft approach, commented, "One of the things we've always valued about Henry Ford is candor." And he said that Ford was "absolutely right in noting that the Foundation should be "on guard against a 'fortress mentality.'" But he declined to discuss Ford's specific criticism in any detail.

Not so diplomatic was John Kenneth Galbraith, a close friend of Bundy's. Ironically, Galbraith was also critical of the Foundation, but from the left, contending that it had "fenced itself off from the really sensitive issues of the society, such as the inequalities associated with income distribution." As for Henry's complaint, it reminded Galbraith of "the old problem" posed by Henry Ford I: the autocrat anguished over his loss of power.

12

IACOCCA OUSTED

FOR LEE IACOCCA, RESIDENT GOLDEN BOY AND, TO THE outside world, the seemingly unchallenged heir apparent to the throne, the end came suddenly, but not cleanly. His ouster as president by Henry Ford II on July 13, 1978, was described on the front page of *The New York Times* as "one of the most dramatic shakeups in the history of the Ford Motor Company." And on the *CBS Evening News*, Walter Cronkite, himself taken aback by the surprising news out of Dearborn, told the nation, "It all sounds like something from one of those enormous novels about the automobile business." And, as usual, truth was stranger than fiction.

Iacocca's dismissal couldn't have come at a more awkward time. Even though sales were excellent, the company was having to cope with several serious problems. Henry himself was facing a grand jury probe into charges that he had authorized a $1 million bribe to Indonesian officials to facilitate the award of a $29 million telecommunications contract, and then had given a $100,000 "bonus" to the dismissed Ford executive who had handled the payoff. And he also faced a stockholders' suit alleging that he had ripped off his own company for hundreds of thousands of dollars, that he had taken a $750,000 kickback from a company supplier, and that he was personally given a $2 million bribe by Imelda Marcos for making an unwise investment in the troubled Philippines. What's more, government safety investigators had charged that the gas tanks on Ford Pintos had exploded on relatively minor impact, causing fatal fires.

Iacocca's ouster stunned the American business community, even though in Detroit there had been rumblings for some time that the number-two man had been losing favor at the number-two auto company. As we've seen, Iacocca was not the first mighty executive to be cast aside by Henry Ford II. Ever since Henry had ousted Ernie Breech in 1960, strong executives had fared badly at Ford Motor. Another celebrated dismissal was that of Arjay Miller, one of the original "Whiz Kids," who had been nudged aside as president in 1968 to make room for "Bunkie" Knudsen, who lasted only nineteen months. Still, Henry knew well in advance that bouncing Iacocca would set off a fire storm, that his normally compliant board of directors would raise hell. So why did he do it? "Well," says Iacocca with grudging admiration, "Henry Ford runs an absolutely czarist company. And the czar can do no wrong."

Henry had set the stage for Iacocca's fall from grace by seeking to humiliate him. First, he had created the Office of Chief Executive, elevating Phil Caldwell to the top ranks as vice-chairman. Then, in June 1978, Henry unfolded a new management realignment that clearly downgraded Iacocca. Caldwell, who had once worked for Iacocca, was made his boss, with the newly created title of Deputy Chief Executive Officer. At the same time, William Clay Ford was named chairman of the executive committee. Thus Iacocca was dropped from third to fourth-and-falling in the corporate hierarchy. But a further humiliation was inflicted when Iacocca was not even informed of the corporate shakeup until just before it was announced.

"I think you're making a serious mistake," Iacocca told his boss, who replied, "That's my decision and the board's."

Of course it was more Henry's decision than the board's. Consisting of twenty members, the board had never defied Henry in any of his wishes. As he had often said, "Let's wine 'em, dine 'em and screw 'em." Cristina, in fact, had once noted, "It's probably the highest paid board in America. Henry buys them with Dom Perignon, new cars every year, and pensions." She wasn't far off the mark. Outside directors earned fees of from $32,000 to $50,000 a year.

For Iacocca, the prospect of reporting to a one-time subordinate was more than his considerable pride could bear. And he began to talk about quitting. But most of the outside directors would not hear of it. And at the regular monthly meeting they urged Henry to reconsider his edict that Iacocca should report to Caldwell. "I think I just lost my board," Henry said.

Under pressure, he agreed to the formation of a three-man committee to examine the issue. The committee consisted of Joseph F. Cullman III, chairman of Philip Morris Inc.; George F. Bennett, president of the State Street Investment Corporation in Boston; and Franklin D. Murphy, board chairman of the Los Angeles Times-Mirror Company.

Iacocca's supporters thought they had gained time in which to try to iron out the conflict. Meanwhile Henry departed for a previously scheduled business trip to the Far East. And Lee flew off to Hawaii for a previously scheduled speech before the Louisiana state dealers' association. This time he did something that was uncharacteristic of him. He took his wife Mary and his daughters Kathi, eighteen, and Lia, fourteen, with him. And even more uncharacteristic, he took a week of vacation, which he spent reading thrillers about Nazis and trying to relax.

On his return he met separately with the three outside directors empowered to examine his case against the new corporate alignment. Using company planes and submitting expense accounts, he flew to Boston, New York and Los Angeles, where he conferred with George Bennett, Joe Cullman and Frank Murphy individually. "Well," one of them observed, "I think this problem can be resolved. After all, Henry can't be that unreasonable."

But Henry wasn't willing to listen to reason. By the time he returned from his Asian trip he had made up his mind to get rid of Iacocca once and for all. And he so informed his outside directors on Wednesday evening, July 12, 1978, in Dearborn. He argued that the "body chemistry" between him and Iacocca "wasn't right all these years." Usually the directors acceded to Henry's wishes without argument. But this time they revolted. Led by George Bennett, the Boston investment banker, the pro-Iacocca forces seemed in the ascendancy. Henry had never before encountered such outspoken dissent from "his" board. According to a participant, Henry, "visibly upset" and "white as a ghost," asked, "What happens to me and my plan for Edsel?" The directors argued that more important was the immediate welfare of the company. They insisted that Iacocca, whom they described as "a great automobile man" who had long demonstrated his loyalty to the company, should be allowed to remain. But Henry wasn't buying any of it. "Either he goes or I go," he finally said.

No formal vote was taken, and the matter was not brought up at the full board meeting the next morning. Henry just assumed—and correctly so—he would get his way. Later that afternoon Henry summoned Iacocca to meet with him and brother Billy in his twelfth-floor suite in the Glass House. Iacocca knew what was coming. The night before he had received word of his impending dismissal from a trade-paper publisher who had phoned him at home. The publisher identified the source of his information as Henry Ford II. As a result, Iacocca spent a restless night waiting for the axe to fall. But the advance warning had done little to cushion the shock.

Mincing few words, Henry came to the point. "You're fired," he told Iacocca.

"But why, Mr. Ford?" Iacocca asked. "I've been with the company for thirty-two years. What did I do wrong?"

"Nothing," snapped Ford. "I just don't like you!"

Then Henry accused Iacocca of "insubordination" in having gone "behind my back" in meeting with outside directors. Iacocca was nonplussed. "But, Mr. Ford, what are you talking about?" he said. "It was you who set up the committee with the understanding that I would meet with them. And it was no secret."

"That's not so," Henry countered. "That's a lie."

Billy Ford, who knew better, became tearful. He knew better because he had been in on the original arrangement for Lee to meet with the outside directors. For some time he had sought to convince his older brother to retire so that he could become company chairman, with Iacocca as his chief executive officer. Vainly he pleaded with Henry to reconsider his Draconian decision. In effect, he argued that the company needed Iacocca. But Henry insisted there was no indispensable man. In the end Billy Ford sorrowfully backed down. Nevertheless the *Detroit News* quoted the younger Ford the next morning as saying, "I'm very sorry Lee had to leave."

The meeting in Henry's office took about half an hour. This time Iacocca had the last word. He noted that under his supervision the company had earned $1.8 billion after taxes the year before. "You'll never make it again," he told Henry.

Iacocca returned to his office, where he began receiving supportive phone calls, many from stunned vice-presidents, who had been immediately notified that henceforth they would report to Philip Caldwell. But most bittersweet of all were the calls from many of the outside directors, who said how sorry they were and that they had had no choice but to go along with Henry. And they hoped he would understand their untenable position. "Of course, I understood," said Iacocca. Driving home that night, Iacocca said to himself, "Thank God the bullshit is over."

But it wasn't. The next day, in an anticlimactic public announcement, the company sought to portray an amicable parting. However, the statements released by Iacocca and Ford indicated otherwise. Iacocca, who said he was resigning effective October 15, his fifty-fourth birthday, had written, "Although I am leaving with many good feelings, one of the considerations leading to my resignation is the fact that I haven't been in complete accord with some of the recent changes in the top management of the company. In any case, I leave amicably."

In his statement Henry paid tribute to Iacocca's "distinguished record of achievement during his thirty-two years with Ford." But he added, "Over the past fifteen months, however, substantial differences have arisen on the subject of how Ford should be organized at the most senior level. In these circumstances, I believe Mr. Iacocca's resignation is in the best interests of the company and himself."

The suddenness of Iacocca's downfall was partly symbolized in the advance press kit that the company had sent out that week for the introduction of a smaller and lighter Mustang for 1979. The kit contained a promotional photo of a smiling Iacocca standing in front of the totally redesigned subcompact. But it wasn't Iacocca who turned up at the Dearborn Hyatt Regency to unveil the new Mustang. It was William O. Bourke, the executive vice-president who was believed by industry veterans to have the inside track as Iacocca's eventual successor. Asked about the way in which the shakeup had been handled, Bourke said: "There might be quieter ways of doing it. Other people set off firecrackers. We drop atomic bombs."

This "atomic bomb" had sent tremors through the ranks of Ford dealers, with whom Iacocca had long been a favorite. Ed Mullane, president of the Ford Dealer Alliance, which represented 1,200 dealers, had tried to change Henry's mind, describing Iacocca as "invaluable" to the company. But Mullane received an answer from Henry "that essentially told me to butt out." And when the deed was finally done, Mullane was heartbroken. "We are in uncharted waters," he said.

The resulting publicity was the worst Henry had ever received, focusing attention on his increasingly autocratic ways. Jack Egan, in the financial pages of the *Washington Post*, reported from Detroit that the feeling in the industry was that "Iacocca's loss could weaken the company, and his method of ouster raises questions about how much an enterprise as large as Ford Motor is run like a private duchy by the whim of one man." And columnist Nicholas Von Hoffman wrote:

> The public at large has been left with the impression that at the Ford Motor Company the reward for doing an outstanding job is getting the gate if the rich, 60-year-old adolescent who inherited the largest chunk of the stock gets up in a bitchy mood some Tuesday morning. . . . Henry Ford II's often grouchy public utterances have left the impression he is mad at the world because

his bodyservants don't keep the silver spoon in his mouth polished. Thus the firing of Iacocca has the look of an act of spite, by a petulantly selfish rich kid. . . . Who has leverage, who has bargaining power, if a Lee Iacocca doesn't?

Actually, it was William Clay Ford who was a bigger stockholder in Ford than either of his brothers or sister. Billy and his wife and children owned over 4 million shares, worth nearly $190 million in 1978 prices. Benson's family had 3.5 million shares and Henry's 2.5 million.

And Billy was sending out signals that he differed with Henry about his brother's eventual successor. Henry's favorite candidate, of course, was his only son Edsel, then assistant manager of Ford operations in Australia. But Billy had some ideas of his own. "Benson has a son, and so do I," he observed. Benson Jr., then twenty-eight, was operating a business in California. William Clay, Jr., twenty-one, was a junior at Princeton and, like Benson Jr., had shown great interest in getting involved in the company. At first the sons of Josephine ("Dodie") Ford expressed no desire to get involved in the company. But eventually the older son, Walter Buhl Ford III, joined the company. The younger one, Alfred Brush ("Alfie") Ford, joined the Hare Krishna movement in 1975. Young Ford, whose religious name was Ambarish, opened a Krishna arts store in Renaissance Center, stocked with an estimated $1 million in antique and contemporary art objects. Previously, Alfie had helped the Krishna movement purchase the East Detroit estate of a long-departed motor magnate. The rest of the money came from Elisabeth Luise Reuther, daughter of Walter Reuther, president of the United Auto Workers who was killed in a plane crash in 1970. Seven years later, his daughter, now calling herself Lekhasravanti, was married at the estate. The groom's best man was Alfie Ford, whose idea it was to have thousands of flowers flown in from as far as Hawaii for the garlands and decorations.

Lee Iacocca meanwhile was saying little for the record. In fact, he sought to downplay suggestions that his dismissal had been rancorous. But he got his dander up when Henry's people began going after him publicly. Two weeks after his ouster a "family spokesman" was quoted in the Detroit press as saying that Iacocca had been sacked because he "lacked grace," was too "pushy," and that "the son of an Italian immigrant born in Allentown, Pennsylvania, is a long way from Grosse Pointe."

Asked about it by Neal Travis of *New York Magazine,* Iacocca bridled. "That is an awful slur. I don't know why the hell they'd come up with stuff like that. It smacks of the royal family, doesn't it? They said I lacked grace and polish. That really hurts me."

That Iacocca should have been surprised by the slur was in itself surprising. For as one of his then closest friends pointed out, Henry Ford II had long believed that "because Lee had an Italian name, he must have been part of the Mafia."

Then Phil Caldwell sought to rewrite history. In an interview he suggested that no one in the company could take credit for any Ford car or design. Thus he sent a signal to subordinates that allusions such as "father of the Mustang" were to be dropped from their vocabularies. As one writer noted, "The Stalinization of the Ford Motor Company had already begun."

And just as in the Stalin era, the purge of Iacocca's protégés had also begun. One after the other, Iacocca's closest associates in the company were being axed for no other reason than the fact that they had been the ousted president's "men." Typical was the summary dismissal of Walter T. Murphy, executive director of Ford's public-relations staff. Murphy, who had been with the company since 1947, received a phone call at home in the middle of the night. It was from Henry Ford II, and it was obvious from the way he was slurring his words that the Chairman had been drinking.

"Do you like Iacocca?" the Chairman asked.

Momentarily taken aback, Murphy thought quickly. He was aware that his relationship with Iacocca was no secret. He was also aware that his role in company affairs was being steadily diminished. A new man, a former ABC television news impresario, William Sheehan, had been brought in to take his place. Sitting up in bed, Murphy said: "Yes, Mr. Ford, I respect Mr. Iacocca. I do like him."

"Then," snapped Ford, "you're fired!"

Meanwhile Iacocca had brought in Bill Fugazy's good friend Edward Bennett Williams, the high-powered Washington lawyer, to work out a financial settlement with Ford Motor. What Iacocca wanted was a deal that would allow him to collect some $2 million in severance pay even if he went to work at a competing company. What Henry Ford II wanted was a deal that would insure Iacocca's getting out of the automobile industry and, if possible, out of the Detroit area. The company would pay him the $2 million only if he refrained "from engaging in competitive activity." For there was increasing speculation that Chrysler was thinking of hiring Iacocca as a means of reviving that number-three company's sagging fortunes. Such an arrangement could provide still another headache for the Ford Motor Company.

Deal or no deal, Lido Anthony Iacocca was restless. Here he was, fifty-four years old and unemployed. And except for a minor case of diverticulitis—"my colon flips now and then"—he was in fairly good shape, anxious to throw his enormous talent and energy into some new challenge. In interviewing him shortly after his ouster, Neal Travis mentioned that Iacocca's story gave him a certain sense of *déjà vu.* "Oh," said Iacocca, "you mean *The Betsy?*" The hero in Harold Robbins' best-selling novel was an Italian-American outsider who moved up quickly in a family-owned automotive giant; presumably he was modeled after Iacocca. "Yes, I suppose it is ironic," said Iacocca. "I must go back and read some passages from that book."

Iacocca never did get back to rereading *The Betsy.* He didn't have time. For Chrysler had come through with an offer and a challenge he couldn't refuse.

13

TROUBLES

On June 16, 1978, the Ford Motor Company reached its seventy-fifth birthday, truly a momentous event in the history of industrial capitalism. But Henry Ford II found very little to celebrate in this diamond jubilee year. His life, in fact, had become even more bizarre than author Harold Robbins could have imagined in writing *The Betsy*.

Whatever personal satisfaction the Chairman may have obtained in getting rid of Iacocca was somewhat dissipated by the extraordinarily bad press he was now receiving. "Management by guillotine" was the way one *New York Times* correspondent had described Henry's technique in ousting underlings. And Henry had thought that by placing Marian Sulzberger Heiskell on the board he would be treated kindly in the pages of that august daily. But it was Mrs. Heiskell, along with several others of his outside directors, who had called Iacocca to voice sympathy.

The kid from Allentown really didn't need any. Even though he had been consigned to a secluded office in a Ford warehouse to await his official day of departure—a final humiliation ordered by the Chairman—Iacocca was feeling free for the first time in years. A new world had opened up for him and he intended to make the most of it. Numerous offers of top jobs from large nonautomotive companies were pouring in. Some were indeed tantalizing. But none was what he really wanted. What he wanted most was to remain in the industry that had been his life for so many years. And though he never said so publicly, what he also wanted now was a chance to compete with Henry Ford II.

One night while at home Iacocca received a call from J. Richardson Dilworth, a Rockefeller family counselor and a board member of the Chrysler Corporation. Chrysler was in serious trouble and needed help, Dilworth said. Which was hardly any secret. The number-three auto company, in severe financial straits, was about to lay off thousands of workers and was generally a basket case. Would Iacocca be interested in taking over? Iacocca said he would think about it.

It took Iacocca several months before he finally made up his mind. After conferring with other Chrysler directors he agreed to join the company as its president and chief operating officer. And the company paid dearly to land him. He demanded and obtained assurances that he could run Chrysler's operations with a nearly free hand. As compensation he received a large amount of cash plus options to buy several hundred thousand Chrysler shares at $10 each, roughly the then current market price. "It's one hell of a challenge," Iacocca told his good friend Bill Fugazy.

Lee Iacocca finally had what he had wanted most of his adult life—a chance to run an auto company. And now he had an added incentive: a chance for revenge. For he did not intend to forgive or forget what Henry Ford had done to him. If he could turn Chrysler around, he could cut into Ford's number-two position in the industry. And he couldn't help but be amused when his pal Bill Fugazy, one of the nation's biggest limousine operators, announced he would replace his highly visible fleet of two hundred Lincolns with Chryslers to serve New York

City's airports and fancy hotels. And he was personally touched when some Ford dealers, including Ed Mullane, announced they intended to seek Chrysler affiliations. This after Henry Ford had taken the unusual step of sending a personal letter to each of some 6,500 dealers on July 14, the day Iacocca's resignation was announced. Seeking to reassure the dealers, many of whom felt the ouster had done damage to the company's top management, Ford wrote that "the company has a strong and experienced management team. Our North American Automotive Operations are headed by talented executives who are well known to you and who are fully attuned to your needs of the retail market."

Two weeks later Henry was notified that his younger brother Benson had suffered a fatal heart attack aboard his beloved cruiser *Onika* in Michigan's Cheboygan River. His death at age fifty-nine added a poignant note to the shakeup in the executive ranks of the company he had joined in 1940 after two years at Princeton University.

His son, Benson Jr., was in Mexico en route to Argentina on a tour of Ford plants when he heard the news. He flew immediately to Los Angeles, where he changed planes for Detroit. That night he stayed with his grief-stricken mother. After the funeral services the next morning the family and close friends assembled at the Benson Ford home. And young Benson recalls the dozens of long black limousines piled up outside, "looking like a Mafia convention." Inside it was more like a party. "Someone yelled, 'Bar's open,' and you would have thought you were at the '21' Club. Maybe I was naive but I thought that the occasion called for some quiet reflection, a few tributes to my dad and so on. Instead, it sounded like New Year's Eve."

Benson complained to his mother, "What is this—a funeral or a social gathering?" And she responded, "This is what your father would have liked, what he would have wanted."

But young Benson still wonders whether his father would have approved of having his brother Henry Ford II rummaging through drawers in his sitting room and cramming his pockets full of expensive jewelry. "First of all, the stuff wasn't his to take," says Benson. "But it does demonstrate the arrogance of

the man. He didn't ask anyone's permission. He just took it."
But why should one of the world's richest men, who presumably has everything, do something like that? "Good question,"
says Benson. "The man is just greedy."

Benson was also annoyed by his mother's refusal to prevent
the looting. And she warned her son not to interfere, saying it
would only make matters worse. So Benson, against his better
judgment, did nothing. "My mother thought Uncle Henry was
God, that he could do any damn thing he wanted."

Also unprecedented was the presence of Kathleen DuRoss.
This was the first time that most members of the family had a
chance to meet the well-publicized woman for whom Henry
had left Cristina. Dressed appropriately for the occasion, she
nevertheless seemed out of place at such a gathering. It was
obvious to Benson that Henry's daughters, Charlotte and Anne,
were treating her coolly. And while almost everyone else "was
drinking up a storm," Kathy DuRoss sat quietly, sipping from
her glass slowly, drinking in an atmosphere she had never
before known. These were the "swells" she had read about for
years. These were the aristocrats who for so long had dominated
the city in which she was brought up. And they seemed no
better, or worse, than the people to whom she catered at her
downtown discothèque L'Esprit.

Cristina, as was to be expected, had not come to the services.
The "pizza queen," as Benson's mother called her, was now
involved with Henry in a potentially costly and embarrassing
divorce action and was expected to seek a settlement dwarfing
the $16 million Henry reportedly had paid his first wife. Cristina
had gone to court seeking to block Henry from selling at auction
what she claimed was "a substantial part of the marital estate."
She testified that on her return from Rome the previous October
she had discovered that at least $2 million worth of rare furniture and valuables had been removed from the drawing room
of the couple's fifty-odd-room mansion in Grosse Pointe. She
broke into tears and had been upset ever since. "I would go in
there and sit and look at all my beautiful things," Cristina said
in Wayne County Circuit Court. "The drawing room was so
feminine, so beautiful—a little corner of Versailles." But no
longer. "I am too proud to show the drawing room bare," she

said. "I felt like a common beggar." And no longer was she doing any entertaining. "I was under Librium, what they give crazy people," she said.

In his petition for a legal separation Henry contended he was under no obligation to "support Mrs. Ford in the life-style to which she is accustomed"—which was one of Cristina's demands. Asked by his attorney, Milton J. Miller, whether she knew what it cost to maintain the mansion—which then had a staff of five inside servants, two gardeners and a security force—Cristina replied she had no idea. But she insisted that without her husband's companionship the home didn't mean much. "I want to live with my husband," she said, near tears. "I was very happy."

In his testimony Henry stated that most of the art objects in question had been acquired before his marriage to Cristina. But that was not what Cristina remembered: "He would say, 'Bambina, look what I have bought for you.' I'd say, 'How beautiful.' He'd say, 'Nothing is too beautiful for my bambina!'"

During nearly four hours on the stand the Chairman of the Ford Motor Company testified that he was trying to "simplify" his life style and make his holdings more liquid. "I'm getting older, not younger. I'm on the downgrade, not the upgrade. I thought it was foolish to have them [the rare furniture and pieces] sitting around. I want my holdings more liquid so my estate is in better shape. I'd like to sell more if I could." The Grosse Pointe home, he went on, "was a 1950–60's house. Things have changed. All our life-styles have changed. The country has changed."

As his former "bambina" listened intently, occasionally blurting out "no" or "yes" to his responses, the Chairman was questioned at length about the financial details of the residences the couple had maintained during their marriage: the $400,000 mansion at 457 Lakeshore Drive, a luxurious country home in England, a "small" four-bedroom residence in London, a $150,000 condominium in Nassau, and a $400,000 sportsmen's retreat in Canada, which Henry said was only for men. In all, he estimated he had at least $18 million worth of valuable objects in these various residences. At least $10 million of these could be found in the Lakeshore Drive residence, including paintings by Picasso, Renoir, and a Bonnard that hung over the family TV set. Though saying he was no "expert," Henry indicated a penchant for collecting antique boxes, which, he testified, he had locked up for some time along with other valuables in the family safe, following the 1967 race riots in Detroit. "I buy what I think to be attractive and what I like," he said. "Yes, they are difficult to replace. They didn't have mass production in the days those things were made."

Judge John Kirwan did not take long in reaching a decision. Apparently impressed by Henry's sworn testimony that "it was my furniture, I bought it and I thought it was mine to sell," the circuit jurist ruled that the auction could take place as scheduled in New York. But Cristina fought on. She appealed the verdict, arguing that the sale would jeopardize her right to a property settlement in an eventual divorce. But the court of appeals turned down her appeal.

And only days later the long-awaited on-again-off-again auction of Ford's possessions took place at Sotheby Parke Bernet on Madison Avenue in New York, which had billed it as "undoubtedly the finest single-owner sale of French furniture to be held in the U.S. since 1972." That was the year Anne McDonnell Ford Johnson, the first Mrs. Henry Ford II, had disposed of the surplus rarities she had kept from her terminated marriage.

As a poker-faced Charlotte Ford sat in a balcony taking copious notes, the auction went off without a hitch. Highest price of the day—$195,000—went for an ormolu-embellished drop-front secretary with an impressive pedigree. The buyer's name, as in the case of most of the other major purchases, was not disclosed. A commode said to have been used by Louis XV went for $31,000. But the biggest applause was for a $100,000 bid on a Swiss enamel-and-gold music box that contained two automated erotic figures. The buyer, it was reported, was either the Shah of Iran or Stavros Niarchos, Henry's former son-in-law.

Less than two hours after the auction began, all but three of the hundred and two lots presented had been sold for $2,048,200. This was $3,500 less than was realized by Anne

Ford six years before. The Chairman, who had earlier told the court that his net worth was $70 million, "give or take $10 million," was now more fluid, but not by much. And "poor little Cristina"—as some Grosse Pointers had taken to calling her—was now reduced to living in one room fewer.

Except for her court appearance, Cristina had maintained a self-imposed silence for over two years, refusing to talk even to old friends in the press. But all the gossip and sniping finally got to her. In June 1978 she agreed to be interviewed at the mansion by Marji Kunz, a staff writer for the *Detroit News*. And she told of the long, lonely hours that had ticked away since her husband walked out on her two days before Christmas 1975.

"I live like a nun here," she said. "I read and I contemplate life. . . . For a year, I was so anguished that I shut myself off from the world. I was grieving so much. I couldn't face people. It came as a shock . . . suddenly . . . without knowing it.

"Now I walk the dogs and contemplate nature . . . I walk and reflect upon all the beautiful days I had with my husband." Her eyes became cloudy. "Then I know I must face the present moment. The thing that kills me most is when I must go into that cold court and have my husband treat me as If I was his enemy. It's shattering."

Also shattering was the fact that some old friends were really not friends. She no longer saw them. "Some people prefer to go where the money is," she said, meaning that they had taken Henry's side of the marital dispute. Nevertheless she still had a few good friends. In fact, she was planning to fly to the Philippines that summer for Imelda Marcos' birthday, as she had done for the past five years. And over the Memorial Day weekend she had attended Nelson Rockefeller's seventieth birthday party at Pocantico Hills, where she had run into the Henry Kissingers. As Secretary of State, Kissinger had once praised Cristina for having the knack of evaluating people accurately. He had said he wished that she were available to fly on his missions abroad as a kind of antenna. At the party Cristina teasingly told Kissinger she was now "available." But Kissinger said it was too late. They had both been replaced.

Now that she had been "replaced," she was through with

marriage. "Me marry? Never!" she insisted. And she thought back to when she had met her husband eighteen years before in Paris.

The world is such a farce. Think about it. When married men court women, they tell them their wives don't understand them...that there is no communication ...they've drifted apart because their tastes have become so different. The man is the victim of the *strega* [witch] at home. We women believe what they say. We tell them how we understand...we know we can change all that and make them happy.

Time goes by and history repeats itself.... The understanding woman eventually becomes the *strega* at home. The man will say those things over and over again to other women. Bingo. He leaves you.

I ask you...Isn't life a farce?

Still, Cristina had learned a great deal from her ill-fated marriage to Henry Ford II. She now had "so much more compassion for weak people." And, she went on, "I think I will go about life with less naiveté—be more aware of people with the Dr. Jekyll and Mr. Hyde personalities."

When Henry read the interview he scoffed. "Some nun!" he exclaimed to a friend. "You should see her bills." Cristina, in fact, continued to run up fairly high expenses on her frequent trips abroad. And she rarely turned down an invitation to some fancy soirée in Manhattan. Typical was the elegant supper-dance for the Claude Taittingers, of the French champagne family, hosted by Celebrity Service's Earl Blackwell in the ballroom of his beautiful apartment on West Fifty-Seventh Street. Cristina, in a slinky black gown with see-through embroidery at the midriff, clearly was the hit of the party. Also there was Ernest Kanzler's widow, Rosemarie, Cristina's old friend and former mentor. Rosemarie, of indeterminate age but still glamorous, was now married to French banker Jean-Pierre Marcie-Riviere. In fact, their wedding had taken place, in happier times, at the Ford mansion in Grosse Pointe. Cristina had insisted on it.

As usual, Henry was saying very little publicly about his

failed marriage. Or, for that matter, about his relationship with Kathy DuRoss, though he never made any secret of his closeness to the former model. Nor was Kathy reticent about her relationship with Henry. Talking with a newspaperwoman about what a "great hostess" Mrs. Max Fisher was, Kathy said, "Henry and I stayed with the Fishers in Palm Beach and we both said it was like staying in your own home. She is so relaxed, she makes running the house, having dinner on the table seem to be effortless, but everything is superb."

Henry plainly missed his own house in Grosse Pointe. He had settled into a hideaway convenient to his firm's Dearborn headquarters. Far from the luxurious accommodations to which he was accustomed, it consisted of only a bedroom, bath, sitting room, dinette and kitchen. He still had his laundry done at the mansion, and very often his breakfast was taken over to his office. "Henry loves that house," said a Grosse Pointe friend. "He's called my wife and said, 'Hey, is Cristina going to be out of town this week? If she is, come over for dinner.'" The friend and his wife would gladly oblige.

Cristina, clearly, was only one of the many headaches besetting Henry Ford II in the diamond jubilee year his company was celebrating. In June the company was forced to recall 1.5 million Pintos and Bobcats manufactured between 1971 and 1976, following a barrage of reports that the location of the gas tanks in the subcompacts made them vulnerable to fires and explosions upon collision. Another potentially severe blow was the report that the National Highway Traffic Safety Administration was about to order the recall of virtually every Ford car and truck with faulty transmissions that slipped from park into reverse, sending the vehicles backward, sometimes over unsuspecting Ford owners and bystanders. Some nine million vehicles were potentially defective. Recalling the nine million cars might have bankrupted the company. Washington finally decided that a letter to every owner warning of the possible defect would be sufficient. Previously the company had been forced to call back 2.7 million four-and six-cylinder engines found to be wearing too fast in cold weather because of a cost-cutting move to eliminate two oil holes in the engine block.

"We've just got to do a better job," said Henry. "We've

had too damn many recalls." At the same time, however, he railed bitterly against federal encroachments on the realm of auto safety. "You can beat a horse to death, but we've just got to have some breathing time. We just now are forced into a position where we've got to meet certain fuel-economy numbers... Then you add airbags on top of that. They just think we can do anything we want as long as they keep our feet in the flames." Henry also noted that while his company was being forced to meet new stringent fuel standards, the Environmental Protection Agency was demanding tough new emissions controls. The difficulty was that the two objectives often cut against each other. And he wasn't all wrong.

Air bags were on Henry's mind. An interviewer noted that in his office on the twelfth floor of the Glass House, a table bore a small needlepoint pillow with the motto "Screw Airbags." Also on his mind was Ralph Nader, the consumer advocate, who had long been especially critical of Henry's posture as a progressive-minded businessman. "He's been very unsympathetic with the consumer laws, and has tried to obstruct them," Nader told Lally Weymouth. "What other corporate executive could be caught driving drunk with his mistress and get away with it? If the president of Chrysler were caught, he would not speak on auto safety. That is the difference between the founding family and the technocrats."

Nader also alleged that Henry had used his influence in Washington to delay the mandatory installation of air bags—devices stowed in the steering-wheel hub and under the glove compartment, designed to inflate on frontal impact. According to Nader, Ford had convinced President Nixon to order Transportation Secretary John A. Volpe "to delay the airbag standard and replace it with the interlock standard." The introduction of the interlock—which made it impossible to start a car until seat belts were fastened—caused a furor among the public and eventually was repealed. Which, said Nader, "set back the cause of the auto-safety movement more than anything in the last twelve years." And, he went on, "the blame lies squarely on the shoulders of Henry Ford II."

Henry had a different recollection about his meeting with the President. "We did go to see Nixon in April 1971, but I have no recollection of any conversation about the interlock." And neither, incidentally, does Nixon. Continuing, Henry said that he and Iacocca visited the President "to talk about inflation, cost increases we were facing, and foreign competition. . . . There might have been a reference to airbags but only in relation to cost increases that might be incurred because of airbags. Iacocca remembers, as we were leaving, the President saying that if airbags become a requirement, please fix me a car without airbags." Henry did not deny he was "pro-interlock" and anti-airbags. "I haven't changed one whit. I said airbags are a lot of baloney and I stick to it."

Perhaps a greater headache for Henry was the federal grand jury investigation that had been launched concerning allegations that the Ford Motor Company had paid a $1 million bribe to an Indonesian general to obtain a $29 million contract to build ground stations for a satellite communications network in his country. What was quickly established was the fact that some Ford officials had indeed agreed to pay the bribe but that, according to company lawyers, the offer was withdrawn. The key question was whether Henry Ford II had known of the bribery plan.

Another question was whether, despite the denials, a bribe hadn't been paid anyway through a subterfuge. In a letter to the Justice Department dated April 6 the Ford lawyers conceded that a key document submitted to the grand jury had been mysteriously backdated. The document also had been altered to make it appear that an additional $900,000 in the final contract was part of the original price rather than excess money that could be used for a bribe. And although company investigators thought the original document had probably been destroyed, the Ford lawyers told the Justice Department only that they could not find it.

The April 6 letter was mentioned in a dispatch by Jo Thomas in *The New York Times* of June 4, 1978. A few days later the letter was referred to in a *Times* column by William Safire, who contended that a "coverup" was involved and that, because Henry Ford II had supported Jimmy Carter for President, the Justice Department was giving "kid-glove treatment to the company headed by the President's friend." Safire also wrote that

ever since the April 6 letter, in which the company conceded
it had previously supplied an "inaccurate record," Ford lawyers
had been negotiating with the Justice Department for "a slap
on the wrist to some mid-level employees."

All of which, needless to say, caused heartburn among Ford's
top executives. They fired off a letter to Griffin Bell asking
the Attorney General to launch an inquiry to determine whether
anyone in the Justice Department had leaked the April 6 letter
to *The New York Times*. "The contents of this letter also appear
to have been known to Roy Cohn at the time of his appearance
at our annual meeting on May 11," the Ford letter to Bell
continued. "We are dismayed that such a highly confidential
communication to the Department of Justice has so promptly
found its way into the hands of third parties."

Then it developed that, after company auditors discovered
the bribery plan in August 1975, an executive vice-president
named Paul F. Lorenz was ousted. In fact, it was Lee Iacocca,
then Ford president, who informed Lorenz he would have to
leave. But something mysterious again occurred. Lorenz was
permitted to remain on the payroll for another year. And, amaz-
ingly, Henry Ford II personally approved a bonus payment for
Lorenz amounting to $100,000. But, the grand jury now wanted
to know, was it a bonus or a payoff?

The biggest headache of all was a $50 million shareholder
suit that alleged, among many charges, that Henry Ford II took
kickbacks from Ford suppliers and squandered company money
to pay for his many personal extravagances. The lead attorney
for the shareholders was the New York barrister Roy Cohn.
Though often dismissed as a publicity-seeker and grandstander,
Cohn was a formidable adversary. And Henry Ford II knew
it. And he also knew that Cohn had been able to latch onto
embarrassing information that could have come only from
sources close to the throne.

Faced with Roy Cohn and his stockholders' suit, a grand
jury investigation into alleged bribes, and litigation charging
that the company knowingly sold unsafe cars (later resolved in
the company's favor), Henry ordered a comprehensive effort
to tighten security at corporate headquarters in Dearborn. Outside attorneys, auditors and investigators, including retired agents

of the Federal Bureau of Investigation, were brought in to prevent leaks of sensitive material and prepare for upcoming litigation. Surprise audits of files and security checks were conducted almost nightly, and regularly on weekends. Although there had been previous internal investigations, including the costly and nonproductive inquiry into the personal and business life of Lee Iacocca, this one—company sources agreed—was the most stringent they could remember. Something of the spirit of the old Harry Bennett days of Grandpa Ford seemed to have returned in a modern guise.

What one executive described as a "siege atmosphere" had taken over the Glass House. No one knew whom to trust as fear swept the plush executive suites. And as rumors circulated that the chairman himself could well be indicted, most frightened of all was Henry Ford II.

14

STOCKHOLDERS' SUIT

RARELY HAD DETROIT NEWSMEN SEEN THE CHAIRMAN OF THE Ford Motor Company so angry. "I have been criticized for a lot of things in my life and most of the time I just don't pay any attention to what was said or printed about me," said Henry Ford II. But, he said, the charges made in the lawsuit filed by Roy Cohn "went beyond the pale as far as I'm concerned."

The suit, filed in Manhattan Supreme Court, was in behalf of John Lang, trustee for a small amount of stock owned by four children of Thomas Bolan, one of Roy Cohn's law partners. It accused the nineteen Ford directors of having acted as "agents of an illegal and fraudulent conspiracy," adding that they had countenanced "gross waste" of corporate assets.

But, as Henry noted, "It is clear that I am the real target of the lawsuit," even though others were named in the action. "So I am speaking for myself about specific allegations against me."

As for the allegations, he claimed they were "totally untrue." And he acknowledged that there had been considerable concern in the upper reaches of the company about his going public on the matter. "There were pros and cons against my saying something and everybody had their say," he said. "But this got to be something of a personal vendetta and I could not stand mute." Asked his thoughts on the motivation behind the litigation, Henry said those he would rather keep to himself.

What surprised Ford watchers was that he had responded at all. None could remember when the Chairman had ever addressed himself to such allegations in public. More characteristic of his usual stance, of course, was the succinct "Never complain, never explain" of 1975.

This time he was complaining and explaining. He appeared to take strongest issue with the allegation that he had accepted $750,000 in kickbacks from the Canteen Corporation, a Chicago-based catering concern, and its consultant Pat DiCicco, in return for an "exclusive concession to provide food and beverages at the company's various offices and factories." In answer to that charge Henry said, "I have never at any time accepted any payoff or kickback from anyone." He said that Pat DiCicco was indeed someone he had known for thirty-five years and that they exchanged gifts every Christmas.

And he went on to explain, in detail, that he had never extended exclusive contracts to companies owned and controlled by Ford family members to furnish and decorate company facilities and personal residences at the expense of the company, as charged in the lawsuit. It was alleged that Ford got "furniture, furnishings and interior decoration for his personal residences around the world." These companies, it was charged, submitted "grossly inflated" bills, which Henry personally approved "to derive considerable personal advantages and benefits."

"I presume this allegation is intended to apply to my brother-in-law, Walter B. Ford," said Henry. The latter Ford headed a company, based in Warren, Michigan, called Ford and Earl Design Associates, Inc. According to the Chairman, it had been retained for many years by the auto company at an annual retainer of $3,000, and in the five-year period 1973 to 1977 it had been paid a total of $1.2 million in additional amounts for work on special projects.

The suit further alleged that Ford Motor had wasted more than $1 million in corporate funds by paying maintenance charges and the Chairman's personal expenses in connection with an elegant six-room duplex apartment at New York's Carlyle Hotel. The co-op, located on the thirty-fourth and thirty-fifth floors, was furnished with French antiques, including a tulipwood desk valued at $82,000 and a chest of drawers worth $31,000. The suit said that "these furnishings were not necessary nor were they used for company business, and in fact the apartment was off-limits to company officials and was utilized by Ford and his family for their personal use." Moreover, all of these expenses were incurred despite the fact that the company maintained other apartments in New York, at the Waldorf Towers and the Ritz Tower Hotel.

Further details on the Carlyle apartment were published in *The Wall Street Journal*. It had been purchased in 1970 for $352,000 by Henry Ford II. But the $80,340 annual maintenance charges were indeed paid by the company. A friend of Cristina's was quoted as saying the Fords used to spend two to three weeks at a time there. "They had social friends over," the friend said. "There were parties there. It was a place that Henry could go to, to get away from business." Cristina, however, rarely fussed in the kitchen. "She isn't much of a cook," the friend confided. Outside company directors, reached by the *Journal,* appeared unconcerned about the propriety of the company's monthy upkeep of the Carlyle co-op. "If Mr. Ford charged the company," said director Carter L. Burgess, chairman of the Foreign Policy Association, "I'm sure it was done in the best standard of business ethics."

At his press conference the Chairman contended that no improprieties existed with respect to his use of the apartment. He insisted that it was used mainly for business purposes. He said that whenever he had used the quarters for personal reasons, he had reimbursed the company. Besides, he went on, he had sold the co-op the year before. But he had no comment to make on the charge that Ford Motor's assets were used to purchase, for his personal use, a mansion in London and an estate in the English countryside, plus lavish furnishings. The estate had been owned by Prince Stanislas Radziwill, the late John F. Kennedy's brother-in-law.

On May 11, 1978, Roy Cohn tangled personally with the Chairman. This was at the annual meeting of the stockholders held in Detroit. Henry had opened the session with a lengthy statement defending himself against the charges filed in Cohn's lawsuit. "But," as a *New York Times* dispatch reported, "many in today's audience of some 1,500 shareholders expressed concern when Mr. Ford and other company officials refused to answer questions from the floor concerning certain allegations in the lawsuit and a reported investigation by the Justice Department into alleged illegal payments abroad."

For the most part, however, Roy Cohn found an unsympathetic audience, particularly when he demanded that Henry explain the company's role in the Indonesian bribe affair. The New York lawyer specifically wanted to know whether the company had sent a letter to the Justice Department admitting that it had earlier submitted documents in connection with the Indonesian investigation that were "forged and backdated."

"There isn't any answer," said Henry. "It's under investigation."

Repeatedly asked for a "yes or no," the Chairman said he was not going to respond because "I don't know the legal answer." Finally he turned the question over to the company general counsel, Henry R. Nolte, Jr., who also refused to discuss the letter, adding, "It is inappropriate to get into the minute details of the matter."

Cohn then asked whether the company auditors had found any questionable matters in company books relating to the Indonesian issue. "This is not a court of law," Henry said from a seat behind a long table on the stage of the downtown auditorium, "and you are not going to get an answer...I am instructing Mr. Nolte and the accountants not to answer."

Cohn's persistence drew loud boos and calls for his removal from the auditorium. As usual in such gatherings, the audience consisted of many present or former employees of the Ford company. Among those present was Henry's longtime friend and retired company vice-president, John S. Bugas, who attacked the lawsuit as "harassment" of the Chairman. Bugas, who owned or controlled 100,000 shares of the company, received an ovation after an appeal for the stockholders' sympathy.

Still, as reported by the *Times,* the often heated exchange between Cohn and Henry and his staff was received with mixed feelings. "I was kind of disappointed that they couldn't get a straight answer on that letter," said Beryl Richter, a stockholder since 1956. "And the business on the recall of the Pintos and Bobcats is troublesome too." Beverly Holbrook, a stockholder for fifteen years, said she was curious to see what more would come out on the allegations of improper payments. "But I'd be really surprised if Mr. Ford took a kickback from Canteen," she added. "I feel he has more integrity than that."

Five days later Roy Cohn turned up the heat. In an amended complaint to his lawsuit he now flatly accused Henry Ford II of having authorized payment of a $1 million bribe in connection with the contract that the company had obtained from the Indonesian government. In an effort to "cover up" the payment, the suit alleged, Henry and others "forged, altered and backdated" certain contracts, books and records.

Henry was further accused of having the company's advertising agencies pay fees to the Leslie Fargo Agency, the model company in which Kathleen DuRoss, "a person in a close personal relationship with the defendant Ford," allegedly had an interest. According to the amended complaint, Henry had authorized the ad agencies to tack on these fees to the bills they submitted to Ford Motor, which the company paid. Such alleged payment was "wrongful, unlawful, and a gross waste of the assets and property of the company." Leslie Fargo, which was named as a defendant, replied that Miss DuRoss had no financial interest in the agency, which provided models to the car companies for shows and commercials. Moreover, the agency said, Miss DuRoss hadn't worked for it for at least two years.

In addition, the suit said that Henry had arranged for some company directors and other company employees to invest large sums in private land-development ventures, including the Renaissance Center and Fairlane projects. It was also alleged that in advance of the investments, Ford tipped off "close personal and business associates," including Max Fisher and Al Taubman, who then allegedly used the information to make advantageous land purchases near the aforementioned projects. In return, Messrs. Fisher and Taubman were alleged to have made available tax-shelter investments to Henry Ford. Neither, however, was named as a defendant. And neither would comment on the allegations.

Nor was there any comment from Coopers & Lybrand, Ford Motor's accounting concern, which was named as a new defendant. According to the suit, the firm "negligently failed to carry out its fiduciary obligations and has, instead, been dominated by" Henry Ford. The suit noted that, at Ford's behest, the accountants had refused to respond to questions at the recently concluded stockholders' meeting. And it also alleged that Coopers & Lybrand had further violated its "fiduciary obligations" by "concealing and destroying financial records" relating "to the illegal, wrongful and unlawful payments in Indonesia."

Asked why Roy Cohn had filed a suit making all these allegations, William Bourke, then executive vice-president of the company's North American Automotive Operations, attacked the lawyer's motives rather than any of his substantive allegations. Bourke accused the New York lawyer of seeking the limelight. "There's no better known industrialist than Henry Ford II," he said. "He's an extremely powerful man and a titan of his time. And here comes Roy Cohn, the giant killer, who thrives on publicity and controversy—the more controversial the better he loves it." Likewise, Ford's outside lawyers accused Cohn of having "engaged in a campaign to smear the company, its chairman and directors with extrajudicial publicity, and to promote his own name."

Roy Cohn denied he had any personal dislike of the Chairman. However, he readily conceded, "I'm anti-Establishment when it comes to people like Ford." With his enormous power, Cohn added, Henry Ford "represents an era of American business that supposedly went out of style at the turn of the century." And he also nourished a "pet peeve against stuffed-shirt Wall Street firms," which, he claimed, charged their clients stiff hourly fees. Representing Ford Motor in the Cohn suit was the

Wall Street law firm of Hughes, Hubbard & Reed. On the other hand, he said, his firm—Saxe, Bacon & Bolan—did not intend to collect a nickel unless the shareholders he was representing won their suit. "We've got a good, solid lawsuit," he went on, "and nothing else."

Still, Cohn was astonished when his opponent violated his own cardinal rule of never complaining or explaining. "If I were in his shoes," Cohn admitted, "I would have either kept quiet or made the usual statement 'the charges have no merit' or 'no comment.'"

Which was exactly the posture Henry assumed as Cohn continued to unloose new charges—one of which was absolutely devastating—against him. Who was feeding all these allegations to Cohn had become "a new guessing game," according to *The Wall Street Journal*. And the unfolding charges of possible hanky-panky in high places inspired William Safire to concoct a plot—pure fiction, he claimed. His *Times* column, entitled "The Manila Envelope," featured a "world famous businessman—an arrogant aging jet-setter, who clings to corporate power because his family name is on the building." The "famous businessman's" enemies, Safire wrote, are "powerful men and glamorous women," plus some "anonymous little people," all of them feeding information to interested parties.

The allegations against Ford, as one might have expected, gave rise to all sorts of gossip. According to *The Wall Street Journal* and the *New York Post*, there was a widespread rumor that an embittered Cristina was providing Cohn with tantalizing tidbits about which only she could have had firsthand knowledge. And it was known that Cristina, in fact, had consulted with Cohn, presumably about her matrimonial problems. The lawyer, after all, specialized in such problems. For example, shortly before his death Aristotle Onassis had conferred with Cohn about arranging for a divorce from Jacqueline.

But Cristina quickly sought to scotch a published "innuendo" linking her to Cohn's $50 million lawsuit. In a letter to the *New York Post* she flatly denied any intention of engaging Cohn as her counsel. "Furthermore, I do not expect to be a witness in the lawsuit. To the best of my knowledge, my husband is beyond reproach in his business matters."

Whoever was supplying Cohn with information obviously had access to supposedly internal documents of the Ford Motor Company. In November 1978 Cohn provided the State Supreme Court in Manhattan with a memorandum marked "privileged and confidential," written by Henry R. Nolte, Jr., Ford Motor's general counsel. In the memo Nolte had advised Henry Ford and other executives of the plan by officials of a Ford subsidiary to include an overpayment of $889,000 in a subcontract to Elnusa, an Indonesian government company. Nolte reported that the full amount of the subcontract had been paid and that records covering it had been altered. What Nolte intended to do, he went on, was to bring these facts to the attention of the Justice Department in a way "that will avoid creating undue concern."

According to Cohn, the memorandum demonstrated that Ford's general counsel had sought to deflect the Justice Department's investigation "by a series of half-truths and outright concealment." But Cohn's request that Nolte be added as a defendant in the suit was rejected by the court.

On January 30, 1979, the group of stockholders represented by Cohn unloosed a series of new allegations. Using a response to legal "interrogatories" posed by the Ford company, the stockholders charged Henry Ford with having improperly diverted corporate funds to pay for political dinners and a host of personal benefits, including opulent office, sauna and gym facilities and private airplane trips and other favors for family and friends.

The legal document, over one hundred pages long, also elaborated on earlier charges. For the first time the dissidents provided details of the alleged bribe paid to Henry by the Canteen Corporation, which this Chicago-based company had denied. They claimed that the negotiations leading to the "sweetheart deals" took place between Henry and Pat DiCicco at the latter's Sutton Place apartment. It was in this Manhattan apartment that the sum of $750,000 allegedly was handed over to Ford, "which monies," it was further charged, "Mr. Ford diverted into a Swiss bank account." Moreover, according to the dissidents, Henry had also created a secret trust arrangement in Liechtenstein in order "to conceal money from illegal sources."

The shareholders also claimed that Henry mixed his love life with business. They charged that the high-living Chairman:

Had used a company plane to fly himself and "his close intimate friend" Kathy DuRoss from London to Palma, Mallorca, on a purely personal vacation trip.

Had used company aircraft to fly personal furniture including an "ornate fireplace," which he had bought for Kathy, across the ocean from Europe.

Arranged for Ford Motor employees to maintain and manicure the lawn at the DuRoss home in Grosse Pointe Woods, "which home was purchased for the DuRoss family by Mr. Ford for approximately $65,000 in cash."

Arranged for the employment of Kathy's daughter, Debbie Evasic, as a supervisor in the Security Department of Ford Motor Company, "although others of far more adequate qualifications were available for far less compensation."

Also hired Tom Kish, Kathy's former bouncer at her disco, L'Esprit, as a director of special events for the company.

The dissidents also charged that Henry had used company aircraft, limousines and personnel to perform personal services for other friends and family members. It was alleged, for instance, that company planes were used to fly his mother's dogs and cats "whenever she felt her pets were in need of a change of climate." Then there was the occasion when, on a return flight from Europe, Henry ordered a plane to land, at a cost of $6,000, to pick up a pack of cigarettes for one of his passengers. In addition, at the Chairman's instructions, corporate planes were used to transport caviar, Dom Perignon champagne, Château Lafite wine and "a special lean bacon" from place to place for his personal use. "In fact," the document further alleged, "Mr. Ford deploys corporate aircraft to maintain his supply of caviar at his office and residences as if the company ran a New York to Detroit air shuttle."

In addition, six to nine corporate limousines and drivers were maintained in New York for the personal use of Henry Ford, company directors and friends of the family, including Henry's daughters, his ex-wife Mrs. Deane Johnson, his "close and intimate friend" Kathy DuRoss, and Pat DiCicco. In Michigan, corporate limousines chauffeured by Ford employees were made available to Kathy as a "regular proposition." Such accommodations were also provided for DuRoss family events, including the wedding of Kathy's daughter, Debbie Evasic. And company limousines plus drivers lined the street in front of Kathy's home at 856 Hampton Road at the time of her father's death. All of which, it was alleged, constituted "an illegal use of corporate assets."

The stockholders contended that for his own comfort Henry ordered multimillion-dollar items to be built into his retirement aerie in a Renaissance Center tower, including a $2.7 million winding staircase to give access from his office facilities to "a suite kept available for his afternoon rest." In addition to "this new recreation area," Henry maintained on a preemptive basis the presidential suite at the Hyatt Regency Hotel in Dearborn for his exclusive use. And while in London, which he visited frequently, Henry never used the elaborate living quarters maintained for company executives in Grosvenor House. Nevertheless he billed the company $300 for every night he slept in his personally owned home. At the same time, Henry had caused the company to purchase an additional mansion on Grafton Street for the sum of $10 million, "which house serves no corporate purpose."

The suit further charged that at his Dearborn headquarters Henry maintained sauna baths at an "astronomical cost" of $250,000, a private gym with a full-time masseuse, and a private dining room, where it cost $200 a person to serve lunch. Many of his guests were "personal, social and definitely not business related." The dining room was staffed by six full-time employees, including a Swiss chef named Joseph Bernardi, all of whom combined "to supply food and service to Ford's special taste and liking, at shareholders' expense." Also picked up by the shareholders were the costs accruing from "misuse" of the company's telephone credit cards by Henry and his family to the tune of $50,000 to $100,000 a year.

Also, according to the charges, Henry directed that $300,000 in corporate funds be used to entertain thirty-two state governors at a personal party at his mother's house in connection with the 1977 national governors conference. If true, the allegation should have raised questions as to whether the party was an attempt by the company to lobby the governors and also whether the company had deducted the funds on tax returns as a business expense.

According to the suit, Henry was receiving an annual salary of $922,000, which was "wrongful, unlawful, exorbitant" and a "waste" of company assets. The suit also claimed that the salary was "substantially a gratuitous payment for which little if any service whatever was rendered or could have been rendered by the defendant." Moreover, Henry was quoted as having said that he had the company directors "in his pocket." According to the suit, each member of the "rubber stamp" board of directors received "anywhere from $30,000 to $50,000 per year (depending upon committee fees), Dom Perignon champagne, two automobiles and through the courtesy of the nonconsenting stockholders a life insurance policy with a face value of $250,000."

But of all the many charges leveled against Henry Ford II, probably the most devastating to his public image was the one that claimed that he had accepted a $2 million bribe—in what William Safire wittily called a "manila envelope," actually an attache case—from Imelda Marcos while she was visiting in Michigan in 1972. The purpose of the bribe was to encourage the building of a costly automobile stamping plant in the Philippines, according to the suit. The record does show that such a plant was indeed built on the Bataan Peninsula in a specially created tax-free manufacturing zone across Manila Bay. But there were denials all around that any bribe was paid. "Can you imagine I would bribe Henry Ford?" scoffed Imelda. "Usually it's the other way around. They call me 'Miss Ten Percent' and say that I am being bribed." But she did admit having cut short a 1979 visit to the U.S.—leaving before she could sign a $100 million World Bank loan—to avoid being subpoenaed.

According to a *Washington Post* correspondent in Manila, there had long been rumors that Imelda Marcos had "cultivated" the friendship of Cristina Ford in part to get her husband to approve the Philippine investment. That investment was important to the authoritarian rule of President Ferdinand Marcos, who had imposed martial law across the country in September 1972. In response to criticism of his policies restricting civil liberties, Marcos noted that they had created a climate that permitted such foreign investments. The Ford plant, which produces body parts for export, incurred a loss of $17 million through 1977, according to the suit.

"Marcos was eager to show his people and the world that martial law could attract investment, and the single biggest investment at the time was Ford's," said Raul Manglapus, a former Philippine foreign minister and a leader of the anti-Marcos opposition. Now living in exile in the U.S., Manglapus said he was aware of the negotiations with Ford, which began in 1971. "But the investment was not put in until 1973," he went on. "And since this was the largest single investment at the time, it enabled the Marcos administration to bring its graph of foreign investment way up in 1973 and to say that its law and order government had attracted investors."

Manglapus had no knowledge that any improper influence had been exerted to attract the factory. But he did tell a story that indicated that Marcos may have been able to influence Henry Ford's actions. When he arrived in the U.S., following imposition of martial law in the Philippines, Manglapus obtained a $12,000 fellowship from the Ford Foundation to participate in the Cornell Southeast Asia Program. Some months later, after the fellowship was already approved, Manglapus heard that Henry Ford himself had contacted the directors of the Ford Foundation about the grant. Asked about this by the *Washington Post,* the Ford Motor Company confirmed that in 1973 the Chairman "did receive an inquiry on Mr. Manglapus and his relationship with the Ford Foundation. He simply referred the inquiry to the Ford Foundation and he did not in any way try to interfere with the Foundation or Mr. Manglapus."

And a spokesman for the Ford Foundation also confirmed the inquiry. Henry Ford wanted to know "what the grant was all about." The inquiry was "not unusual, not uncommon and did not constitute any interference." At any rate, the Foundation did give Ford the details of the grant, "and," added the spokesman, "there was no change in the grant." However, Manglapus did find it somewhat curious that his fellowship, amounting to $12,000 out of total disbursements that year exceeding $100 million, had been personally reviewed by Henry Ford II.

On top of all this, William Safire had become interested in

. the misadventures of "one of the last of the corporate autocrats."
In several columns in *The New York Times* the Pulitzer Prize-
winning writer reported an amazing story. He told that Henry
Ford had personally visited Frank Sinatra prior to a concert in
Detroit. According to Henry, it was purely a "social call."
Safire, however, speculated broadly that Henry hoped that Sinatra's alleged gangland contacts would get to Cohn's underworld law clients and persuade him to lay off. This Ol' Blue
Eyes vehemently denied. What was established, though, was
the fact that Sinatra did fly to New York, where he met with
Cohn at a restaurant misspelled "Seperate Tables." And according to Cohn, "The meeting was arranged to discuss an
offer to settle the Ford suit. I waited for the settlement offer,
but it turned out that Henry Ford asked Sinatra to ask me to
take a dive. I told Frank to stop kidding and I went home."

Sinatra later told friends he had "stumbled" into the dispute
between Ford and Cohn. What had happened was that Hugh
Carey, New York Governor then dating Henry's daughter Anne,
had asked him to see the auto magnate. Henry appealed to
Sinatra for help, claiming that Cohn was "doing a number" on
him. Sinatra said he'd see what he could do. So he set up the
meeting with Cohn. And the meeting backfired.

As we shall see, the allegations against Ford were never
examined in court. They were to remain allegations, neither
proved nor unproved.

In March 1979 Roy Cohn got an assist from a fairly surprising quarter: Henry Ford's nephew. Benson Ford, Jr., twenty-
nine, involved in a legal battle to gain control of a $7.5 million
inheritance, including roughly $6 million in Ford stock, an-
nounced that he had retained Cohn as counsel in several suits
against Ford officials and family. "I picked Mr. Cohn because
he is one mean son of a bitch," young Benson said. And Cohn
described his new client as yet another stockholder "who wants
to end the autocratic regime" at Ford.

15

BENSON FORD, JR.

HENRY FORD II HAD NEVER EXPECTED OPPOSITION FROM ANY
of his nephews or nieces. All of a sudden, however, he found
himself in a raucous, public dispute with the son of his late
middle brother. And to make matters worse, Benson Ford, Jr.,
had joined forces with Roy Cohn, whose unremitting series of
charges had patently rattled the Chairman of the Ford Motor
Company.

At the heart of Benson's complaint was his belief that he
was being euchred out of his rightful legacy by a scheming
uncle. He was incensed at the way he claimed the family lawyer
had persuaded his father to change his will to place the voting
power of a huge block of stock ultimately in Henry's hands.
And he was convinced that Uncle Henry would do anything to
assure his son Edsel's accession to the throne, even though
there were nephews hoping to play major roles in the company.

Not all nephews, to be sure. Alfred Brush Ford, then twenty-eight, had never shown any interest in automobiles other than riding in them. One of two sons of Henry's only sister, Josephine, and her husband Walter Buhl Ford II, Alfie had become enmeshed in the theological thicket of Hare Krishna. Alfie's older brother, Walter Buhl Ford III, had for a time been involved in making a film about a noble proletarian. But in 1978 Buhl, as he was called, went to work for Ford's parts and service division. Which left Benson and William Clay Jr., both of whom were also quite willing to compete for eventual leadership of the Ford Motor Company. Twenty-one-year-old Billy, a Princeton man, had spent a summer working in his father's product-design department at Ford. And Benson, described in the *Detroit News* as "the under-the-hood type, interested in mechanics," had already begun an informal training program designed by his father and Lee Iacocca, then Ford's president (and, said young Ben, "like an uncle to me"). As for the top job, Ben put it bluntly: "If and when the opportunity arises, I'd like a crack at it. I don't want to be ruled out."

Which sounded like heresy in a family in which disputes rarely became public. But, then, Benson had always been considered something of an outsider. He did not quite fit the mold of other fourth-generation Fords, who seldom caused waves. Of course there was Alfie, whom the family had written off as merely eccentric, not threatening. He was forgiven his religious deviation, largely because he claimed Hare Krishna had saved him from heavy involvement in the drug scene. Besides, Alfie had not gone all the way in his new religion. He did not observe all the communal rituals of his faith. For example, he did not shave his head. But he did wind up selling Buddhist *objets d'art* in his incense-filled shop at Renaissance Center. And on weekends he would usually fly out to his condominium in Malibu, where he spent most of his time looking out at the sea. Once Benson asked Alfie for his phone number. "No, I don't want anyone to know I'm here," Alfie said. "I don't want the sort of publicity you've been getting."

When they were youngsters, Benson had been close to Alfie and Edsel. They would see each other regularly, stay over at each other's homes, and generally raise hell. Edsel, particularly, was a "fun guy." But as they grew older they went off to separate schools and saw each other only infrequently. Benson, however, has done a lot of thinking about Edsel. And he believes that the "Crown Prince"—as he calls him—has never been bloodied in the harsh world of reality. "Until you lose some blood and draw some blood," he says, "I don't think you know what you stand for or what your limitations are. My cousin Edsel doesn't know what his limitations are. I think he'll learn—if he ever gets out of the nursery. Maybe that will happen some day. It seems to me he's going through life with the Muzak turned up."

Benson thinks he knows his own limitations. And he also speaks frankly about the bleak life of a very rich kid who had everything handed to him.

"Until I was fourteen I was always in a car with a god-damn guard or a governess. My parents were usually traveling. I'd go to school in Grosse Pointe for six months, then to a school in Palm Beach for three or four months in the winter. I had to repeat the third grade and flunked the seventh. So they shipped me off to Fessenden, a snatch-proof pre-prep school in West Newton, Massachusetts. It was quite a shock. I was fourteen and had never before been out of protective custody. Now I was in an environment where you had to fight to survive. They took fourth-grade boys and made them into tough little bastards by the time they were in the eighth grade. They had a head start on me. I started in the seventh grade."

His living quarters at the dormitory consisted of a cubicle no bigger than a closet. It contained a cot, a bureau for clothes and a tiny table on which to do class assignments. What he missed most were the pet dogs he had left at home. At the first opportunity he went downtown and purchased a goldfish "to keep me company." After class one day he returned to his cubicle to discover his little companion nailed to the wall. "That really broke me up," he says. At first he would write his parents almost every day, circling the tearstains on the letters, hoping to get some sympathy. But that ploy didn't work.

The first year at Fessenden was sheer agony. "It was like being in prison," Benson says. "You wake up by a bell, go to sleep by a bell, eat by a bell, go to the bathroom by a bell, and wake up by a bell." And one of his masters "must have been trained by the Gestapo," he says. "He was forever looking for transgressions." Once, when Benson had been in a brawl with a classmate, the master grabbed the heir to one of America's great fortunes by the ear and threw him against the wall. He then gave two heavy books to Benson and said, "For the next hour, you stand at attention, your arms outstretched, holding the books. And I don't want to hear them fall." Every ten minutes or so the master would come out to check on him. Finally Benson's arms got so tired he dropped the books. Wham! But apparently the master did not hear the noise. "If ever I hated anyone, it was him," says Benson. "I hated him with a deep passion." Finally Benson arranged to move to another dormitory.

Benson became a troublemaker. "I was trying to fight the system, trying to revolt." And that's when he got caught cheating on an examination and received seven demerits. "I thought it was the end of the world, that I would be expelled." But Benson was unduly apprehensive. For it took twenty-eight demerits to get kicked out of Fessenden. One student who was expelled was the school bully, a stocky youngster who had taken particular pleasure in harassing Benson. Once, Benson recalls, he was late for class because the bully knocked his books out of his hands, threw him to the floor and kicked him in the rear.

"By the time I left Fessenden, I had one hell of a tough hide," he says. From Fessenden, Benson went to Suffield Academy, a small prep school in Connecticut. "That was much better for me. I'd had the advantage of having attended a kind of high-class juvenile reformatory. Some of the kids who hadn't were in pretty grim shape and would make suicide attempts. I got into sports. It was the alternative to going stir crazy. There weren't any girls. I guess soccer is upper-class saltpeter."

As a graduation present his parents gave Benson a trip to Europe. All expenses were picked up. Cars were waiting for him in England and on the Continent. In addition, he received $10,000 in spending money. "Don't spend it in one place," his dad had admonished, "but have a good time." And for two months that was precisely what Benson did. Joined by two buddies from Suffield, he traveled wherever he wanted. And for the first time in his life he felt really free. "I was on my own," he says, "and I discovered I could manage."

In the fall of 1969 Benson drove out to California, where he enrolled in Whittier College. His father had wanted him to attend a school back east, but Benson dreaded eastern winters. More important, Whittier—Richard Nixon's alma mater—was the first warm, small college with girls on the campus to grant him admission. And the first year was "party time." Having more money than other students, he paid for the beer. "The kids would get roaring drunk and tear up the dorm," he recalls. "Finally, I got fed up with that kind of nonsense and moved out."

Benson at first did not work too hard on his studies. In fact, he took up drama, because, as he says, "I didn't want to rack my brains too much." It was while he was working the lights for the campus version of *Cabaret* that he became friendly with Elliot Kaplan, who was also "having a ball" at Whittier. And it was Elliot who introduced Benson to Louis Fuentes, the owner of a psychological clinic across the street from the campus. Of Mexican origin, Fuentes was born and raised in the eastside barrios of Los Angeles. Educated in California colleges, he had made a great deal of money from his extensive outside interests in real estate in the Los Angeles area. But his first love was psychological counseling.

Most of his patients were adolescents or young adults. He says:

> . . . most of them were unhappy kids with good intellects who came from wealthy homes. And I knew a lot of my friends' kids who had nothing to do with my practice. One of them was Elliot Kaplan, whose father, a cardiologist, was a good friend of mine. But he and Elliot were not getting along. Finally, Dr. Kaplan asked if Elliot could live with me and my family while continuing

to go to Whittier College. We have a very large house
so it was no problem fitting Elliot in with my two older
sons, who were teenagers then. He'd been with us for a
few weeks when he asked me to talk to a school friend
whom he described as being *really* screwed up. The
friend was Ben Ford. Ben was living in an old frame
house with five or six other guys, not eating, putting
down a lot of booze and not paying much attention to
school. One more mouth to feed was nothing to my wife
and me. Just another potato in the oven.

For a time Benson dropped out of school and went to work
in a plastics factory. "I just wanted to get out and get my hands
dirty," he says. "So I went from being a rich little Ford to
making trash cans for three bucks an hour." Working mainly
with Mexicans, Benson learned a great deal about manual labor.
But after a year of getting his hands dirty Benson decided to
go back to school. He had had a long talk with Dennis Murray,
then vice-president of Whittier College, who convinced him of
the necessity of obtaining a degree in business. Murray helped
arrange a part-time schedule that enabled Benson to work on
the outside.

About this time Benson's father arranged for him to meet
an old friend, Bill Stroppe, who was a well-known figure in
off-road racing. This was the increasingly popular sport in
which specially modified trucks and other vehicles match speed
and endurance across the desert or through the washes and
gullies of Baja, California. After observing his first race Benson
was hooked. So hooked, in fact, that he became the first member of the Ford family since his great-grandfather to drive in
races. His codriver was Elliot Kaplan, by then Benson's close
friend, roommate and unofficial bodyguard. "It was exhilarat-
ing," Benson recalls. "It's your challenge against the elements."

Bill Stroppe had a small California business modifying vehicles for off-road racing. And as he informed young Ford and
Fuentes, he needed cash to expand the company. Would they
be interested in a partnership? Yes, they said. So, in late 1972,
Bill Stroppe Associates Inc. was formed, with Stroppe, Ford

and Fuentes each holding a third of the stock. Because Benson was not yet in control of the money left to him by his grandparents, he borrowed $100,000 from Fuentes to help pay for his share.

Actually, all Benson was getting from home was $1,000 a month, but he added to his income by working on the side. And when he complained to his parents, they said not to worry, if he needed any extra money they would send it to him. But that wasn't good enough. "Here I was supposed to be a Ford, one of those people you read about at glamorous parties, wearing fancy duds, and living it up," says Benson. "But I was being kept on short rations."

At Fuentes' suggestion Benson retained the well known Beverly Hills lawyer Harvey Fierstein to look out for his interests. Through Fierstein and his associate Mike Blumenfeld, Benson requested that his personal wealth—from a series of earlier trusts already his—be transferred from control of the family's lawyers in Detroit to his bank in California. This request prompted an almost Dickensian rebuke from the longtime top family lawyer Pierre (Pete) Heftler. In a March 1973 letter to the young heir Heftler wrote:

It is very understandable that every young man wants to become the master of his own affairs and it is well that those who, like you, are destined to have substantial wealth should lose no time in learning how to handle it. If your fortune were of your own making no one would ever criticize you for wanting to be the complete master of it, even to the exclusion of those closest to you.

However, the fact is that not one cent of this fortune is due to your own efforts; it is a family fortune which has come to you through the efforts of others.

In effect, the letter suggested that Benson, then twenty-three years of age, was not capable of handling vast sums of money. And this infuriated Benson even more. He insisted on a meeting to thresh the matter out. Along with Fierstein, Benson met in a downtown Detroit legal office with his parents and family lawyers, including Heftler. "What they wanted to know was why I wanted the money," recalls Benson, "and I told them it was my money and I had absolutely no idea of what I was going to do with it. They seemed stunned by my abrupt response. Then they warned me that I would have to be responsible for paying taxes. I told them no sweat." After three hours the meeting ended. Benson Ford, Jr., finally had obtained about $4 million of his own money, part of which he was to use as capital in his ventures with Louis Fuentes.

Meanwhile the partnership with Stroppe had soured. According to Benson, Stroppe was spending money "like there was no tomorrow." Almost every week, said Benson, "he'd ask us for $50,000 to meet the payroll." After which there was a parting of the ways and lawsuits began. All of them were won by the two investors or settled. One cross-action suit filed by Stroppe, however, is still pending.

> When the litigation with Stroppe started [Benson says] I tried to talk to my father about it. He said he didn't want to hear about it, that it upset him. I never brought the matter up again. Later, after my father died, I found he had been paying Bill Stroppe's legal fees in the litigation against me. He had been brainwashed into thinking I was unbalanced, that I was under the evil influence of Lou and Elliot, whom they called "the ruthless Californians." They wanted me back in the juvenile cage in Grosse Pointe, and if it took busting our little California company—so be it. Losing a million or so would teach me not to go sailing off on my own.

(Obviously, Benson thought, whether accurately or not, that the lawsuit was intended to break him financially.)

According to Benson, a great deal of "misinformation" about him had been fed to his father by Neil G. McCarrol, a Los Angeles lawyer. McCarrol had been asked by his old friend Pierre Heftler to represent Benson when the young heir had been arrested for erratic driving. As it turned out, Benson was exonerated. But afterward McCarrol surreptitiously kept an eye on him anyway. He was in constant touch with Bill Stroppe, who alleged all kinds of personal and business wrongdoings on the part of young Benson and his associates. The allegations then were passed on to Heftler and Benson Sr. in a series of letters.

In May 1973 McCarrol wrote that "young Ben is apparently under the complete domination of Fuentes, Fierstein and Kaplan. My first impression is that they have been 'milking' him." Fuentes, in particular, was painted as trying to get his hands on Benson's fortune. Which, in retrospect, was nonsense. The record shows that in partnership with Fuentes young Ford has done very well indeed. That partnership, Fuentes-Ford Enterprises, owns a huge sheep ranch in Wyoming, two other ranches in Mexico, silver mines and a construction company below the border, a tire company in Arizona and two industrial companies in California. One of those companies, Luben Industries, manufactures automobile parts—such items as roll bars for recreational vehicles. Employing over seventy people, Luben has been grossing over $10 million a year and, says Ben, has been exceedingly profitable.

Despite his wealth, Benson lives a fairly unostentatious life. Unlike his more celebrated relatives, he's not one for fancy parties and his name rarely appears in the social columns. Not that his tastes are entirely simple. He travels a good deal, particularly on business, likes good restaurants, and enjoys female companionship. His home near Whittier is a hilltop, Spanish-style spread. There is a well-equipped darkroom, an elaborate hi-fi system, two large telescopes pointed at the sky, shelves of racing trophies and helmets, and an aviary populated by several squawking African grays and red-and-yellow macaws. Ferocious-looking guard dogs prowl the grounds. His is an ideal place for privacy, and Benson likes his privacy. All through his student years he turned down repeated requests for interviews, saying he was just another private person. Whittier College officials always stood between him and the media, asking that he not be singled out "for security reasons."

In May 1978, when Benson finally received a B.A. degree, no one was more pleased than his father. Much of the bitterness over the Stroppe affair seemed to have been dissipated. Benson Sr. now knew that, despite all the alarms, his son had done quite well for himself in the business world. But, more important, he knew how anxious Benson Jr. was to get involved in the affairs of the Ford Motor Company. In fact, he had helped arrange for his son to take an indoctrination tour of Ford plants in Europe in the summer of 1977. And following his graduation from Whittier, Benson was to visit various Ford Facilities in Latin America. Eventually Benson Jr. wanted to get into the company's product-planning and development division. And he agreed with his dad that he would have to work five or six years in various countries abroad before coming to Dearborn in an executive position.

"My father couldn't have been happier," says Benson. "And then, suddenly, he passed away."

And Benson Sr. passed away before he could do anything—that is, if he had wanted to—about the will he had revised three years earlier, according to Benson Jr. at the strong urging of family lawyer Pierre Heftler. According to terms of the will, half of a $100 million estate, of which about $85 million was in Ford Motor stock, was left to his widow, Edith McNaughton Ford. The remainder, after payment of $35 million in taxes, was to be divided into two trusts for Benson Jr. and his sister, Lynn Ford Alandt—each trust valued at $7.5 million.

In November 1978 Benson Jr. filed suit in Detroit to contest his father's will. At stake was voting control of 913,628 shares, or 6.5 percent of the family-held class B stock in Ford Motor Company. Benson Sr. had left the stock in trust to his ailing wife and his children, but he had specified that in the event of his wife's death, voting control of the stock would pass to his brother Henry Ford II.

Young Benson claimed that his father had been "brainwashed" into mistrusting his only son and leaving him without any say in Ford Motor Company affairs. He insisted that his father had not understood the implications of the will and that his mother's powers were being usurped by Pierre Heftler or even by Henry Ford himself. "I have reason to believe," said Benson, "that Heftler, using Los Angeles attorneys and investigators, piled up an unbelievable file on both Fuentes and me. Then they advised my parents to rewrite their wills and tighten up the trusts. My dad was told I was completely dominated by big, bad Lou, who was out to bilk me out of my last dime."

And then, in a move that further rattled the Glass House, Benson sent a "Dear Uncle Henry" letter to Dearborn, asking the Chairman to nominate him for election to his father's seat on the board of directors of the Ford Motor Company. He cited his considerable holdings of Ford stock, his deep devotion to family enterprises, and his own ten-year experience in profit-making ventures.

"I know that my father would have wanted me to have his director's seat," says Benson. "I also know that he was planning my future with the company when he passed away."

One of young Benson's staunchest allies was none other than Lee Iacocca, the new head of Chrysler. Iacocca had been a friend of Benson's father for fifteen years. At the father's request, he had long advised and counseled young Benson. In response to questions, Iacocca indicated he had only a general knowledge of Benson's legal action. But he made it clear he believed the late Benson Ford's "dream and ambition" was eventually to see his son have a "responsible position with the company" and "represent his side of the family" and its vast holdings of Ford Motor stock. Iacocca said that he and the late Benson Ford had often discussed the subject. Which was what made it so "shocking" when he was told that Benson Ford's will "doesn't seem to read that way."

Yes, Iacocca went on, he had met recently with young Benson at an auto dealers convention in Las Vegas. But he did not want that meeting to be interpreted as being related to his falling out with Henry Ford. "I am friendly with a lot of Fords," he said. "I didn't stop talking to them the day somebody ripped my epaulets off."

Asked about his nephew's request for a directorship, Henry said that the matter would have to be taken up by a nominations committee, of which he was the chairman. When asked how he himself felt about it, the Chairman said tersely that he hadn't made up his mind. But he had, in fact, made up his mind. "That kid has as much chance of getting on the board as I have of becoming adviser to the Pope," he said.

Not long afterward, Benson contends, he became the target of a smear campaign. "There were rumors that I had tried to commit suicide on several occasions," he says. "Then I was supposed to be a homosexual." But his cause wasn't helped any when in January 1978 he was arrested on a charge of possessing a small amount of cocaine and hashish.

The drug bust issue was raised in the case of the will in chambers of Judge Ira G. Kaufman in Wayne County Probate Court. Benson's California lawyer, Harvey Fierstein, strongly objected to the matter being raised, noting that he could also cite rumors about more prominent people using drugs. When the judge protested this line of argument, Fierstein said he was merely relaying gossip he had heard to illustrate hearsay that "had as much reliability as the newspaper accounts about Benson." Later, in open court, Fierstein demanded that the judge disqualify himself for having made prejudicial remarks about his client. Judge Kaufman overruled the motion.

That the court fight would prove to be an embarrassment to the Ford family, airing its dirty linen in public, was further borne out by an affidavit submitted by young Benson. In it Benson described his father as an "alcoholic who drank as much as a fifth of liquor a day" and was not mentally competent when he redrafted his will in 1975. The affidavit went on to tell of his mother's response when Benson asked why his father agreed to the new provisions of the will: "She shrugged her shoulders, pointed her index finger toward her temple and rotated it in the usual manner of indicating to me that she believed that my father was not of sound mind."

The affidavit, however, was ruled inadmissible, the judge contending that it was filed too late.

For several months Benson had tried to iron out the dispute with his mother, who, as executor of her husband's huge estate, was the nominal defendant in the action brought by her son. The last thing Benson wanted was to cause her anguish. "Every time I talked to her, she would say, 'Do what you believe is right, Benson.' Then the questions were bucked to the Ford lawyers, and everything flew apart. The lawyers were listening to the man on the twelfth floor in Dearborn, not to my mother."

At Christmas 1978 Benson telephoned his mother and sister "just to say hello. . . . The servants said they were out. They never called back. I guess it's unanimous in the big, warm-hearted Ford family that I'm the renegade bastard who's rocking the boat. Everyone digs the old family square dance but Benson. . . . When my father died, there was a lot of chatter about my being the man of the family. What that means is waiting for Heftler to give me a blueprint and *do it* the way the print says. *Not me.*"

According to Benson, his sister Lynn objected vociferously to what he was trying to do. Lynn no longer listened to her brother as in the past. At his suggestion, she had attended Whittier College, but after a year or so she had returned to Grosse Pointe to get married. Benson was and still is fond of Lynn. He recalls the "great time" he had at his sister's coming out party in June 1971. It was a debut that rivaled those of her cousins Charlotte and Anne Ford. It had a three-ring-circus theme, with jugglers, sword-swallowers, and several bands to entertain the 650 guests.

There could be little doubt about the pivotal role Pierre Heftler played in the affairs of the Ford family. According to papers filed in probate court, documents the family would rather have kept private, Heftler had drafted wills, overseen the trusts and acted as a friend and confidant to the Ford family for over three decades. It was Heftler, a senior partner in the Detroit firm of Bodman, Longley, Rogle, Armstrong and Dahling, who ran Ford Estates Inc. The court documents also provided a small glimpse into how Ford Estates, an unincorporated agency in Detroit, had invested the fortunes of family members in housing projects in various major cities to provide tax shelters and to obtain substantial tax write-offs. One such investment was in South Common Stage III, a large housing project in Chicago, which had run into trouble. The group of Ford family members who had investments in it, including Benson Jr., had to put up more money through Ford Estates. When young Benson's bookkeeper asked questions about it, Heftler pointed out that for an investment of $85,000, young Benson had reaped tax savings of $200,000 over four years.

"Would you believe," says Benson, "the almighty Ford family getting tax writeoffs from some tenements in Chicago?"

In the midst of all the legal byplay, Benson received a letter inviting him to talk things over with Uncle Henry. Benson decided not to go, however, after the newspaper publicity of quotes from family members which, he claims, "put me down and questioned my motives." A few days before the 1979 stockholders' meeting, Roy Cohn met with Benson in the latter's top-floor suite in the Detroit Plaza Hotel. Roy had just come from a meeting with Max Fisher, who had reported that the Chairman was willing to discuss settlement with Benson. The young heir was not convinced. But Cohn insisted that he see his uncle. "Max claims that everything has been arranged," the lawyer said. "You have no alternative but to call him."

Benson called for an appointment. The next day he was alone with his uncle in his imposing suite in the Glass House.

"How are you doing, Benson?" the Chairman asked.

"Fine, Uncle Henry." Benson replied. "It's nice to see you."

"Well," the Chairman went on, "what are you doing here?"

Benson, taken aback, recovered quickly. "I was given to understand you wanted to talk to me," he said.

"I have nothing to talk to you about. If you have any ideas for a settlement, forget them," he said. "I don't like your friends on the West Coast. I think they're taking advantage of you."

"Listen, Uncle Henry," Benson replied, "you've got your friends and I've got mine. You don't say anything about my friends and I won't say anything about yours."

The meeting, lasting half an hour, was neither friendly nor bitter, Benson later reported. His uncle, he said, gave him "a clear picture" of where he stood with him, saying that if Benson ever wanted to occupy the Chairman's chair in that office, "you must do it on your own." Since he had not brought up the chairmanship, but had renewed his request for his father's seat on the board, Benson thought the remark significant. Benson felt that Uncle Henry's attitude was obviously conditioned by the fear that young Benson constituted a threat to his plan for his son Edsel. As he departed, aware a private settlement was impossible, Benson told his uncle that he would have to proceed with the two lawsuits he had filed. Henry replied, "Che sera, sera."

One suit, of course, was the one filed in probate court, and a decision on whether Benson would be allowed to challenge his father's will was expected momentarily. The other, filed in Detroit's Federal Court by Roy Cohn, was against Ford

Estates Inc. In it, Benson was asking for $2 million in damages, alleging that two officers of the private corporation (not including Heftler) had breached their fiduciary duties. To defend the family's interest in the suit, Henry Ford had retained Edward Bennett Williams, the Washington lawyer who had represented Lee Iacocca in negotiating his severance from the Ford Motor Company.

Thus a dramatic confrontation between two of the nations' more colorful lawyers—Roy Cohn and Edward Bennett Williams—seemed in the offing.

Then, in a "Dear Benson" letter, Henry Ford advised his nephew that his request for a directorship had been discussed by the company's Organization Review and Nominating Committee, which, he said, "has unanimously declined to recommend your nomination to the board." The committee, Henry went on, "does not regard your ownership of Class B stock as a necessary criterion for election to the board."

The news hardly came as a surprise to Benson. For at the private meeting he had attended with other members of the family, Uncle Henry had made it perfectly clear there were no "Crown Princes" in the Ford Motor Company. Also at the meeting, held in William Clay Ford's home in Grosse Pointe, the argument had been made to Benson that he should disassociate himself from Roy Cohn in the Ford Estates case, since the lawyer also represented a group of dissident stockholders and the two actions weren't easily distinguished in the public eye. This, Benson said, he would not do.

At another point in the meeting the family had discussed their private use of company aircraft and limousines. The perquisite had been criticized by Roy Cohn in his stockholders' suit. Also criticized, as we've seen, had been Henry's use of company money to maintain a luxurious apartment in New York's Carlyle Hotel. The Chairman disclosed he had reimbursed the company with a payment of more than $34,000. But, he insisted, most of that money related to personal use of the suite by his estranged wife Cristina and her friends.

There was no discussion of other problems bedeviling the Chairman. One of the more embarrassing, certainly, was the grand jury investigation into the alleged Indonesian bribe. Already two company officials had given testimony under grants of immunity from prosecution. One of them, Paul Lorenz, told the jurors that Henry Ford II was not among those who had devised the plan to pay a $1 million bribe and, in fact, had been involved in scotching it before the bribe was paid. Lorenz further testified he knew nothing about any overpayment of $889,000 to an Indonesian subcontractor. As far as he was concerned, there was no coverup.

Lee Iacocca, talking to prosecutors voluntarily, told how he had personally dismissed Lorenz after being instructed to do so by Henry Ford. Iacocca said he had known nothing of the original bribe offer, having been absent from the meeting at which the offer had been authorized. According to Iacocca, Henry was at that meeting. But, after Iacocca had fired Lorenz, Ford told him that he felt sorry for Lorenz, wondering whether Lorenz had misunderstood the Chairman's instructions for handling the Indonesian contract. At any rate, Iacocca was later surprised to discover that not only was Lorenz permitted to remain on the payroll for another year but was granted a $100,000 bonus.

Then word leaked out from the Justice Department that though there were inconsistencies in testimony, it did not appear likely that any top officer of the Ford Motor Company would be prosecuted in connection with the Indonesian bribe. In fact, according to a Jo Thomas dispatch in *The New York Times*, "the Ford case had lost momentum" and had come at a time "when the Justice Department appears understaffed and ill equipped to grapple with criminal investigations involving large corporations." Which was pretty much what Bill Safire had predicted almost a year before—that Jimmy Carter's Justice Department would "give kid-glove treatment to the company headed by the President's friend." And, as it turned out, the Justice Department dropped the case.

Then there was the ruling in probate court that denied Benson Jr.'s petition to reopen his late father's will so as to gain voting control of the family's Ford Motor stock. Judge Kaufman found that the heir had ignored opportunities to contest the will before the filing deadline. Benson's lawyers had insisted that he had not been given proper notice of the proceedings. But the judge contended that Benson was given "repeated and ample notice of the proceedings" and that his failure to file timely objections "wasn't inadvertent but deliberate."

Benson, who sat glumly facing the judge as he read his ten-page opinion, left the courtroom stunned. For he knew that his campaign to get a role in the affairs of the Ford Motor Company had been dealt a severe blow.

Faced with mounting legal costs, Benson eventually dropped his Ford Estate's suit. But he pursued his action on his father's will, a still pending matter.

Meanwhile there were chuckles on the twelfth floor of the Ford World Headquarters. For, finally and at long last, things appeared to be going the Chairman's way.

16

CHANGINGS
OF THE GUARD

MEANWHILE THE LEGAL SAGA OF GROSSE POINTE'S BEST known couple continued. After Cristina had filed a suit for separation in December 1977, Henry Ford initiated action for divorce the following month. And, as he said, he wanted to get it over with quickly. But that was not to be. For the case was moving at a snail's pace compared to the divorces of more typical couples.

A year and a half later the case was even further complicated when Cristina suddenly decided to replace her team of New York lawyers with attorney A. Robert Zeff of Detroit. Zeff, of Zeff and Zeff, specialized in malpractice as well as divorce and slander suits. He had won spectacular judgments, chalking up a total of $9.7 million for three clients during one four-month period. He had also won a $5.5 million verdict for Barbara Posselius Ford in her divorce suit against Henry Ford's nephew Walter Buhl Ford III, called Buhl, after the judge ruled that their thirteen-year marriage broke up because of Buhl's affair with a cocktail waitress. That eight-day hearing, which ended with the settlement, disclosed some interesting details about how the rich live in Grosse Pointe. The Buhl Fords customarily spent $5,000 a year to rent new movies for private showings at home, and a year did not pass in which they did not spend at least $6,000 for cut flowers for their home.

In June 1979 Henry Ford's lawyers protested that, by changing counsel, Cristina was seeking to stall the case. All their client wanted was to get on with the proceedings, they said. Cristina, however, was not in court. And neither was Henry. Purely by coincidence both were vacationing in Italy, though miles apart from each other. But the arguments in their behalf in a Detroit court were tough and to the point.

Henry's chief lawyer, Milton J. Miller, argued that his client should not be penalized because his estranged wife had retained Robert Zeff. "This woman has consulted every lawyer from A to Z," he said. "The scales of justice are large, but they can't accommodate that many lawyers."

"She is bathing her bruised ego in the blue waters of the Mediterranean," Miller added. "Maybe her fingers are going through the Yellow Pages of the Italian law directory." And he concluded: "This divorce case is liable to last longer than the marriage."

The case was scheduled to go to trial in the fall. Zeff, however, told the judge he needed more time to prepare for it and to determine the extent of Henry's holdings.

Eventually the trial date was set for early in the following year. Cristina's new lawyer, however, said that he hoped the case could be settled without going to trial. "If we can't get what is a reasonable settlement, then the only recourse we have left is court," he added.

But Henry was not willing to pay the amount of money Cristina wanted in order to settle the case out of court. All Henry was willing to pay was a sum reported at $5 million. As far as Cristina and her lawyer were concerned, that wasn't enough. After all, Henry's first wife had walked off with a reported $16 million, and that was before inflation.

Then the lawyers for both sides began to do battle over pretrial statements sought from each of the principals in the divorce action. Also sought was a statement from Ford's long-time companion Kathleen DuRoss. Other potential witnesses decided to extend their vacations away from the Detroit area. Max Fisher's wife, Marjorie, according to *The Detroit News*, found even the bad weather in Palm Beach more inviting than a possible subpoena from Cristina's lawyer. Not that she couldn't be called to testify. But getting her to Detroit would require complicated legal maneuverings.

For hours on end the lawyers argued about whether all the dirty linen of the marriage should be permitted to be aired in open court. His lawyers were willing to stipulate for the record that Henry Ford was responsible for the marriage reaching the point of no return. Then all the court would have to decide was how many millions should be turned over to Cristina. But Cristina's lawyer said nothing doing. Bob Zeff said his client felt that all the stories, embarrassing as they might be, should be entered on the record in order to demonstrate "the degree of responsibility" for the breakup.

What Henry's lawyers particularly wanted was to protect Kathleen DuRoss by keeping her off the witness stand. No way, said Zeff. She was to be subpoenaed along with seventy other witnesses, whose testimony, the lawyer said, was most relevant. The witnesses were a diverse group, ranging from Detroit columnist Shirley Eder to Henry's nephew Benson Ford, Jr.

All of which had become a matter of enduring fascination for many Detroiters. Then, almost on the eve of her divorce trial, Cristina helped fuel still more Motown gossip when she filed a slander suit against her onetime best friend, Rosemarie Kanzler Marcie-Riviere, the jet-setter who had introduced her to Henry. In the suit, filed on February 15, 1980, Cristina accused Rosemarie of defamation by telling people she was "committing the crime of blackmail" toward Henry in the pending divorce action.

However, the terse two-page legal complaint offered no details of the "defamatory statements" Cristina claimed her former chum Rosemarie had allegedly made "in the year 1979, on the European continent and the American continent." And Cristina's lawyer, Bob Zeff, refused to elaborate on the slander suit, which sought damages of $10,010,000 for the "injury to [Cristina's] good name, fame and reputation."

First inkling of the suit, which is still pending, had come from "Suzy" in the New York *Daily News*. The society columnist reported that Rosemarie was preparing to fly over from Paris to testify in Henry's behalf at his forthcoming divorce trial in Detroit. As for reports that Cristina might file a slander suit against her, Rosemarie was described as being practically overjoyed. "She'd be absolutely thrilled to be sued by Cristina," "Suzy" reported. "Then Rosemarie could *really* let fly. Not that she won't anyway. That trial will be some sizzler."

The main event, of course, was the long-awaited divorce trial. Paradoxically, the trial was scheduled to begin on February 19, 1980, the Fords' fifteenth wedding anniversary, in the Wayne County Circuit Court, several blocks away from the Renaissance Center, which was one of Henry's pet projects. At about 8:30 A.M. Henry arrived, accompanied by Rosemarie Marcie-Riviere, whose presence was described by local reporters as a "surprise." A crowd of photographers and TV cameramen swarmed around them. Numerous print journalists from around the world were also there to record every juicy detail of what was expected to be one of the most sensational divorce trials of all times. And the trial was expected to last at least four to six weeks, according to Zeff.

The minutes ticked away, but no Cristina. At 9:30 A.M. Henry's chief lawyer, Milton J. Miller, quipped, "Late for her wedding; late for her divorce."

When Cristina finally made her entrance, over an hour late, electricity surged through the courtroom. Her hair cascading below her shoulders, she was dressed in an oatmeal-color wool suit and suede boots and wore little jewelry. "The suit is from Balestra—he's a well-known Italian designer," she told an inquirer. She was accompanied by her chief lawyer, Bob Zeff, looking camera-ready in a natty pin-striped suit. Seated next to her in the front row was her niece, Paola Tanziani, an aspiring actress, who had flown over from Rome. "You know," said Cristina, "I'm a woman alone here."

Only a few seats separated Cristina from Henry. But neither looked at the other. Henry, paunchy, balding, in a smartly cut gray suit, spent his time chatting and laughing with Rosemarie Marcie-Riviere. The essence of Parisian fashion, Rosemarie wore a black Yves St. Laurent suit and a tricornered hat atop her blond hair. From time to time she made notes on a yellow legal pad. She too avoided looking at Cristina.

Also in the courtroom was Alejandro DeTomaso, who, as he said later, "just happened to be in Detroit that day" and had come to see the fireworks. Though unknown to the press, DeTomaso was recognized by his former employer. Turning away quickly, Henry seemed shaken at seeing the Italian auto maker. And DeTomaso couldn't have been happier about the situation.

Judge John R. Kirwan took the stand. The judge was no stranger to either Cristina or Henry. They both appeared before him after Cristina filed a motion asking that her husband be prohibited from selling numerous French antiques he had taken from their Grosse Pointe home. Kirwan had ruled in Henry's favor.

In the small wood-paneled courtroom, packed with witnesses, lawyers, reporters and spectators, the proceedings finally began. But they began with a whimper rather than a bang as the first day's session bogged down in procedural wrangling. One of Henry's lawyers immediately asked the court to quash a subpoena for records of the Irvine properties—the huge California landholdings in which Henry was an investor along with Max Fisher, A. Alfred Taubman and others. The lawyer was informed he would have the chance to make his plea later—should the issue arise at the trial.

At that point Zeff asked and obtained permission to go into chambers to discuss preliminary matters with Henry's lawyer and the judge. Everyone else remained in the courtroom. About the only exciting thing that then occurred was the wheeling in of a hand truck filled to the top with boxes of papers and documents. Then came a recess, and as Cristina came out of the courtroom, she said of Marcie-Riviere, "And that was my best friend!"

With reporters hanging onto her every word, she said in

disgust, "Men! I never want to see another one!"

Among the witnesses whom Zeff had subpoenaed were a number of Ford Motor Company executives, all looking uncomfortable in the unfamiliar surroundings. But Zeff had also subpoenaed many of Henry's personal friends. Among them were people whom the motor magnate had met through Kathleen DuRoss. They included Roy Zurkowski, a former Mr. Illinois who was now president of Vic Tanny International; his wife Lucia, a former Leslie Fargo model and DuRoss' best friend; and Lucia's brother, Dominic Loretti. All three were described as members of Detroit's fast set with whom Henry had been spending a good deal of time socially in recent years. All sorts of bizarre rumors spread through the courtroom. [The most bizarre report was that Cristina's counsel was prepared to ask the judge to appoint a doctor to examine the physical state of Henry's nostrils.]

Suddenly Henry had a change of heart about fighting the case. During the lunch hour he informed his lawyers to seek a settlement. This surprising change in strategy was not made known to the sharp-eyed newspeople, who returned to the courtroom only to learn that the judge had decided to dismiss the witnesses for the day, admonishing them to be available for the next morning's session at 9:00 A.M. Attorneys for both sides were going into closed-door meetings in order to "narrow the issues" for a possible "shortening of the trial," the judge explained. The principals, however, remained. Henry did not leave the City-County Building until 7:00 P.M. A tired-looking Cristina finally left at 10:30 P.M. Asked if they were going to trial, her attorney said, "Looks like we are."

And for a few minutes the next morning it appeared that Zeff had been right. The lawyers for both sides, followed by aides carrying suitcase-size briefcases filled with documents, entered the courtroom. Cristina and her husband arrived separately, again avoiding each other's eyes and not speaking. The fourteen seats of the jury box had been commandeered by the press. Other newspeople had grabbed seats on hard wooden benches in the spectator area. Most of the witnesses were back again, and there were more than the usual contingent of curiosity seekers.

At 9:15 A.M. Judge Kirwan took the bench. Henry's lawyer, Milton Miller, informed the judge that negotiations for a settlement were "progressing in good faith. It is a very difficult matter. We ask your indulgence to see if we can effectuate a settlement." The judge gave the lawyers two hours. As the day wore on he granted further extensions. All day long the elevators were busy as the lawyers and their aides kept traveling between their outpost hideaways and the judge's chambers, with reporters, photographers and TV cameramen at their heels.

At 5:55 P.M. Judge Kirwan again took the bench. To the disappointment of the packed courtroom, attorney Zeff announced that "an amicable settlement" had been reached. Cristina was then sworn and put on the witness stand. She was asked whether there had been "a breakdown of the marriage relationship to the extent that the objects of matrimony had been destroyed and there remains no reasonable likelihood the marriage can be preserved."

"Yes," she replied, nervously playing with her large lightly tinted sunglasses.

"Mrs. Ford," Zeff asked her, "have you reached a fair and satisfactory settlement of real and personal property?"

"I have," she said.

Zeff handed her the thick financial agreement. She said she had read it "paragraph by paragraph" and had signed it "voluntarily" and of her own free will.

Her testimony lasted about five minutes. Then Henry's lawyer asked the sixty-two-year-old multimillionaire to stand at the defense table to be sworn. As he rose, Cristina walked slowly to her seat and covered her eyes with her sunglasses.

Looking gray-faced and unhappy, Henry responded to his lawyer's questions concerning the settlement. In the end, Miller asked, "Are you bound to this agreement?"

"I am," said Henry.

With both Henry and Cristina seated, the judge granted the divorce. Cristina's eyes filled with tears. Henry, his arms crossed across his chest, lowered his head.

According to agreement, no details of the out-of-court settlement were to be made public. However, some details soon leaked out. It was reported that Cristina had received at least

$16 million and, as she put it, "a little house in London." Henry, however, regained the Lake Shore Drive mansion, from which he had walked out on his wife in 1975. But he agreed that his ex-wife could live there for a short time while she looked for another house.

After the judge granted the divorce Henry slipped out of the courtroom through a rear door, but he was unable to escape pursuing newspeople. "I wish her good luck in the future," he said of Cristina. About his own future he said, "I haven't thought beyond today." Then, as he got into an elevator with his lawyers and bodyguards, he turned to the reporters and said, "Bye, bye."

Cristina, however, remained behind. She told reporters that she was "sad but relieved." Her turquoise eyes flashed with anger when she spoke of Rosemarie Marcie-Riviere, who had spent many hours chatting with Henry in the courtroom. "She was my best friend," Cristina said, "and here she comes to get publicity and to say slander about me! She said these bad things because she was jealous I married Mr. Ford. I am very hurt and I hope she reads this in the papers. If you want to know more, ask me more about it. I could write ten books about it."

That "the divorce could have been nasty" was reported by Pete Waldmeir, the *Detroit News* columnist who knew both the principals. He continued:

Both sides had come to court armed with enough ammunition to blow the other's reputation to kingdom come.... It was obvious from the outset that neither Ford, 62, nor the lovely Cristina really wanted to kick the pile and make it stink. They both had too much to lose. But in the end, Cristina's attorney Bob Zeff reasoned correctly that Ford could ill afford not to settle, particularly since it only cost money. For Ford, there were more than personal considerations.... Cristina doubtless could catch any bombshells Henry had to pitch and allow them to go off with acceptable losses. But Ford and the company which he still chairs plainly didn't need any more bad ink.

Which was the main reason that Henry Ford had also decided to settle the stockholders' suit that had so plainly embarrassed him. On January 11, 1980, the Ford Motor Company announced in Detroit that it was paying a total of $260,000 in fees and expenses to Roy Cohn and another attorney involved in the suit. Nothing was paid to the company or the shareholders. The announcement said that both sides had agreed "not to continue in Michigan courts or elsewhere," but this did not mean that the shareholders could not recommence the suit, but only in Michigan. Thus far, it has not been recommenced. In New York, Cohn said he was "satisfied with the settlement," noting that Ford was no longer the chief executive officer of the company. Some months later Cohn announced that he had withdrawn as counsel for Benson Ford, Jr., in the suit in which Henry's nephew had accused his family's financial managers of breach of trust. The long-awaited court battle between Roy Cohn and Edward Bennett Williams had died aborning.

Ford Motor, however, continued to suffer "bad ink." Sales were declining steeply. Then there was the unprecedented criminal trial in Winamac, Indiana, in which the company was accused of reckless homicide in the deaths of three teenager girls in a fiery Pinto crash in 1978. They were the fifty-seventh, fifty-eighth and fifty-ninth victims of fatal accidents involving the subcompact, which Ford had begun to manufacture in 1971. The prosecution set out to prove that the Ford company had known that the fuel tanks of the early Pintos were dangerous, but that after a cost-benefit analysis had decided against installing a $6.65 part that would have helped protect the tanks. The company did do something about it later under government pressure, finally recalling 1.5 million Pintos for modification—too late, in this case, to matter.

The trial in the isolated Hoosier farm community drew worldwide attention. Almost regularly, television newscasts featured the latest developments. For Ford the story was a running public relations fiasco. Also at stake in the trial was far more than the potential penalties of $30,000 in fines. A guilty verdict could expose the company to untold millions of dollars in punitive damages in the nearly forty Pinto cases still pending. No wonder, then, that the company was reportedly paying over $1 million to a defense team headed by Nashville attorney James F. Neal, who had prosecuted the major cases resulting from the Watergate scandal. In addition, the company assigned public-relations men and other officials to cover the trial. By contrast, the state was represented by a part-time county prosecutor, Michael Cosentino, and a platoon of volunteer lawyers and experts, including several former industry executives who knew something about auto safety.

After ten weeks the trial ended on March 13, 1980. The jury, which had deliberated for twenty-five hours, voted to acquit the Ford Motor Company of reckless homicide. A relieved Neal said the decision vindicated Ford and its Pinto, which he believed had been "maligned by one-sided articles" in the national media. Prosecutor Cosentino said that, despite the acquittal, the trial should serve as a lesson to corporations that "they can be brought to trial and have twelve citizens judge their actions."

By coincidence, the Ford directors were meeting that very day around the horseshoe-shaped table in the board room on the twelfth floor of the Glass House. When the news of the acquittal was announced, the usually staid directors broke out in cheers.

But the loudest cheers were for Henry Ford, who, after thirty-five years, retired that day as the company's boss, to be succeeded as chairman by Phil Caldwell. The management shakeup was completed by the unexpected appointment of Donald E. Petersen as president and chief operating officer. Also unexpected was the "resignation" of William O. Bourke as executive vice-president for North American operations. After Iacocca had been fired two years before, the outspoken Bourke had said he would like to succeed him as president. Now he had become still another victim of Henry Ford's sudden-death management style. No reason was given for Bourke's forced departure. But it was known that Henry had objected to Bourke for "talking too much." Bourke was to be succeeded in what had clearly become the toughest assignment in the company— recapturing Ford's share of the domestic market—by Harold A. Poling, a financial expert who had been executive vice-president for corporate staffs.

After the board meeting Henry met with the press. He said he would have left the chairmanship the previous October except for what he called "a lot of things facing the company then." Asked for examples, Henry replied with a chuckle, "Such as lawsuits."

He suggested that he would retire completely when he turned sixty-five in three years, except for maintaining his name on the product and his sizable holdings. But he said there were ways for him to remain "useful" until then. "I have always valued what I think of as the 'outside eye' and I shall be looking in, but at the same time participating in what I think is now a more fitting role for me."

And no one doubted that from his new vantage point, his aerie atop the Renaissance Center, he would keep his "outside eye" on things in Dearborn. After all, he remained the head of the board of directors' powerful finance committee. More important, he controlled the family's huge stockholdings. Which meant he could still veto money for future projects and, if he chose, dismiss chairmen and presidents. So while it made worldwide news that the Chairman had retired, he hadn't really. As his longtime confidant John Bugas had previously put it, "If he's in good health, I see him staying in close touch with the important policy issues of the company." And his daughter Charlotte added, "I don't think he'll be able to cut it off completely, and I don't think he'd want to."

As for Henry's health, the angina that had once plagued him seemed to have eased. However, he had become afflicted with another problem. "I'm getting deaf," he had said earlier. "Can't hear. And there's nothing they can do for me medically."

Before leaving the press conference, amidst the applause of some of the reporters, Henry disclosed that the Justice Department had dropped its investigation of the alleged company scheme to bribe an Indonesian general. Caldwell said later that the Justice Department had informed the company about a month before that "it planned to take no further action because it saw no need for further action." However, Caldwell conceded that he did not know the status of a related investigation being conducted by the Securities and Exchange Commission.

Meanwhile, ever since his divorce, there had been speculation that Henry would soon marry Kathleen DuRoss. Rumors
grew when he purchased a new home, a scaled-down version
of his red brick Lake Shore Drive mansion, just around the
corner on Provencal Road. But, as Eleanor Breitmeyer later
reported in the *Detroit News*, "Kathy had told friends she wasn't
moving in unless she was Mrs. Ford."

Just two days after he had said that reports of an impending
marriage were "a bit premature," Henry did it. On October 13,
1980, the sixty-three-year-old auto magnate swapped rings with
Kathy DuRoss. The marriage—a short civil ceremony—took
place before a justice of the peace in Carson City, Nevada.
Snapping pictures during and after the five-minute ceremony
were DuRoss' two daughters, Kim DuRoss and Deborah Evasic,
and her son-in-law, Mark Evasic. Also present were Thomas
P. Kish, a Ford aide, and lawyer Dennis Brynaert, who acted
as witnesses.

Conspicuous by their absence were Henry's three children.
Edsel, of course, was still in Australia and had a good excuse
for not attending. But Charlotte and Anne, living in New York,
were described by "Suzy" as not fully approving of their new
stepmother. It was the *Daily News* society columnist who had
first broken the story of the forthcoming nuptials.

After the wedding the bride's daughters threw rice on the
couple as they left the courthouse. At the airport, crew members
provided the newlyweds with a surprise cake when the couple
boarded a Ford company plane. They then flew to New York,
where they changed planes for a flight to Spain. In Spain they
attended two balls, one given by the Duchess of Alba and the
other by the Duchess de Cadaval. The following week they
flew to England to stay in the country house they had enjoyed
for several years. Their plans included a hunt with Prince and
Princess Michael of Kent.

On his return from his honeymoon Henry was greeted with
even more depressing statistics concerning the increasing ill
fortunes of the Ford Motor Company. And while he was concerned about the bad numbers, he appeared even more troubled
about his eventual plan to install his son Edsel, now thirty, as
chairman of his great-grandfather's company. He was no longer

worried about Benson Ford, Jr. But he was concerned about a
new threat. His other brother's son, William Clay Ford, Jr.,
was now working in the marketing-research department and
design center and, from all accounts, was doing quite well.
And why not? He had recently graduated from Princeton University with honors and was considered one of the brightest of
the young male heirs. Moreover, he was making no secret of
his desire to play a major role in the company some day.

While driving with Benson Jr. to a Detroit Lions football
game in Pontiac, William Jr. compared notes with his cousin
on Uncle Henry's behavior. Benson related how he had tried
to make peace with his uncle, only to be told, in effect, "to
get lost." This was a far different approach than that taken by
William Clay, Sr., who was more sympathetic. "Come talk to
me whenever you want to," Uncle Billy had told his nephew.
"Whatever Henry does, he does on his own. You are still my
brother's son and my door is always open."

Young William had had another kind of experience with
Uncle Henry, he told Benson Jr., one that had truly shaken
him up. At a birthday party for Alfie, the Hare Krishna cousin,
Uncle Henry had shown up "drunk as a lord," according to
young William. "At one point in the party, Uncle Henry took
me aside, shoved me against the wall, and waving a finger in
my face, said angrily, 'If you ever do anything to hurt Edsel,
I'll get you!'"

But as the new year 1981 began, questions arose as to
whether any Ford heir, let alone Edsel, would ever be able to
assume the top position in the Ford Motor Company. For the
company was in dire straits. In late February the company
announced that its losses for 1980 totaled $1.5 billion, the
largest ever for an American corporation. The fact that Chrysler
was also a big loser was hardly any solace. By urgently playing
catch-up in developing smaller, fuel-efficient cars, Ford nearly
doubled its debt in 1980, while working capital declined an
unprecedented 79 percent. And chairman Philip Caldwell made
this gloomy prediction: "Recovery from the present depressed
level of operating results will be slow."

In the face of potential disaster Henry forsook the Renaissance Center to spend more time in the Glass House. To all

intents and purposes he was again running things. Phil Caldwell's days were clearly numbered. In fact, in March 1981, there was a flurry of rumors that the new chairman was about to leave for a post in the Reagan Administration. The reports, which found their way into print in Detroit and elsewhere, claimed that Caldwell had lost the confidence of either the entire board or, more pointedly, Henry Ford II. The issue was threshed out at a board meeting in Washington. Henry finally agreed to a reprieve. And when asked about the rumors, Henry was quoted by a spokesman: "The board has total confidence in Philip Caldwell."

Nevertheless, the rumors persisted despite official denials. An irritated Caldwell called both Detroit newspapers to deny he was leaving for a job in Washington. Similarly, Walter Hayes, Ford's vice-president for public relations, characterized newspaper articles to the contrary as "utter rubbish." Asked about the persistence of the reports, Hayes said: "Detroit is a small town, an incestuous, gossipy place. The atmosphere is like a beleaguered city, and the thing that grows fastest is rumors."

More than rumor was talk that the Ford Motor Company might soon be seeking federal loan guarantees à la Chrysler.

But the Reagan administration, seeking to effect drastic cuts in the nations' budget, clearly was in no mood to entertain any such proposal. Besides, bailing out failing companies went against the President's deep-seated philosophy. More likely the administration would insist on a merger of Ford and Chrysler, thus giving the new combined company a better chance to survive.

For Henry Ford II, whose grandfather had revolutionized the world with the Model T, such a prospect would be truly dismal. For not only could that mean that his name might no longer be on the building, but it would also probably result in Lee Iacocca's taking over as boss of the combined operation. And that would be the unkindest cut of all. The immigrant's son from Allentown, Pennsylvania, whom Henry Ford had so publicly humiliated, would have the last laugh.

More than anything else, that possibility soured prospects for a Chrysler-Ford merger, at least temporarily. On April 10,

1981, the Ford Motor Company announced its rejection of the merger proposal. It was clear that a major factor behind the rejection was the enduring bitterness between Chrysler's chairman Lee Iacocca and Henry Ford II, his former boss. In fact, Henry had made it clear that he would have no part in "resurrecting" Iacocca. And the Ford board of directors, as usual, followed Henry's lead. Such was Henry's continuing power even in a company in rapid economic decline.

EPILOGUE

EVEN IN CONTEMPORARY DEPRESSION-RIDDEN DETROIT, POWER is still the prize. The long knives flash and the great ones clash and fall. Which was what nearly happened to Phil Caldwell, chairman and chief executive officer of the Ford Motor Company, in March 1981. Only a last-minute reprieve by Henry Ford II at the board meeting prevented an ignominious departure by Caldwell from the company that he had supposedly taken supreme control of only the year before.

Still Caldwell's uncertain future demonstrated anew the basic weakness inherent in a company so dependent on the capricious whims of a single individual. Because his family owned forty percent of the voting stock and, not so incidentally, because his name was on the building, Henry Ford II—despite his ostensible retirement—still made the major decisions.

As the Ford Motor Company moved into the eighties, its

future looked grim indeed. A $1.5 billion loss in 1980 appeared to be the beginning of the end. But company officials were blaming everyone but themselves. They blamed the Government for holding down gasoline prices, thus creating a "false" demand for big cars that dissipated when gas shortages appeared and prices rose. They blamed "do-gooders" in Washington for insisting on expensive add-ons designed for safety and to combat pollution. And they blamed the Japanese who were capturing a larger share of the market than either Ford or Chrysler.

But there were those in the industry who thought that Henry Ford II must shoulder a lot of the blame. "When you have a personality-dominated company, you get a system of insiders built up around the boss," said Eugene A. Jennings, professor of management at Michigan State University. "Ford has never been able to keep its first team intact." In a personality-dominated company, there can be only one dominant personality. There can be no room for any Bunkie Knudsens or Lee Iacoccas, bright, aggressive men who knew more about the business than the boss. Knudsen's departure, of course, was softened by his eventual replacement by Iacocca. But Iacocca was not replaced by anyone of similar take-charge ability. And the fortunes of the nations' second largest auto-maker soon began a precipitous decline.

In large measure, that decline was occasioned by another of Henry's unfortunate decisions. Disregarding Iacocca's strong pleas, the Chairman vetoed a proposal to begin downsizing its products to compete with General Motors, which had already begun to do so. It may have been Henry's biggest mistake, even bigger than his promotion of the ill-fated Edsel. For many Americans had rid themselves of the habit of buying Ford products, preferring instead to purchase Japanese imports, which they considered to be more fuel-efficient, of better quality and cheaper.

And mistakes in the automobile industry have had serious consequences elsewhere. With one in seven jobs in the nation's economy tied directly or indirectly to the industry, a Detroit on the skids always means trouble for many other businesses— and the current crisis is already rippling through rubber plants in Akron, steel mills in Pittsburgh and the hundreds of smaller companies that supply the assembly lines.

Not that Henry Ford II can be blamed for everything that has gone wrong in Detroit. What at least he can be blamed for is the disarray in a company leadership that he had dominated for decades and for his unwillingness to relinquish control. Gone are the days when a family dynasty can continue to dominate one of the nation's most important public companies. Now, more than ever, it is necessary for Ford Motor to move from a family enterprise to one more structured to cope with the contingencies of the times. But this would mean bringing in strong executives. And this, in turn, could well work against Henry's ultimate desire—to have his son Edsel eventually work his way to the top of the company.

All of which has raised serious questions concerning Henry's stewardship of the Ford Motor Company. Impetuous and arrogant, Henry continues to act as if the company is his own personal fiefdom—even though it has been publicly owned for over two decades. This conduct, though infuriating, could be forgiven in his grandfather. For whatever else may be said of Henry Ford I, the old man was an industrial genius and an idealist in his often eccentric ways. The Ford Motor Company was his company in the most real way. He built it with his intelligence and vision, skewed as that vision may sometimes have been. It was his, truly his to do with as he pleased.

After World War II, young Henry Ford seemed to be taking his grandfather's enterprise into a new era, one that would benefit both the company, the nation's economy and its transportation needs. Whether Henry would have been able to run the gigantic enterprise on his own is doubtful, but he did have the executive ability not to stand in talent's way. Thanks to the coaching of Uncle Ernest Kanzler and the presence of a team of progressive executives, Henry came to be looked upon as an industrial statesman. And he began to believe his own public relations. So much so that, eventually, it became difficult for him to take advice. In running the company, he began to act more and more like his grandfather. He refused to share his power, riding roughshod over any dissent within his corporate structure.

But no longer. With stockholders increasingly interested in

what is taking place behind closed doors of plush executive suites, it is highly unlikely that any superannuated playboy could now get away with, say, firing a brilliant executive officer because he didn't like him. Not in these days of great financial losses. Nor is it likely that stockholders would accept without cavil the financing of an unprofitable Renaissance Center in place of fuel-efficient, front-wheel-drive cars.

In all probability, therefore, Henry Ford II is the last of a kind.

SELECTED BIBLIOGRAPHY

Books

Amory, Cleveland. *Who Killed Society?* New York: Harper, 1960.

Bender, Marilyn. *The Beautiful People*. New York: Coward-McCann, 1967.

Bennett, Harry, as told to Paul Marcus. *We Never Called Him Henry*. New York: Fawcett/Gold Medal, 1951.

Birmingham, Stephen. *The Right People*. Boston: Little, Brown, 1958.

Burlingame, Roger. *Henry Ford*. Chicago: Quadrangle, 1970.

Conot, Robert. *American Odyssey*. New York: Morrow, 1974.

Fay, Paul B., Jr. *The Pleasure of His Company*. New York: Harper & Row, 1966.

Herndon, Booton. *Ford*. New York: Weybright & Talley, 1969.

Lilly, Doris. *Those Fabulous Greeks: Onassis, Niarchos, and Livanos*. New York: Cowles, 1970.

Marquis, Henry S. *Henry Ford: An Interpretation*. Boston: Little, Brown, 1923.

Nevins, Allan, and Frank Ernest Hill. *Ford: Decline and Rebirth 1933–1962*. New York: Scribner's, 1962.

Richards, William C. *The Last Billionaire*. New York: Scribner's, 1948.

Safire, William. *Safire's Washington*. New York: Times/Quadrangle, 1980.

Sward, Keith. *The Legend of Henry Ford*. New York: Rinehart, 1948.

Tobias, Andrew. *Fire and Ice: The Story of Charles Revson—the Man who Built the Revlon Empire*. New York: Morrow, 1976.

Wik, Reynold M. *Henry Ford and Grass-Roots America*. Ann Arbor: Univ. of Michigan Press, 1972.

Periodicals

Burck, Gilbert. "Henry Ford II." *Life*, Oct. 1, 1945, pp. 109–110 ff.

Cheyfitz, Kirk. "Can Ford Put It Back Together?" *Monthly Detroit*, April 1980, pp. 43–48 ff.

———and J. Patrick Wright. "The Rise & Fall & Rise of Lee Iacocca," *Monthly Detroit*, Feb. 1979, pp. 38–53.

Cordtz, Dan. "Henry Ford, Superstar." *Fortune*, May 1973, pp. 188–192 ff.

"Cristina Ford." *Harper's Bazaar*, Aug. 1973, pp. 62–63.

"Detroit Dynast." *Time*, April 21, 1947.

Erhlich, Henry. "Charlotte: The Latest Model Ford." *Look*, Aug. 12, 1969, pp. 62–68.

"End of an Era at Ford." *Time*, May 21, 1979, pp. 66 ff.

"Ford After Henry II." *Business Week*, April 30, 1979, pp. 62–65 ff.

"A Ford & an Austin." *Time*, Aug. 16, 1963, p. 36.

Ford, Henry II. "My Turn: The Crisis-Crash Syndrome." *Newsweek*, Aug. 6, 1973, p. 7.

"The Ford Heritage." *Fortune*, June 1944, pp. 138–144 ff.

"Ford in Russia's Future?" *Time*, April 27, 1970, p. 87.

"Ford's Secret Probe of Iacocca." *Time*, Aug. 7, 1978, p. 63.

Galbraith, John Kenneth. "The Mystery of Henry Ford." *Atlantic Monthly*, March 1958, pp. 41–47.

Guzzardi, Walter Jr. "Ford: The Road Ahead." *Fortune*, Sept. 11, 1978, pp. 36–48.

"Help Russians Build Trucks? Ford's Policy." *U.S. News & World Report*, May 18, 1970, p. 102.

"Henry Ford." *Journal of Negro History*, July 1947, pp. 398–401.

Keerdoja, Eileen, with Lea Donosky and James C. Jones. "Separate Ways." *Newsweek*, Aug. 22, 1977, p. 10.

Koether, George. "Benson Ford: Old Henry's Second Grandson Moves Up in the Auto World." *Look*, Oct. 18, 1955, pp. 89–94.

"Life with Henry." *Time*, Oct. 8, 1951, pp. 101–104.

Lurie, D. "The Fabulous Life of Mrs. Henry Ford." *Ladies' Home Journal*, Sept. 1969, pp. 94–95 ff.

———, and Alfred Eisenstaedt (photographer). "The Sunshine Days of Cristina Ford." *Life*, June 4, 1971, pp. 46–52.

McCarthy, Joe. "The Amazing Mansion of Henry Ford." *Saturday Evening Post*, May 16, 1953, pp. 38–39 ff.

———. "The Ford Family." *Holiday*, June 1957, pp. 68–73 ff; July 1957, pp. 60–63 ff.; Aug. 1957, pp. 64–68 ff.; and Sept. 1957, pp. 72–78 ff.

"Mister Ford: They Never Call Him Henry." *Time*, July 20, 1970, pp. 66–67.

"Mrs. Henry Ford: Contagious Joy." *Vogue*, July 1972, pp. 72–75.

"A New Look at Ford." *Life*, May 25, 1953, pp. 134–144 ff.

Nicholson, Tom, James C. Jones and Melinda Beck. "Ford Fires Again." *Newsweek*, July 24, 1978, pp. 65–66.

Nicholson, Tom, and James C. Jones. "Ford's New Trimotor." *Newsweek*, April 25, 1977, pp. 65–69.

"'Nyet' to Ford's Future in Russia." *Business Week*, May 23, 1970, p. 40.

Real, James. "There's a Ford in Your Future." *New West*, March 26, 1979, pp. 29–36 ff.

"The Rebirth of Ford." *Fortune*, May 1947, pp. 82–89 ff.

Rothenberg, Al. "An Informal Visit with Henry Ford." *Look*, May 28, 1968, pp. 92–96.

Serrin, William. "At Ford Everyone Knows Who Is the Boss." *New York Times Magazine*, Oct. 19, 1969, pp. 25–27 ff.

———. "Ford's Iacocca—Apotheosis of a Used-Car Salesman." *New York Times Magazine*, July 18, 1971, pp. 8–9 ff.

"'77 Ford Trimotor." *Time*, April 25, 1977, pp. 76–77.

Sheehy, Gail. "Conversations with Iacocca upon Facing the Axe." *Esquire*, Aug. 15, 1978, pp. 77–80.

Sheils, Merrill, and James C. Jones. "The Shape of Cars to Come." *Newsweek*, April 28, 1980, pp. 60–61.

"Split: Cristina Ford's Drawing Room Is Bare, But Her Estranged Husband is $2 Million More Liquid." *People*, March 13, 1978.

Tracy, Eleanor Johnson, et al. "In the News: New Models in the Ford Line." *Fortune*, March 26, 1979, pp. 15–16.

———. "In the News: 'Somebody Called Ford.'" *Fortune*, Aug. 14, 1978, pp. 13–14.

Travis, Neal. "After You've Been President of Ford, What's Left?" *New York*, Aug. 21, 1978, pp. 27–30.

"Trouble in the House of Ford." *Time*, April 9, 1979, p. 65.

"Upheaval in the House of Ford." *Time*, July 24, 1978, pp. 60–61.

Weymouth, Lally. "Tycoon: The Saga of Henry Ford II." *New York Times Magazine*, March 5, 1978, pp. 12–17 ff., and March 12, 1978, pp. 22–25 ff.

"Young Henry Takes a Risk." *Time*, Feb. 4, 1946, pp. 75–80.

"Young King Henry Ford II." *Newsweek*, April 21, 1947, pp. 70 ff.

Newspapers

Apcar, Leonard M. "Ford's Hot Seat: Harold 'Red' Poling Has Task of Reviving North American Sales." *Wall Street Journal*, May 7, 1980.

———. "Founding Families: As Henry Ford's Reign Fades at

Ford Motor, Clan Is in Transition." *Wall Street Journal*, May 10, 1979.

Curtis, Charlotte. "Capote's Black and White Ball: 'The Most Exquisite of Spectator Sports.'" *New York Times*, Nov. 29, 1966.

———. "Kissinger and Mitchells Enliven a Party." *New York Times*, Jan. 20, 1973.

———. "Noblesse Oblige at a Vegas-on-Sea." *New York Times*, June 3, 1966.

———. "Party on the Riviera Is More Than a Fling." *New York Times*, Aug. 20, 1969.

Flint, Jerry. "Ford's Man of the World." *New York Times*, March 13, 1977.

Lewis, David L. "Henry Ford, Publicity and a One Million Dollar Libel." *Public Relations Journal*, Aug. 1969, pp. 21–24.

McGill, Andrew R., and Barbara Young. "One Man Shakes a City: Henry Ford Has the Power." *Detroit News*, Oct. 8, 1978.

Nemy, Enid. "Behind the Masks." *New York Times*, Nov. 29, 1966.

Pearlstine, Norman. "The Road to the Top: Ford Motor's Mr. Ford, Savvy Industrial Prince, Is One of Last of Breed." *Wall Street Journal*, Sept. 20, 1971.

Safire, William. "Return Fire." *New York Times*, March 29, 1979.

———. "Son of 'Big Shot Crook.'" *New York Times*, June 5, 1978.

Smith, Liz. "The Fords: From Model T to Jet Set." *New York Daily Column*, July 1-3 and 5, 1968.

In addition, the following newspapers were used: *Chicago Tribune, Detroit Free Press, Detroit News,* New York *Daily News, New York Journal-American, New York Post, The New York Times,* Richmond *Times-Dispatch, The Wall Street Journal, Washington Post, The Washington Star* and *Women's Wear Daily.*

Index